CULTURE**SHOCK**!

A Survival Guide to Customs and Etiquette

BORNEO

Heidi Munan

Marshall Cavendish
Editions

This edition published in 2006 by:
Marshall Cavendish Corporation
99 White Plains Road
Tarrytown, NY 10591-9001
www.marshallcavendish.us

Other Marshall Cavendish Offices:
Marshall Cavendish International (Asia) Private Limited. 1 New Industrial Road,
Singapore 536196 ▪ Marshall Cavendish Ltd. 119 Wardour Street, London
W1F 0UW, UK ▪ Marshall Cavendish International (Thailand) Co Ltd. 253 Asoke,
12th Flr, Sukhumvit 21 Road, Klongtoey Nua, Wattana, Bangkok 10110, Thailand
▪ Marshall Cavendish (Malaysia) Sdn Bhd, Times Subang, Lot 46, Subang Hi-Tech
Industrial Park, Batu Tiga, 40000 Shah Alam, Selangor Darul Ehsan, Malaysia

Marshall Cavendish is a trademark of Times Publishing Limited

ISBN 10: 0-7614-2489-X
ISBN 13: 978-0-7614-2489-5

Please contact the publisher for the Library of Congress catalog number

Printed in Singapore by Times Graphics Pte Ltd

Photo Credits:
All photos from Heidi Munan, Hedda Morrison and Dennis Lau, except pages
120–121 (Photolibrary.com). ▪ Cover photo: Photolibrary.com

All illustrations by TRIGG

ABOUT THE SERIES

Culture shock is a state of disorientation that can come over anyone who has been thrust into unknown surroundings, away from one's comfort zone. *CultureShock!* is a series of trusted and reputed guides which has, for decades, been helping expatriates and long-term visitors to cushion the impact of culture shock whenever they move to a new country.

Written by people who have lived in the country and experienced culture shock themselves, the authors share all the information necessary for anyone to cope with these feelings of disorientation more effectively. The guides are written in a style that is easy to read and covers a range of topics that will arm readers with enough advice, hints and tips to make their lives as normal as possible again.

Each book is structured in the same manner. It begins with the first impressions that visitors will have of that city or country. To understand a culture, one must first understand the people—where they came from, who they are, the values and traditions they live by, as well as their customs and etiquette. This is covered in the first half of the book.

Then on with the practical aspects—how to settle in with the greatest of ease. Authors walk readers through topics such as how to find accommodation, get the utilities and telecommunications up and running, enrol the children in school and keep in the pink of health. But that's not all. Once the essentials are out of the way, venture out and try the food, enjoy more of the culture and travel to other areas. Then be immersed in the language of the country before discovering more about the business side of things.

To round off, snippets of basic information are offered before readers are 'tested' on customs and etiquette of the country. Useful words and phrases, a comprehensive resource guide and list of books for further research are also included for easy reference.

CONTENTS

FOREWORD

Travel is one of the boons of the 21st century. Never before has it been so easy, and safe, for people from all parts of the world to visit faraway countries, interact positively and learn from each other.

All travellers, however, carry invisible luggage in the form of their own culture and habits. They may find themselves disoriented in a new environment. Local customs may seem strange, even threatening, to the unprepared newcomer.

Heidi Munan's book *CultureShock! Borneo* introduces the newcomer to this hospitable island and to the details of life in East Malaysia and Brunei. While specifically designed for people who intend to spend more than a pleasant holiday here, it is of interest even to the serious-minded tourist who wants to understand more than the surface of a country he visits. It is too easy to be confused by the cultural, social and natural diversity of Borneo!

In reality, it is the diversity which makes our lives so interesting. Our multi-tribal festivals, customs and cuisine alone will warrant a weeklong stay at least!

Heidi Munan is making a sincere effort to lessen the impact of culture shock for the unwary visitor, to prepare the traveller for the unexpected aspects of the Borneo environment, and to create understanding and respect for a vibrant, alien culture.

Heidi has had her share of culture shocks, having arrived as a total stranger at a time when the only source of information about life in Sarawak was the local newspapers and a few official statistics! What she put into this book is 'all the stuff I wish somebody had told me when I first got here, many years ago…', her readers gain the benefit of Heidi's many faux-pas, shocks and near-disasters. Having learnt to see both sides of the picture, Heidi now writes with some authority, but never without understanding and humor.

In fact, I sometimes am put to shame, considering that Heidi, in her quest to find out more on Sarawak's potpourri of culture and *adat* (local customs) knows so much more than we locals do! Being local, we tend to take many things for granted—our wonderful foods, the fascinating places to go, our people etc. Through Heidi's book, I too have learned to appreciate what travellers to our country would expect or look forward to experiencing, and what may surprise them, just as it happened to Heidi many years ago!

For the first-time traveller, I suggest this book as part of your 'survival kit' alongside your maps, sun block, raincoat, sandals, Vicks and insect repellant! Have a wonderful experience in Sarawak!

Gracie Geikie
CEO, Sarawak Tourism Board

MAP OF BORNEO

FIRST IMPRESSIONS

'I AM USING ANTI-PERSPIRANT!'

'That the first sight of Borneo should have
inspired a romantic disposition, I can well understand. When,
on the 16th January 1852, I for the first time
steamed past Tanjong Datu in the Hon.East India Company's
war-steamer Pluto, I beheld with delight the country
which was for so many years to be my home.'
—L V Helms, *Pioneering in the Far East*;
Helms was the first manager of Borneo Company

WELCOME TO BORNEO!

As you step off the plane, you will notice one thing: the heat. In the major airports, it will not hit you until you leave the air-conditioned building, but it is there, and it is going to stay. You have to adapt.

Wear comfortable clothing (cotton is preferable) and use a hat or sunshade if you are going to be in the open. Long sleeves which keep the sun off your skin are cooler than no sleeves.

Go for a few short, gentle strolls in your neighbourhood. No need to rush—you'll only get hot—but look around, take in the sights and sounds and get a taste of your new home.

A Walk in Town

Random observations of foreigners taking their first walk in an East Malaysian town: everybody seems to loiter; there are an awful lot of men around on a workday morning; boys giggle at foreign women; it is hard to get orientated among all the lanes (especially in Kuching), and what happened to the tails of all those cats?

Animals in the Street

Last question first. Nothing happened to the tails of all those cats. By some genetical quirk, nine out of ten kittens are born with bobbles and knobbles at the end, bent and double-bent tails of the weirdest shapes.

While it is quite true that boys do ill-treat animals, with minimum interference from adults, they are innocent in the case of the mistailed felines. The tale of the butcher in Miri who cut off the tails of cats stealing gobbets of meat is just that—a tale.

Cats are not the only animals seen in the streets. There are dogs, skinny pariahs mostly, that flit around out of people's view and kicking range, foraging for bites of food.

Foreigners are distressed at the way animals are neglected in Borneo. Even if a dog 'belongs' to a household, it may get fed once every few days; rare indeed is the local family that will take a sick pet to a vet.

An exception is made for valuable pedigree animals, kept for security and prestige reasons by the well-to-do. These superior canines give a new meaning to the term 'a dog's life'!

Ignore all the above when it comes to fighting cocks. There is no more pampered, preening pet on earth than the common Borneo Fighting Cock, a handsome fowl tethered to a shady tree for its morning airing. The favourite cockerel gets carried in arms like a baby, has better housing than the family in some squatter settlements ('it wouldn't do to get the fighting cock wet, my goodness!') and travels the rural air services on its owner's lap.

These truly beautiful birds can be seen on any walk in town, carefully fastened by one shank to a shady tree, condescending to a lusty crow from time to time, preening in the filtered sunlight in anticipation of a bloody end in a swift, cruel cockfight.

Loitering

Why do people loiter? They do not. You are rushing.

There are some places where idling around out of doors results in frostbite. Borneo is not one of them. Local people walk slowly to prevent getting overheated, and so should you. Do not stride. Walk. You will get there just the same, nay better, for who wants to do their shopping red-faced and puffing?

Shops

A first glance at some Borneo shops, especially those in the old parts of town, can be disappointing. The sundry goods shop is just that: everything from fine tea to garden hose is sold by one *towkay* (shopkeeper) in rolled-up singlet and long shorts.

Some establishments look scruffy, not too clean, 'sinister' to quote one foreign lady who was not used to incense clouds billowing out at her from a hardware shop. It was some god's birthday, but how was she to know that?

Markets

The open markets (wet markets) are generally clean. Still, the shopper used to cellophane-wrapped foodstuffs may find the feather-flying poultry stall, the beef market with fresh buffalo heads on the floor picturesque rather than appetizing.

Shopping Malls

These are greeted by the foreign traveller as a familiar sight—or depreciated as un-cultural. Much depends on your viewpoint. There are shopping plazas in all East Malaysian towns, even the larger villages. They are air-conditioned, multi-storeyed and look and act like their counterparts anywhere in the world. The local McDonald's,

WHERE'S THE MALL?

Pizza Hut or Kentucky Fried Chicken is usually found in the mall.

Liquid Intake

The town is dotted with foodstalls and restaurants. For a newcomer, bottled drinks or hot coffee/tea are preferable to the wonderful concoctions the ice-man and the soft drinks-man exhibit for sale. Give your system time to acclimatise.

It is good to have a drink from time to time while strolling in a bazaar. Even a slow walker perspires, and the liquid thus lost has to be replaced. All hotels have coffee houses where you may sip a cool drink in air-conditioned comfort. If you buy a drink en route, stick to packaged or bottled. Keep an eye on the waiter's hands while he pours your Coke; old-fashioned establishments add a pinch of salt.

Girl Watching

It is true that boys—and those who should be old enough to know better—stare, giggle, leer and call out to foreign women. If it is any comfort, they do it to all females, though they recognise a certain age limit for local ladies.

Boys are cheekier with foreign women because, unlike local ones, they often walk on their own. This is considered a come-on sign. A 'decent' girl is not often seen in public without a sister, cousin or girl friend.

Some foreign women are 'shamelessly' attired in sleeveless dresses, in shorts or strapless tops, low-slung skirts or pants and the like. Silly remarks like 'I love you baby!' may be met with a friendly 'Hello!' from an unsuspecting lady tourist. This proves beyond doubt that she is immoral and therefore fair game!

Local girls, even if they are dressed the same as these 'shameless' foreigners, know how to take care of themselves. They usually move around in groups of two or three at the least, and simply ignore over-friendly fellows—noses in the air—if any heave into view!

Beggars

You may be amazed to see beggars in the streets. They are not numerous, but they are there.

The presence of beggars does not mean that the country is going to rack and ruin. They are part of the street picture in most Eastern countries, and in Borneo, they are not usually troublesome.

The 'classic beggar' is blind or handicapped, seated near the entrance of a mosque, quietly chanting. His presence permits the faithful to carry out their religious obligation of giving alms to the poor; of course he will not object to 20 cents from a non-Muslim, but he does not expect it. This man, a *haji* as often as not, is never in any way obtrusive or cheeky.

More enterprising blind persons have formed themselves into musical groups and busk around large shopping centres or other busy public places. Some of them appear to believe that volume is more important than harmony. Amplifying apparatus is alas easily available these days. In a shopping mall where half a dozen record shops are blaring out what purports to be music, the addition of 20-decibel buskers can be a bit of a trial to the sensitive ear drum.

Few shoppers complain about the noise nuisance, and many dole out a few coins or a RM 1 note. It is hard enough for sighted, healthy youngsters to find work in some parts of Borneo. These musicians are at least not living off welfare funds.

Another sort of beggar is the vagrant, often mentally disturbed. This one, fantastically or very scantily dressed and given to eccentric behaviour, may frighten foreign visitors.

Patrons of open-air food shops may find the presence of a persistent beggar embarrassing. Giving alms in public is a matter of personal preference. Some foreigners absolutely hate the idea; a word to the owner of the premises is usually enough. Twenty cents will get rid of the fellow too, but he will recognise you the next time you come to the place!

"Is this sort of thing safe?" they ask, and "why isn't he put in a proper institution?"

Asylums for the mentally ill are not numerous in Borneo. Unless a madman is dangerous, he is left to wander, talking to himself, fighting imaginary enemies, or politely shaking hands with all comers. While schoolboys sometimes make fun of a vagrant and get whacked for it, adults ignore him politely.

Do not comment on these strange apparitions if it can be avoided. There is a sneaking belief in most people's minds that a madman is under divine protection. One puts up with his pranks as far as possible; only a very extreme case would be forcibly restrained. If one actually bothers you or your family, call the police.

Sabah has a kind of beggar only seldom seen in Sarawak and Brunei, the illegal immigrant or 'refugee'. He is what used to be called a 'sturdy beggar', a strong healthy man or big boy who demands rather than begs.

A transient population has moved around the Sulu Sea area for generations. The number of those now trying to settle in Sabah is estimated to be between 300,000 and 500,000. The Malaysian authorities are attempting to control this influx, insisting that immigrants who come here to earn an honest living must go through proper immigration formalities and get work permits. Some of them, unfortunately, prefer to make it around the fringes of society. If one is in trouble with the police, he can rely on his friends to quietly ship him back to the Philippines or Indonesia.

Local residents will brief the newcomers on the areas of town to be avoided after dark, and what home safety measures to take.

The Eye of the Law

The presence of soldiers in uniform is a common sight in the streets of East Malaysia. No, the country is not at war.

Civilians have nothing to do with soldiers unless they happen to be manning road blocks, in which case they would request to see drivers' licences or identity cards. This is unusual; most traffic matters are handled by the ordinary police.

The policeman, *mata-mata* (eyes) in common parlance, wears dark blue and a uniform cap. Policewomen sport blue dresses and a nattier version of the male headgear.

One section of the police, the 'Field Force', wears jungle green. They are not seen around town much, but may be met with upcountry. An upriver traveller lost for directions will get better information from a Field Force man than from a regular soldier, because many of the Field Force personnel are locally recruited.

AN OVERVIEW

CHAPTER 2

3 Sept 1893: 'Old Saart much concerned about
cattle who sleep on the beach although he constantly
drives them inland, the cause of his anxiety is the
number of crocodiles about the shore just now; he has seen
one very large one and another minus a tail. A crocodile
carried off a cat and a dog yesterday and he thinks one
seized one of the cattle as there was a noise, he want out
and made demonstrations so the animal was released.'
—Ada Pryer, wife of William B Pryer,
lived in North Borneo (Sabah) 1884–1894;
she wrote about her experiences in *A Decade in Borneo*

"You're getting that promotion all right, Smith. I'm sending you to our Kuching branch."

"???"

"Kuching, Sarawak, Borneo. Big island near Singapore."

"Oh. Kuching. Yes, of course. An island south of Singapore."

Later.

"I'm getting that promotion after all, Mary. I'll be manager of the Kuching branch."

"???"

"Kuching, Sarawak, Borneo. You know, one of those islands..."

"Oh, Sarawak. Isn't that where the White Rajah lives?"

"Wouldn't be surprised. We're getting this huge house..."

And within weeks it was known to all of Smith's friends that he was to be transferred to Singapore to live in a Rajah's palace.

Borneo deserves better.

Considering the size of Borneo, it is surprising how very little the rest of the world knows about this island. Our Wild Man and the White Rajah have had a fascinated bad press for most of the 19th and early 20th century. And since any writer who could not be bothered doing research set a wild adventure story in Borneo. His editor would not know the difference; the public would swallow anything primitive and topless.

But there are *facts* about Borneo.

NAMES

Simple names like Sarawak, Sabah and Brunei will do for everyday use. To write about these balmy lands, more poetical expressions are necessary.

Land Below the Wind

Sabah (formerly North Borneo) has a start on the other two here. Known to sailors on the old China-India route as lying just south of the hurricane belt that spans the South China Sea, it was referred to as the 'Land Below the Wind', a place to anchor safely while the annual storms blew themselves out over the Philippines.

The modern tourist trade has pounced upon a simple meteorological description and declared it to be lyrical!

Land of the Hornbills

Sarawak clearly could not lag behind. 'Land of Headhunters' is definitely not on, 'Land of the White Rajahs' is no longer on. What remain are the hornbills, a fairly elusive species of wildlife seen on the wing by very few, but on postcards, pamphlets, photos, souvenirs and logos by everyone.

Upraised to an eagle pose, the ungainly fowl graces a state crest, and Sarawak proudly calls itself the 'Land of the Hornbills' (once slightly misinterpreted by an intrepid T-shirt manufacturer as 'Land of Horn Bill').

Negara Brunei Darussalam

There used to be Brunei the town and Brunei the state, which made life simple for the compilers of maps and airline timetables, and third-form geography students.

To distinguish between the two, the town was renamed Bandar Seri Begawan ('town of the retired nobleman') upon the accession of the present sultan, in honour of his then retiring father. Since Brunei gained independence in 1984, the state's name has been improved to Negara Brunei Darussalam, 'Brunei Abode of Peace'.

Compilers of maps and airline timetables and third-form geography students just have to put up with it!

GEOGRAPHY

The world's third largest island after Greenland and New Guinea, Borneo covers more land than all of Great Britain, about 750,000 sq km (284,000 sq miles), but has a population of hardly 20 million.

The land mass rises into a mountain chain running roughly north-south, culminating at the peak of Mount Kinabalu (4,101 m/13,454.7 ft) in Sabah, one of the two East Malaysian states. Two mountain ranges run east-west; the northern one forms more or less the watershed and boundary between Indonesian Borneo (Kalimantan) and Sarawak, Brunei and Sabah.

Rivers drain the central mountains and plateaux towards the coasts. The longest of them is the Kapuas, which flows west to the old port and sultanate, Pontianak. The Barito flows south towards the trading centre of South Borneo, Bandjermasin. The Mahakam and Kayan drain to the east coast, the Rejang flows north-westward through much of central Sarawak.

Borneo's remarkably low population figure is explained by geography. 'The interior is too steep, and the fringes too

The monarch of Borneo, Mount Kinabalu.

swampy for much farming,' as an agriculturalist quite glumly puts it. Miles of coast are mangrove swamp, vast tracts of the interior is virgin forest, trees 40–60 m high. This forest holds the soil; any interference with it imperils the delicate ecosystem that is used to nourish wild beast and man alike.

Man has to fight nature for his living. Borneo's position astride the equator permits humans to survive with minimum shelter and clothing; it also means they have to defend scanty plantations and houses from pelting tropical rainfall, suddenly swollen rivers, landslides and floods.

Kuching in Sarawak has an annual rainfall of over 400 cm; Kota Kinabalu in Sabah has 260 cm. The Borneo jungle isn't called 'rainforest' for nothing!

The main centres of population are along the coasts, grown up around the germs of old trading settlements. For centuries, the rivers were the highways of Borneo. Early seafarers found shelter and trade in these rivermouth townships. More than one is called 'Labuan' or 'Labohan', meaning anchorage.

Starting nearest to Singapore and moving around the island anti-clockwise, the main towns in Kalimantan are Pontianak, Pelangkaraya, Bandjermasin, Balikpapan, Samarinda, Tanjung Selur and Tarakan. The next towns are in Sabah: Lahad Datu, Sendakan, Kudat, Kota Kinabalu and Beaufort. Bandar Seri Begawan is the capital of Brunei, next door to the eastern Sarawak town of Miri; Kuching on the Sarawak river closes the round.

Kalimantan, under the names South, East and West Divisions, was part of the Dutch colonial empire and is now part of Indonesia. Sarawak and Sabah, and to a lesser extent Brunei, have been under British influence of an irregular kind.

HISTORY

Borneo is situated on the south flank of the India-China seaway. The island's coasts have yielded evidence of early Hindu and Chinese contacts, but few of any systematic colonisation. Borneo was a stopover, a shelter from the fury of the monsoon. Trade with the natives was conducted on the beach.

Early Chinese records mention birds' nests and hornbill ivory. Trading centres asserted themselves: Brunei, Sambas, Sukadana, Landak and Bandjermasin evolved as independent principalities between the 12th and 14th centuries. Muslim traders from India brought their religion to the area a little later. When the Portuguese arrived in these waters, they found trade routes dominated by coastal states each with a chieftain or sultan.

A good description of Brunei was written by A Pigafetta, a member of Magellan's expedition, in 1521. He probably rounded up figures when he described Brunei as 'a town of 25,000 fires' (families). His eulogy of the sultan's state and wealth was obviously aimed at his compatriot merchant captains.

For the next 250 years, Portugal and Spain kept up desultory trade contacts with various ports in Borneo. Neither of the great rivals could ever bring the huge isle under their influence, though the Spanish—settled in the Philippines—tried more than once to get a firm foothold in Brunei.

With the formation of the Dutch East India Company came yet another European power that showed interest in Borneo. The Dutch had settlements on the south coast through their influence with Javanese sultanates under their control, but they found little profit and much vexation in these ventures. Their attempts at creating a monopoly of the Borneo spice and jungle produce trade were foiled, time and again, by Chinese junk captains.

Sarawak, first mentioned in western writings as 'Cerawa, the place antimony comes from', was vaguely part of the Brunei sultanate. After the rise of Singapore provided a new, easily accessible market, a few Brunei nobles decided to go into the antimony trade.

Their less than tactful conduct led to a local revolt. An English gentleman-adventurer named James Brooke happened by in his private yacht and helped the Brunei Viceroy put down the rebellion. In recognition of his services, he was awarded the government of the troublesome province in 1841.

This, briefly, is the origin of 100 years of White Rajah rule in Sarawak. Sir James was succeeded by his nephew, Sir Charles Brooke, a Victorian eccentric of the best kind, a strict but fair ruler with a penchant for territorial expansion—at the expense of his titular overlord, Brunei.

The Dutch started to extend their East Indian empire from the 1840s onwards. They considered the whole mass of Borneo as a natural part thereof. Complaints about British expansionism in general and the Brookes in particular turned up in the diplomatic correspondence of the later 19th century with commendable persistence.

Sir Charles' son saw his country overrun by the Japanese Imperial Army in 1941. For a variety of reasons, he abdicated in 1946 and handed Sarawak over to the British Crown.

The area of present-day Sabah has an equally colourful history. An Austrian baron in partnership with a British firm founded the North Borneo Company in 1877, on leases of land from the sultans of Brunei and Sulu respectively. Official recognition in 1881 upgraded the venture to a Chartered Company, and under this style, it ruled the 73,300 square kilometres of North Borneo until the Japanese invasion.

Both Sarawak and North Borneo were British colonies from 1946 until the formation of Malaysia in 1963. Since then, they are integral states of Malaysia, each with its own chief minister and cabinet. Special safeguards for East Malaysian rights were built into the constitution; one that still remains is the Borneo States' control of immigration. To most travellers' surprise, they are required to show their passports upon entry into Sarawak or Sabah, even if their point of departure was Kuala Lumpur!

Sabah is the subject of an old controversy: the Philippine republic, as heir to the long-defunct Sulu sultanate, lays a vague claim to parts of the state's territory. There is lingering disagreement as to whether the sultan of Sulu ceded or leased his section of eastern Sabah to Baron von Overbeck, and whether the payments made to the late sultan by the North Borneo Company were meant as tribute due, or gift. The claim is not vigorously pursued. In the regional press, it takes the place of a Loch Ness Monster when the news scene is a bit slow; the whole business is in the process of being settled by diplomatic means.

The Dutch divided their part of Borneo into a Western Division centred on Pontianak, a Central Division administered from Bandjermasin and an Eastern Division governed from Samarinda.

The interior of all parts of Borneo—Dutch, English, Bruneian—was hardly touched by anything that could reasonably be called administration until the 20th century. Many people of the interior only learned about the Japanese invasion when their usual sources of the cloth and salt trade dried up!

This is but the briefest outline of a history of Borneo. The student of this absorbing and colourful subject may refer to the Further Reading section at the end of the book.

TOWNS

An East Malaysian town is small by world standards. It is quite possible to take in most of the central district in a morning or an evening walk.

As of 2005, Kuching had about 570,000 inhabitants, Kota Kinabalu 457,000, Miri 228,000 and Sibu 198,000.

The towns of Indonesian Borneo are larger: Bandjermasin had 580,000 people, Pontianak 450,000, Samarinda 355,000 and Balikpapan 433,000. The last two, on the east coast, have tripled and quadrupled within the last 20 years, due to timber and oil exploitation in the region. The sultanate of Brunei is home to some 350,000 inhabitants.

Borneo towns bustle with life and activity, those of Malaysia and Brunei with capacity motor traffic as well. Kuching has the advantage of being a quaint old town, but that includes quaint old lanes in which one wrongly-parked vehicle can hold up all traffic.

Visitors remark on the historical beauty of Kuching: the old Fort, the Astana etc. New parts are often overlooked while the Round Tower, the Square Tower and the Fish Market are nostalgically admired. Why is it that Kota Kinabalu and Miri look so new and 'unhistorical' by comparison?

Those two towns were bombarded flat during World War Two. War came from the east; the heaviest damage was done to Sabah and Miri. The conflict had been decided by the time the invading troops in 1941, or the liberating force in 1945, reached the western part of Sarawak. Kuching, where a large internment camp housed prisoners-of-war

Crooked lanes of Kuching, Sarawak.

The Round Tower is a well-known building in Kuching.

and civilian detainees, was treated with more caution by the Allies to avoid casualties.

After the horrors of war, reconstruction followed. This gives Kota Kinabalu the advantage of being a clean-cut modern town, planned to function as a state capital. Roads are wide and generously laid out and public buildings have enough space around them to allow for movement. Green strips and parks divide built-up areas, and the whole town is open to the sea.

RELIGION

The official religion of Malaysia is Islam, but the constitution guarantees religious freedom to other faiths.

Some visitors are surprised to see churches and chapels dotted throughout East Malaysian towns and villages until they find out that many of the indigenous people, collectively called 'Dayak', are in fact Christians. Animism, their old religion, has comparatively few adherents nowadays, although some vestiges of it have been preserved especially in connection with the rice farming rituals.

In Brunei, Islam is the religion of the majority of the population. Some of the most impressive works of modern Islamic architecture are in Brunei; the Sultan Omar Ali

Saifuddien mosque inagurated in 1958 and the Jame Asr Hassanal Bolkiah Mosque are not just places of worship, they are major tourist attractions.

Visitors to mosques are reminded to cover up decently, and to take off their shoes before entering. In Brunei, dust coats and head scarves are provided for ladies who forgot to bring their own.

PEOPLE

'I have lived with communities of savages in the East who have no laws or law courts but the public opinion of the village, freely expressed. Each man respects the rights of his fellow, and any infraction of those rights rarely or never takes place. There are none of those distinctions of education and ignorance, poverty and wealth, master and servant, which are the product of our civilisation.'
—A R Wallace, *The Malay Archipelago*

LO, THE CUTE NATIVE!

In Malaysia and Brunei, the word 'native' has never carried the pejorative connotation it may have elsewhere. A person born and bred of indigenous stock is a native. He is proud of the fact. In modern days, it entitles him to certain quite tangible economic privileges from which the more recently immigrated Chinese are excluded.

The word now mostly used is the Malay *bumiputra*, literally 'offspring of the soil'. In East Malaysia, this means the Borneo people collectively styled 'Dayak' and the Malays, Bajaus and other indigenous Muslim groups.

The world in general perceives the Borneo native as a Dayak, a noble savage picturesquely clad in loincloth and lots of feathers, beating a gong, while Dayak maidens in the background wear artistically handwoven petticoats, beads and feathers—and little else. Picture postcards and posters with this sort of illustration are very popular in tourist promotion drives.

Borneo sees the Dayak tilling his fields in tattered shorts, old police uniforms, worn shirts and any kind of shady headgear but no feathers; his wife is covered from top to toe in khaki, a faded *batik sarong* (long piece of cloth wrapped around the body and tucked at the waist or armpits) or her daughter's jeans. She too wears a huge hat to keep the sun out.

Come Sunday or a visit to the bazaar, he wears a pair of slacks or good jeans, a long-sleeved shirt and Japanese

Everyday work in the fields of Sarawak.

rubber sandals. She is decked out in a blouse and slacks, maybe a smart dress, or a *sarong* and finely embroidered muslin blouse pinned shut with three gold brooches. The daughter sports a skirt and blouse of current fashion, a dress, a pair of pre-faded jeans riding low on the hips and a T-shirt emblazoned with UCLA or some uplifting slogan. The teenage son is dressed in a more with-it version of slacks and shirt.

Malay men wear essentially the same things as Dayaks for field work or fishing. Their womenfolk are usually seen in the *baju kurung*, a knee-length long-sleeved blouse. This may be worn over a matching *sarong*, or a *batik* one. Some Malay women cover their heads; a gauzy muslin veil is still popular with the older generation. Many ladies follow a new fashion that makes them look like gaily rainbow-coloured nuns.

Look where you may, loincloths and feathers are about as common as kilts in the Edinburgh business district on a workday morning!

In a town or bazaar, most people look and dress more or less the same. Distinctions are by age and income group rather than by race. Yet Sarawak, Brunei and Sabah have some 30 major races between them. And that is not counting the sub-groups and the sub-sub-groups, though such distinctions are of considerable local importance.

The following brief notes are a general guide, not an exhaustive and definitive catalogue. Muslims may consider themselves 'Malay', even if they are descendants of native people who have embraced Islam.

Iban

The Iban in a Nutshell

The Iban have cultural and traditional affinities with the Batak of Sumatra. Now found in Sarawak, Brunei and some parts of Kalimantan, the Iban were concentrated on the Kapuas basin in West Kalimantan at one time, strengthening the theory that they crossed the sea from Sumatra. They spread all over Sarawak, and began moving into the upper reaches of the Rejang River within the last 120 years, despite edict after edict issued by the Brooke government to contain Iban migration.

Often referred to as 'Sea Dayak' in older books on Borneo, the Iban are found in Kalimantan, Brunei and East Malaysia. They are the largest single native group in Sarawak, accounting for one-third of the state's population. In the past, they were much given to wandering and settling where they pleased. If this brought them into conflict with other people ... the Iban were known and feared as reckless headhunters until the late 19th century.

They are a comparatively homogenous group; while there are dialect variants, they all understand each other's speech quite well.

Iban longhouses may now be seen by the roadside; traditionally they were always built by a navigable river. The Iban excel in the building and management of river craft, from tiny dugouts to seaworthy war boats. Their longhouses were built to last as long as rice farming in the vicinity was good, usually up to 10–15 years. For safety's sake, these houses used to stand on very high pillars.

Iban women are Borneo's most skilled weavers. They produce artistic masterpieces on the simple backstrap loom. Some gifted weavers have recently switched from homespun cotton to silk thread, which gives added value and brilliance to their plant-dyed textiles.

Unlike some Borneo people, Iban society is democratically regulated. Some families may be richer or more influential than other families, but no man is barred from leadership, advancement or fame by his descent. The *tuai rumah* (longhouse elder) governs the community by his personal skill and prestige, and not on the strength of any aristocratic ancestry.

Bidayuh

The Bidayuh in a Nutshell

The Bidayuh (Land Dayaks) live in western Sarawak and Kalimantan. Neighbouring people have often expanded at their expense; the Bidayuh were pushed into the mountainous and inaccessible back areas.

Formerly known as 'Land Dayaks', these groups inhabit western Sarawak and Kalimantan. There are several distinct linguistic groups among them: in Sarawak, the main ones are Bukar-Sadong, Jagoi, Singghi, Biatah and Selakau.

The Bidayuh live in longhouses, often finished with slit and flattened bamboo tubes as walls. One distinctive feature of the various Bidayuh groups is their traditional community house ('headhouse', the war trophies were kept there) where bachelors and visitors sleep, big ceremonies are held and matters of importance are thrashed out. A few well-preserved headhouses may be seen in the First Division of Sarawak.

Bidayuh longhouses or *kampongs* could be near a navigable river, or a long hike off the beaten track. Bidayuh are sure-footed and tireless walkers—there was some justification for the old name 'Land Dayak'!

Orang Ulu

> ### The Orang Ulu in a Nutshell
>
> The people loosely termed 'Orang Ulu' (upriver people) in
> Sarawak have slightly mongoloid features, and are considered
> to have come from mainland Asia by some scholars. Once
> confined to the inaccessible heartland of Borneo, the Orang
> Ulu have been moving down the major rivers in search of new
> territory and farmland.

The Kayan, Kenyah, Kajang, Kelabit, Lun Bawang and their
many sub-groups are collectively termed 'Orang Ulu' in
Sarawak and 'Ot Danum' in Kalimantan (upriver people).
They live along the upper reaches of Borneo's major rivers
in the central highlands.

Together they are known for their tall stature and fair skins,
their use of and interest in antique beads, the hornbill feather
dances and the beauty and solidity of their longhouses.

The Kayan are a fairly homogenous group, sharing
language and customs which readily identify them with their
fellows from other parts of the country. The Kenyah have
quite distinct sub-groups. The Kelabit are closely related to
the Lun Dayeh and Lun Bawang people, sometimes known
as Murut in Sabah and Brunei.

The Orang Ulu societies are aristocratic, observing strict
class distinctions until the fairly recent past.

Melanau

> ### The Melanau in a Nutshell
>
> The Melanau, an ethnic group related to some Orang Ulu people,
> are now concentrated in central and eastern Sarawak. There are
> traces of Melanau customs among many coastal communities;
> many Malay fisher-folk are of Melanau origin but consider
> themselves Malays since their conversion to Islam.

Mostly found in the coastal areas of Mukah, Oya and Bintulu
in Sarawak, these fishing and seafaring people are related
to several inland groups. The Melanau prefer eating sago to

rice, and their version of raw fish, *umai*, is second to none. Many Melanaus are Muslim, Christian, or adherents of the old animist religion.

Kadazandusun

The Kadazandusun in a Nutshell

The Kadazandusun are Sabah's largest indigenous community. Traditional shifting cultivators, they are now turning to intensive farming of tobacco and a large variety of temperate-climate vegetables which thrive in the high altitudes around Mount Kinabalu.

Some natives of Sabah are connected to the original inhabitants of the southern Philippines. The main group are the Kadazandusun, skilled rice farmers and artisans formerly called Kadazan or Dusun, depending on location. They distinguish a number of sub-tribes by variations in dialect, costume and customs.

The Idahan of eastern Sabah are an Islamised group of Kadazandusun. The Bajau, known as the 'cowboys of Sabah', are of Filipino descent.

Penan

The Penan in a Nutshell

The Penan, nomadic hunter-gatherers, may be the original inhabitants of Borneo. They are found in the jungle-covered interior parts of Sarawak, Sabah and Kalimantan, where a few small groups still follow the nomadic lifestyle.

Nomadic people who are found in small groups in the deep jungles of central Borneo, the Penan, Bukitan and Ukit are often considered to be the last of the island's original inhabitants. They live by hunting and gathering, usually keeping up trading ties with one or several of the settled communities within their range. Their womenfolk are expert reed workers; some of Borneo's finest mats are of Penan manufacture.

Buffaloes working the fields of Sabah.

Modern government policies promoting settled agriculture and systematic logging are gradually encouraging these forest dwellers to adopt a new lifestyle.

Lun Bawang (formerly known as Murut)

Lun Bawang are found in eastern Sarawak, Brunei and Kalimantan. In western Sabah, members of inter-connected groups are called Lun Dayeh or Lun Lod. They are related to the Kelabits of the highlands, and may dwell both near the sea or in the interior.

Ngaju and Maloh

The main native groups of Indonesian Borneo are the Ngaju of central and southern Kalimantan and the Maloh of the middle and upper Kapuas. The Maloh, skilled silversmiths, used to visit parts of Sarawak as itinerant craftsmen.

OTHER INHABITANTS

Malay

About a fifth of Sarawak's and Sabah's inhabitants call themselves 'Malay' on the strength of their religion, Islam. Indeed, the common phrase for 'embracing Islam' is 'to become a Malay'. Ethnically speaking, many of these Malays are natives who were converted by Indian or Arabic missionaries over the last few centuries. Brunei lays claim to being the oldest Islamic sultanate in Borneo.

Borneo Malays are considered to be descendants of immigrants from the Malay Peninsula and Sumatra. Traces of language and custom suggest historical links with Johor, Aceh and Minangkabau.

Chinese

While the bulk of Borneo's present-day Chinese population arrived within the last 100 to 200 years, traders and settlers from the Middle Kingdom have known the island for many centuries as P'oni. In West Borneo, Sambas and the lower Kapuas, there have been Chinese gold-mining settlements since the 18th century. Self-governing groups, these miners pursued their dangerous trade, tolerated by the coastal sultans with whom they had made tribute arrangements.

When the Dutch decided to consolidate their policy in the 'Outer Islands', the 'Chinese kingdoms' tried to fight for their independence, but they eventually collapsed. Many of the gold miners from Sambas fled across the mountains into Sarawak, to prospect for minerals there or take up farming.

Today, about one-third of East Malaysia's population is Chinese. An industrious and able people, they have taken to business from small shopkeeping to multi-million import-export companies. Many Hakkas and Foochows are market gardeners and farmers, Henghuas are often fishermen, while Teochews and Cantonese often operate cookshops and restaurants.

THE LONGHOUSE

In the past, all Borneo natives lived in longhouses. This is no longer the case. One of the reasons for such communal dwellings was their safety in times of war; this precaution has not been necessary for the last 100 or so years.

Borneo natives who embraced Islam nearly always opt for *kampong*-style housing—single houses built close to each other along village lanes. In Brunei and along the east coast of Sabah, villages are even built just off the banks of the shallow river and sea. Access to these 'water villages' is by gangways from the land, or by boat.

Married offspring of longhouse folk may prefer to build one-family houses. It is not unusual to see a venerable longhouse surrounded by a clutch of little houses and huts, rather like a mother hen with chickens. The reason given for this preference is the risk of fire. If fire breaks out in a longhouse, the whole building—this means the whole village!—will go up in flames.

In Indonesian Borneo, people have been actively discouraged from building new longhouses. In Sarawak and Sabah, they are left to their own devices. In areas of government-sponsored land development, a surprising number of re-settlers opt for longhouses. And longhouses they get.

Built to official specifications, these solidly-constructed new timber houses feature the traditional front verandah as a meeting place and thoroughfare, well-ventilated family rooms, functional kitchens and sanitary facilities and proper drainage. A 'New Longhouse' may not be as photogenic as the old one, but its inhabitants are proud of it.

A New Longhouse

I had known this family in their old longhouse, half a days' paddling and pushing upriver from the small pasar of Lubok Antu. On my first visit to the new 'resettlement longhouse', I was taken straight to the kitchen by the resident grandmother.

"Look at this!" the old lady said radiantly, leading me to the stainless steel sink and turning on the water tap. "Water! Clean water! And it will continue running until I turn this handle off again!"

In her lifetime, this old lady had spent countless hours carrying water for her family; no male will help with this task if there are any women within hollering distance. Now these 'woman hours' of labour can be put to better use!

Old or new, a longhouse is in effect a whole village and street under one roof. The visitor lands at the jetty and is invited to walk up one of the staircases to the outer verandah. 'Staircase' may be a notched log, with or without handrail, hard to negotiate in solid footwear. Helping hands drag and push the uninitiated up—he may well give a fleeting thought to how he will get down again!

The Verandah

The steps usually lead to the outer verandah. This wide expanse of timber slats is used for drying clothes, *padi* (rice still in the husk) or cocoa seeds, for carrying out coarse work or storing farm implements under the eaves of the house. It may be fairly rickety; self-preservation rather than modesty keeps a visitor's eyes to the ground as he walks.

Doors lead from the outer to the inner verandah where most of the community life takes place. This is considered indoors; shoes are taken off and left near the door. Any man carrying a long *parang* knife takes it off as he enters the house, and hangs it near the door, in token of the peaceful nature of his visit.

The verandah is wide, under the roof, and at its far end are the doors. (A set of rooms—usually two and a kitchen—is called a 'door'.) Unless visitors are close family members, they will be asked to take a seat outside, and mats are rolled out for them.

A girl or woman brings a drink and some of the older men will sit with their guest for a chat to find out what's new in the world and what might be the purpose of this call. Even if the visitor is the district officer on a duty tour, he engages in polite small talk before entering upon the business at hand. Any women in the party will sit at a little distance from the men, talking to the ladies of the longhouse.

People of the one or two adjoining doors will show a mild interest in the visitors; on the other parts of the verandah, life goes on as usual.

Some women are making mats, baskets, weaving, embroidering beadwork or pounding rice for the evening meal. Old men may be mending farm implements, making fish traps or heavy-duty baskets or carving utensils or magic charms.

Hordes of little children run up and down, fighting cocks tethered by their owners' door raise a lusty crow from time to time. These unconscionable fowls crow at any one of the 24 hours, to the chagrin of a visitor who tries to snatch a few hours' sleep at night.

Pigs grunt and wallow under the house, chickens scratch hopefully through the refuse thrown down from the kitchens, skinny curs slink around in the hope of a bite and are casually kicked aside. A longhouse is never dull and never completely quiet, at any hour of the day or night.

Longhouse Meal

Towards evening, the farmers return from their work. The women have brought jungle vegetables like fern tops, mushrooms and young leaves for the evening meal. Some men may have fish or meat to contribute to the pot. After a bath at the jetty, the women get busy in the kitchens, each mother cooking for her family, or putting the finishing touches to a meal started by granny.

Visiting ladies are invited to sit inside the rooms, where they may watch the housewife squatting before the clay hearth. Male visitors do not come into the family room or kitchen until they are invited in for the evening meal.

An ordinary longhouse meal is a simple affair. Seated in a circle on a big mat, each person has a plate of rice. Dishes of jungle vegetables, the products of the day's hunting or fishing and home-made preserves or shop-bought tinned stuff are put in the centre. The rice is taken by hand, small amounts of meat or vegetable added with a communal spoon which nobody eats with. Water is drunk after the meal, then the men excuse themselves and withdraw to the verandah to continue their gossip. The women wash up, tidy and clean the rooms, then sit in a circle for their own chat, or take up some handiwork.

Evening

This is the time when friends visit each other; nubile young ladies may decide to work on a mat too large for the privacy of the family room. She has to bring her handiwork out into the open verandah, where she can see and be seen while plying industrious fingers.

The older folk sit together and talk about matters concerning the community's welfare; girls and boys are in groups, segregated but acutely aware of each other. Eventually it is time for lamps-out, though a few old men are likely to sit over small fires in the verandah until nearly dawn.

Male visitors are allocated sleeping places on the verandah; ladies share the family room. A night in a longhouse is never silent: the murmur of the old men goes on, an old lady coughs persistently, babies wake up to be fed, some misguided fighting cock crows, immediately answered by his ill-timed fellows, the mangy dogs fight over something or other, a pig below the house grunts and rubs against the wooden support pillars, and there is the stealthy tread of a young fellow on a night visit to the lady of his heart.

FAMILY CYCLE
Pregnancy and Birth

Children are among the Borneo people's most treasured possessions. Every blessing, prayer or invocation includes a petition for healthy progeny. Parents, grandparents and the community at large desire children, indulge and cosset them, and are prepared to make sacrifices for their sake.

A pregnant woman is subject to various taboos. She is not allowed to eat certain foods, kill animals such as fowls, cut meat, plait her hair or sew. A light may not be passed behind her back. She is not supposed to look at monkeys, or other animals considered ugly, for fear that her unborn baby might absorb some of the bad influence. The jury is still out on the effect of horror films on TV, which are very popular in Malaysia! Among many communities, a father-to-be has his activities restricted, too. He may not go hunting (because this would involve killing), do some kinds of woodwork, see a corpse and tie or mangle anything.

Many taboos are rooted in sympathetic magic. If labour is unduly long, the woman's family members start to uncover jars and baskets and untie whatever strings may be knotted in the house, with the idea of allowing the baby to 'get out' or 'come unstuck'. In a really serious case, all the boats in the jetty will be set adrift, usually in the care of a few lads who will paddle them safely back a few hours later.

If a child is born defective, the parents' conduct during the mother's pregnancy is scrutinised minutely by a self-appointed committee of grandmothers. Usually they pinpoint the 'sin' that is responsible for the mishap.

After the baby's birth, the mother is in confinement for a number of days. She is considered to be 'cold' and may be made to sit in front of or on a rack over a fire to recover proper warmth. This practice is dying out now; a few middle-aged or elderly women still bear burn scars on their backs.

Recent improvements in health care have brought trained midwives to more and more outlying areas. Village girls themselves know how to circumvent some of the more hazardous customs (such as vigorously massaging or even standing on the labouring woman's body!) while turning a blind eye to the more harmless ones. To replace the fire for 'warming' purposes, various kinds of tonic wines are popular these days. The proud father who brings the stuff home may permit himself a sip or two, just to test it...

Many babies are provided with ritual protection against evil influences: a black cloth is tied around their tiny wrist, with a silver capsule containing some sacred words scribbled on paper. The Selakau women of western Sarawak wear their beautiful blue beads while suckling a baby so his tiny fingers may touch them, strengthening his soul and thus improving his chance of survival.

> In some families, mother, baby and bed linen are stained bright yellow. In this case, the grandmother or midwife is a believer in Malay medicine and has rubbed the happy pair with a mixture of spirits, pounded turmeric and wild ginger root.

Childhood

Many indigenous groups do not name a baby until he is learning to walk, at the age of about one. He has nicknames until then, designed to put off the evil spirits—'Worm' is one of the more respectable!

Once little Ringgit has a name, his parents abandon theirs. Henceforth they will be known as Father of Ringgit and Mother of Ringgit.

If he is a first grandchild, the grandparents may choose to become Grandfather and Grandmother of Ringgit as well. Toddling little Ringgit is the hero of the household, the centre of attraction, the apple of everyone's eye.

He knows it. Longhouse children, boys in particular, may do exactly as they please. They are sure of the tastiest morsel, of sufficient food at a time of scarcity; they may refuse to eat what they do not fancy and will be offered something else.

Adults interrupt their conversation to attend to a child's demands or questions. '*Enggai*!' ('Don't want!') is accepted as the final answer from an Iban three-year-old. Mother complains that Ringgit is really too naughty for words, but only an outsider would suggest she reprove or punish him.

"I can't do that, he would cry!" she will say, aghast, and Ringgit continues his merry pranks.

Education, compulsory for all Malaysian children over the age of six, is making inroads into the longhouse youngsters' freedom. Children from remote areas, too far for a daily trip to school which may involve shooting rapids or walking for hours, are given places in school hostels. They go to school on Monday, stay in the boarding house for the week and go home on Friday.

Fond parents though they are, upriver people are occupied outdoors on most days. Small children are left in the longhouse or farm hut, in the care of elder brothers and sisters or grandparents.

'Elder' sibling is a relative term here. A tiny girl may be seen staggering under the weight of an infant not much smaller than herself. Her efforts to keep him clean and contented are nothing short of heroic. At mealtime, she will carefully feed him with her fingers. She supervises his extended baths and romps to the utmost of her limited strength.

Brothers, too, are amazingly capable and patient babysitters. A small child gets away with tricks that would earn a friend of the same age a cuff over the ear from any spirited lad.

Courtship

Much has been written and said—indignant, salacious or scientific—about 'the Borneo mode of courting'. The longhouse view is simple: courting leads to marriage, without which the community would soon die out.

Native marriage is fiercely monogamous. Adultery could be punished by a particularly horrible death in the old days! So it seems only fair that the young should choose their partners with care. A girl's parents are very well aware of what goes on, and do not hesitate to put a stop to the night visits of a man whom they consider unsuitable.

It is not until an outsider with no intention of marriage abuses the confidence of a girl that trouble starts.

Of course a young woman may be pregnant by the time she gets married. What if her lover has absconded? An illegitimate birth brings divine displeasure down upon not just the mother, but the whole community. This is the main reason why old-fashioned free-and-easy courtship is now condemned by native leaders, and actually outlawed in many communities.

Young couples intending to marry have to seek their senior relatives' permission. This is a matter of form. Few Iban suitors would heed even their own parents' objections to the lady of their choice, but custom must be observed.

Elders in the Longhouse

The preferred baby nurse is the granny. Young women feel easier about working long hours in the fields if they know granny is in charge at home, looking after the children, putting on the rice, making mats and baskets, doing as many of the hundred and one household chores as her strength permits.

Grandfathers are less likely to mind little ones, though they do it very capably. At busy times, a man wants to be seen pulling his weight in the fields. During slack periods, he will go off hunting or at least fishing if he possibly can.

Younger people may make the occasional remark about grandpa's fancied prowess, but on the whole they are deferential to their elders. When it comes to questions of customary law, endless land disputes or the proper conducting of ceremonies, who would know better than the old?

Death Rites

Borneo natives show respect to their elders and great circumspection in the disposal of dead bodies, but they cannot be considered ancestor-worshippers.

The Orang Ulu built magnificent tomb huts or tall carved burial poles for their late leaders, in keeping with their family's status. The best artist was called in to decorate such monuments and great feasts were held to commemorate the deceased. For the wealthy, it would be shameful not to splurge on a grave monument and funeral festivities. The living, in the form of critical neighbours, were feared more than a possibly vengeful spirit.

Whether a body was deposited in a tomb hut, elevated coffin or punctured ceramic jar, the bones would eventually be collected and treated to a secondary burial. Ancient monuments are preserved by some societies, neglected and allowed to fall to ruin by others.

The coastal Melanau shared with the *ulu* people the custom of sacrificing slaves at the funerals of great people. These unfortunate dependants were tied to the richly carved burial poles and left to die. The Bidayuh of western Sarawak used to cremate their dead, a custom seen as an indication of their link with ancient Hindu culture.

Today, earth burial is the norm for all societies. All communities hold a wake, grand or simple as the family's means permits, while a body is in the house. Custom demands that relatives and guests be offered a meal when they pay condolence calls. In longhouses and *kampongs*, a well-organised network of voluntary kitchen helpers is available for such emergencies.

Where shirts and blouses are worn, a black patch or band on a sleeve indicates that the person is in mourning; it is polite to inquire and offer murmured sympathies.

Iban graveyards are lonely, ghost-ridden places only visited by burial parties. The occasional very brave man, determined to wrest a lucky omen from an ancestor, will spend a night there. Such daring is rare and talked of long after.

FITTING IN

CHAPTER 4

'Never speak disrespectfully of Society, Algernon!
Only people who can't get into it do that.'
—Lady Bracknell, in *The Importance of Being Earnest*
by Oscar Wilde

THEM AND US

The people you meet in the streets, in the shops, in the bazaars, on buses and boats, are the Local People. And what they see in you is the Foreign People, often known as 'expats'.

Both definitions are about as right and as wrong as such generalisations can be.

Locals

The Local People, as will be explained in more detail in its proper place, are a variegated lot: many races, many social and religious groups, many different levels of education, outlook and individuality.

When we say 'the local people are offended by a woman wearing low-slung jeans that expose half her buttocks in the streets of a town', we mean the hypothetical average local person.

There are a few who drool at the sight of a large woman with an unrestrained plop-plop-plopping bosom in a muslin blouse; there are those who have just returned from Australia and do not even notice her. And then there are those who are genuinely offended.

There are locals who believe in every ghost they ever heard of and a few they have not, and those who would not leave town without first consulting a temple medium or a *bomoh*; then there are others who walk under ladders even on Friday the 13th and think nothing of it.

Some locals revel in the ceremonious courtesy demanded by a formal situation; others find it irksome.

Culinary and medical authorities agree that, for reasons of enzymes, many South-east Asians cannot digest milk products. Small matter, they do not like them anyway. But there are any number of locals who drink milk, butter their bread and relish a toasted cheese sandwich. And children, regardless of race or creed, LOVE ice cream!

When we refer to local beliefs, superstitions, mores, customs, aversions and predilections, we mean that which generally applies to the locals, that which most of them would profess when they are in a conformist mood. You will get to know them personally and realise that they are many individuals, not only 'a people'.

Expats

When the locals see you in the street, in the shop, in the bazaar, on a bus or boat, they see you as an expat. This applies to Europeans mainly, because they are conspicuous; Japanese, Koreans and even West Malaysians share to some extent the dubious pleasure of being looked at and commented on.

The general consensus among locals is that foreigners are rich, very free (and this includes morals!), clever—though easily fooled in some ways—loud-spoken and very large.

Foreigners all like and dislike the same things. They overpay and underwork their servants, they must have electricity and a club. All foreign women drink, they do not know how to cook or do any housework. The compliment 'Did you bake/cook this *yourself*?' can take on a dubious note when asked in a voice of utter astonishment.

An Australian who prided himself on being unconventional and individualistic in his home country is speedily pressed into a mould. Here, he has got to do as Australians are perceived to do, upon the authority of the last Australian who came to his local friends'cognisance. One Danish lady does not drink alcohol. "Oh, is this the custom in your country?" And woe betide the next Dane who turns up and wants to indulge!

Each foreigner is taken to be the pattern of his nation, sometimes ludicrously so. Every time you think or hear 'All locals...' remember, they think 'All expats...' too!

In the pages of this book, you will often be warned that you must never say or do this or that because it annoys the locals. What I really mean is: do not say or do this unless and until you are among close friends. They do things to mutually annoy each other too!

To quote GB Shaw: 'Do not do unto others as you would have them do unto you—their tastes may be different.'

Obliging, thoughtful people go out of their way to do things which they think will keep another person happy.

I remember being given a chair to sit on, years ago. Anybody knows foreigners need chairs. This would have been fine, but nobody else had one! They all sat contentedly around my knees—until I slipped off my perch and joined them on the mat. It would be a moot question to determine who got the biggest culture shock out of that, but it is how one learns to interrelate.

Friends

After a period of adjustment, you will have a circle of friends here, people with whom you can talk freely and seriously. You will learn from them, they from you. Both sides will gain.

The new arrival must not rush in wildly, but feel his way around. Formal gatherings, for all the pain in the neck they can be, provide a setting in which one can put out a few cautious feelers. Ladies have their coffee mornings, bridge parties, needlework circles and 'play groups', consisting of five toddlers and ten mothers (and 55 toys, of which only one is in demand by all five darlings).

There is no need to turn up an intellectual nose at these meetings; they are often the first contact a newcomer makes. Proceed to matters that specifically appeal to you at your own speed.

Foreign men in East Malaysia usually have their work to do; their wives have the harder job of coming to terms with life on their own.

Experiencing Culture Shock
Everyone has to adjust, even local girls!

A young woman from upcountry Sarawak married a government officer from her home village. His first posting was in their own district and all went well.

Then he was transferred to Kuching. The young wife, now a mother of two toddlers and a baby, found herself living in a terrace house between two families whose language she could not speak. Her husband bought a car, but she did not drive. He did all the shopping, took the eldest child to 'kindie' in the morning and arranged for return transport.

The young woman spent 24 hours a day in her little house. She did not so much as go for a walk, being convinced that the neighbours were laughing at her, and talking about her each time she ventured outdoors.

Once in a while, friends from her home area dropped in for a chat, giving her a chance to vent her feelings about this horrid, dreadful, inhospitable, insufferable place fate has condemned her to live in.

THIS is culture shock!

BORNEAN SOCIAL CIRCLES

The strong family bond described in the chapter on longhouses is not confined to Borneo's indigenous tribes. Everyone is tied to a family in a way outsiders simply cannot understand. *Kampong* shacks or palatial mansions are inhabited by a family; a foreigner's casual remark that he does not know all his second cousins elicits incredulous stares.

Everyone is his brother's keeper here, and 'brother' is very liberally interpreted to include cousins and uncles, in-laws and related matters. No one in East Malaysia gets lost and abandoned unless he himself wishes it.

The misfortune or disgrace of a relative is deeply felt by all members of the widest kin; the good luck and prosperity of one are shared by all.

In the West, a company manager thinks twice before awarding a top job to his own cousin because 'people will talk!' In East Malaysia, a manager hastens to provide his relatives with respectable jobs because if he was seen to neglect them, his mother and all the aunts would want to know why, and 'people will talk!'

Some managers would mind the loss of 'face' incurred by leaving a known relative unprovided for. Some find the rough edge of heckling female tongues more than they can take. So young Minah, armed with only a typing certificate, does get a job in some vague junior capacity—just to keep the aunts quiet.

The Universal Aunt

The foreigner who has read stories about shy, servile females cringing along the fringes of Eastern society has not met the Universal Aunt.

She is middle-aged and stout-hearted. If she's conservative, she wears a flowery cotton *sarong* and a fine muslin blouse pinned shut with a set of three gold brooches, though you see aunts in silk pantsuits, fine linen chemise-dresses or jeans and T-shirts nowadays. Having successfully reared her own brood to maturity and matrimony, the aunt is now occupied with supervising the smooth functioning of the wider family, the neighbourhood, the municipality and the country.

Aunt knew the general manager since he was only this high. If he is an obstinate case, she knew him when he used to catch tiddlers in the drain without his pants on, which makes her the obvious person to ask for favours, or rather to inform him what he had better do next for the health and well-being of the family.

Aunts have duty rosters for illness, death and emergencies of all kinds, including wedding festivities.

Aunts descend in thick droves upon any young woman in her first pregnancy. They regale her with horror stories of what could go wrong if she does not take all the evil-smelling concoctions and potions they ladle into her day and night. Aunts institute baby-minding relays, they keep a sharp eye on everybody's household helpers, budget, teenage daughters and middle-aged husbands on a spree in Singapore. Aunts know everything about everybody. Believe me, aunts are a wide-flung network!

Interfering busybodies...or ministering angels? It depends on how the object of their attentions feels about it. But they are a fact of life in the East.

A foreigner should not take lightly the invitation from a local friend's mother to call her 'auntie'. It means she will

take a motherly interest in his life henceforth; there are times when he may be grateful.

Courting or engaged couples call each other's parents 'uncle' and 'auntie' respectively.

Togetherness

Family closeness is not confined to East Malaysians of any one race. Despite the climate, we all like nest warmth.

Girls seldom stroll downtown without a sister or a cousin. Boys go hunting or fishing in threes and fours. Young men travel out in search of work in groups. The women who come to help in the kitchen during weddings or funerals arrive and depart in bunches.

"How can I go to the kampung next week? I haven't got a friend to come with me!" is a final refusal.

Single foreigners are often amazed, or touched, at the concern their local friends feel for them.

"You must miss your mother!" they say, pityingly, and a smart answer like "Oh, I can't put enough miles between myself and the old bird!" is not appreciated. Fancy talking like that about your mother!

This does not mean that there are no misunderstandings between the East Malaysian generations. There are. Plenty. But one does not talk about them, certainly not to anybody whose good opinion one values.

A foreign man is sometimes asked, when family matters in general are under discussion, how much money he sends to his mother each month. Here a little exaggeration is recommended if he does not wish to be regarded as an unnatural monster unworthy of having a female parent.

"I send her about as much as I can manage!" indicates tact and modesty and satisfies his local friends (who are at times very insistent about exact figures). It is technically not a lie either.

A foreign bachelor of whatever age may be asked point-blank why he is not married. Just as a matter of interest; the speaker need not have unmarried nieces in reserve! Such a question is not meant to be personal, though it appears so to the newly-arrived manager of a big foreign business firm who has it sprung on him by an eager reporter.

"Mind your own bloody business!" is the worst possible answer. Try something like, "I just haven't seen the right girl yet. Who knows, I may meet her in Sabah!" This sidesteps unwarranted curiosity without making an enemy on your first day on the job!

Alternative Lifestyles

There is no 'gay scene' in East Malaysia or Brunei; the official view is very conservative. It should be noted, however, that Malaysia's first 'same-sex union', involving a bride who had undergone surgical sex change, was solemnised in Sarawak in October 2005. The civic authorities hastened to point out that while this might be a 'marriage by mutual consent', it could not be legally recognised.

Lonely Lady

"You live alone! Without a friend?" is what a female foreigner living in a flat or terrace house hears again and again.

All sorts of helpful suggestions are made, spare nieces and cousins are offered as companion-chaperones. The lady's protests that she likes to live alone are either disregarded or taken as a sinister indication that all is not as it should be.

Depending on how one takes it, this can be amusing or infuriating. A woman living on her own, unless she be over 60 and more than commonly plain, is considered to be looking for adventures of the amorous kind. She will not just be gossiped about, she will be actively propositioned! She may get phone calls, self-invitations from male colleagues or acquaintances who think they are on to something easy.

This sort of attention is worst in the first few weeks, before a foreign bachelorette's impeccable demeanour has had time to speak for itself. She is settling into a new environment, anxious to appear friendly and have a kind smile for everybody. A number of somebodies are going to misunderstand completely, and become anything from very attentive to plain pestering.

"What do you take me for!" the frustrated, angry young lady asks, rhetorically.

"A woman living on her own—we know what that means!" East Malaysians of both genders drawl, insinuatingly.

After a tedious start, most lonely ladies learn the fine art of being friendly in a firm way. Many of them decide to share quarters with another girl, local or foreign. This often has economical and practical advantages. Housekeeping cost is shared; it is better worth employing daily help for two than for one solo.

Call Me Joe

East Malaysians are sensitive about their names. Most of them would rather you ask twice than half-understand a muttered introduction and get the name wrong.

The elegant way out, if you have forgotten a name and have to introduce the person to somebody else, is to whisper confidentially, "How exactly do you pronounce your name?" He will tell you, slowly and distinctly, to make sure you have it right.

Nobody likes it if you burst into howls of laughter or stifled sniggers and then explain that his name means this and that in your own language! That may be so; your name possibly means something bawdy or outrageous in the local tongue, but East Malaysians will not mention it except in an extreme case.

By Any Other Name

With all the best intentions in the world, misunderstandings about names can arise.

One such case was a Canadian gentleman who called his wife Barbara 'Barbie'. He did not pronounce the 'r', and to East Malaysian ears it sounded exactly like *babi*, 'pig', an abomination to Muslims and a rather strange name for a wife to anybody else.

The matter was serious. Much behind-the-scenes discussion ensued. It was finally solved by a middle-aged Malay lady asking her Chinese friend to mention to Barbara that it would be so much nicer if her husband called her full name all the time. It is suspected, though not known, that the Chinese lady did bring some basic Malay into the discussion. To everybody's relief, 'Ba'bie' became 'Barrrbie' henceforth.

NAMES/FORMS OF ADDRESS

Borneo natives name their children at birth or at the age of one, depending on local custom. Some infants are given temporary baby names which are later discarded; in many native groups, parents of a first child abandon their own names and take on the proud little 'father of' or 'mother of' the little one.

Parents name a baby for what is to them good reason. One father may take the weather prevailing at the time of the birth as an omen. He was banished outdoors each time his wife went into labour, so the weather at the material time is something he knows about! That way, you get a family of Gelumbang (waves), Ujan (rain), Pasang (high tide) and Rangkang (low tide). Another parent prefers the radio to make the choice: Stalin, Winston and Hitler are elderly men now, Ramos and Nixon are in their 50s, Malaysia is a staff nurse, Jimmy is getting married soon. Shakespeare is alive and well and working in the Kuching Water Board.

The system functioned well enough before the days of law, order and red tape. But in the civilised 21st century, if a child is registered with a baby name at three weeks of age, this name will appear on his birth certificate and on every personal document for the rest of his life.

Not that this hampers anybody much. Names may be changed by family and friends, or by the owner himself. Those who have to do with teenagers, as in a school, are well advised to ask for identity cards when compiling the attendance register.

I remember teaching a classroom full of Elvis Tans, Cliff Ahmads and Lulu Balangs in the 1960s; nowadays it is Posh Wee and Jacko Rimbas.

Such self-assumed names are respected by the person's own group, though school certificates and other important documents will feature Tan Ah Meng, Jamil bin Ahmad, Weng Balang and Wee Moi Moi. The person you meet as Mr Robert Sumpit may have 'Boy anak Sumpit' in his passport—his birth was registered while he still had only a baby name.

Introductions

Grown-ups are introduced as 'Mr and Mrs Peter Bangau'. He is Peter anak (son of) Bangau, she is Mrs Peter but not Mrs Bangau. Bangau is her father-in-law.

The lady's own name is Mary Bulan, called 'Madam Mary' or 'Madam Bulan' at work. She is 'Mrs Peter' in the social context. Many women retain their own names for professional purposes. To make life more complicated, the Bulan in question may be Mary's father, i.e., she is Mary anak Bulan. You cannot be expected to know all this in advance, but it is perfectly all right to ask.

You meet the Bangaus at a cocktail party.

"Mrs Brown, I want you to meet Mary, my wife."

"How do you do, Mrs Peter?"

"Oh, call me Mary!"

"I'd be delighted to. Funny enough, my own name is Maria."

And after some talk about names, ask her: "What is your full name, Mary?"

"Mary anak Bulan. My father's name means 'moon'."

"And he chose to give you just one name?"

"Actually, I'm Mary Nulang, but I hardly ever use it."

And there you have an interesting conversation going. Next time around, you will introduce her as Mrs Peter or Madam Mary.

As you get friendly with Peter and Mary, they may invite you to visit their longhouse on the occasion of the big Gawai. Do not be surprised to hear them called 'Apai Gromi' and 'Indai Gromi' (father and mother of Gromi) after their little son, Gromi. You cannot call his father 'Bangau' either, but address him as 'Apai Peter'. As the festival gets under way and you begin to feel at home among your hosts, they may drop the Mr and Mrs Brown too and dub you 'Apai Jason' and 'Indai Jason' after your eldest boy.

In town, such modes of address are used between close relatives only. With outsiders, they feature as a bit of a joke, like calling your young daughters 'Miss Brown and Miss Caroline' in order of birth.

Chinese Names

The Chinese you meet have three names (occasionally two) of which the first is the surname.

Wong Ah Meng is Mr Wong. You may call him that even if he does not understand English. Within the family, he must be addressed according to his relative status, but that doesn't concern an outsider.

Mr Wong's wife is Mrs Wong, or Madam Wee Ah Moi. Chinese ladies retain their own name after marriage; the title 'Mdm' indicates the owner's married estate. This explains why you may meet a Mr Tan who introduces his mother as 'Mdm Hon'. She is Mrs Tan senior, but as there is now a Mrs Tan Jr in the house, it is easier all around to call her Mdm Hon.

Many younger people ask you to 'Call me Joe!' This indicates their desire to be friendly, and you respond by inviting them to call you Jack. But be sure to get Joe's full name. When it comes to returning a business call, addressing an invitation or trying to get him through a large switchboard, you would have to know he is Joseph Wong Ah Hiang!

Muslim Names

Malays and indigenous Muslims usually have recognisably Arabic names such as Mohammed, Hamid or Roslan.

But not always! In East Malaysia, a non-Muslim or Christian native may be called Hamdan or Jamil; many use 'bin' and 'binti' ('son of' or 'daughter of') too! On the other hand, some native Muslims have kept their traditional, pre-Islamic names.

The infix 'bin' or 'binti' usually indicates that the person is Muslim, but not in all cases. In practical terms, religion does not matter such a lot. If you invite people for a meal, you have got to know whether your guest can eat pork or beef; for casual conversation and social contacts, it makes no difference!

A Muslim man is called 'Rahim bin Rustam', Rahim son of Rustam. You address him as Mr Rahim or Encik Rahim depending on whether the conversation is in English or in Bahasa Malaysia. Many people use 'Encik' throughout.

His wife may be called Mrs Rahim if you are all talking in English, but this neologism betrays the speaker's ignorance. She has her own name, 'Salbiah binti Jalil', Salbiah, daughter of Jalil. She is addressed as Mdm Salbiah or Puan Salbiah. If she were unmarried, she would be Cik (pronounced 'chick') Salbiah.

Titled Muslims

There are some hereditary titles among some Borneo Malays, especially in Brunei: Abang, Awang, Awangku, Pehin and Pengiran for men, Dayang or Dayangku for ladies. If a person is introduced by such an honorific, use it.

Speaking to and of Abang Yusuf, use the term 'Abang' or 'Abang Yusuf'. It is considered a shade uncouth to use personal pronouns in Malay: this speech habit has carried over into East Malaysian English.

"Cik Ramilah, could I speak to Abang Jamil? Oh, Abang's not in? What time is Abang expected back? Please ask Abang to ring me up when he has time."

A really polite counter clerk telling a customer that he has no small change puts it thus, "If Encik (the gentleman) has only got a large note, I'm afraid Encik will not be able to pay Encik's bill. Would Encik care to wait till a few more people have paid theirs, then I will be able to accommodate Encik..."

Luckily, most of us are a degree or two below ideal standard; still, do not address people as 'you' more than can be avoided.

Muslims who have performed the pilgrimage to Mecca are called 'Haji' (men) or 'Hajjah' (women) followed by their names. A man wearing a white embroidered skullcap may be addressed as 'Tuan Haji' on sight, even if his name is not known to the speaker.

There is an international aristocracy of Muslims who claim descent from the Prophet Muhammed. These are addressed as 'Sharif (Serip)' and 'Sharifah (Seripah)'. In some societies, a young man is called 'Wan', amended to 'Tuanku' in middle age or after he has performed the pilgrimage to Mecca. All these honorifics belong to a person's name, and are commonly used when addressing letters, on business cards, etc.

You may have an appointment with a new business contact whose name you only know as 'Abdul Rahim'. Ask his secretary discreetly whether her boss is a Haji; if yes, walk in with a hearty "Good morning, Tuan Haji!" In conversation, it is 'Haji Abdul Rahim' or 'Tuan (Sir) Haji Abdul Rahim'.

If your gardener, driver, or any other employee is a Haji, that is what you call him.

"Please have the car ready at 7:00 sharp, Haji Ahmad!"

Also refer to him thus. Do not ask the *amah* to keep the driver's dinner hot, ask her to keep Haji Ahmad's dinner hot. It is the sort of courtesy that costs nothing, shows respect for a man's religion and permits him to keep his proper status in society. It preserves 'face'. Wildly 'democratic' foreigners who insist their household staff call them Jack and Ethel and merrily address them by nicknames may lose some very good servants!

Of Gongs and Handles

The state and federal governments award decorations to the deserving. They are conferred by the sultan or governor and are taken very seriously. The lower degrees consist of a number of letters after the recipient's name. These must be used for formal correspondence and invitations. The highest distinction the state can award carries the title 'Datuk', with the courtesy title 'Datin' for the wife. In Sarawak, there is a gradation of Datuk Patinggi, Datuk Amar and the 'plain Datuk'. There are a few female Datuks elevated in their own right.

Federal titles are Datuk, Tan Sri (and Puan Sri) and Tun (and Toh Puan). The foreign resident here is well advised to peruse the newspaper the day after the governor or sultan's birthday and check which if any of his business acquaintances have been decorated. A card or brief message of congratulations is in order, and do remember to call him 'Datuk' or whatever next time you meet!

COME TO THE HOUSE!

On festive occasions, East Malaysians like to fill their houses with friends and celebrate. Each community gets its star turn when the others come to visit and convey the compliments of the season. Foreigners are invited by the all-embracing phrase: "Come to the house!"

In this context, it means roll up any time after 10:00 am. Put on your prettiest clothes and bring the whole family and any visitors who may be staying with you at the time. We love a crowd!

You arrive, greet the host and hostess with the salutation appropriate to the season and sit down. You will first of all be offered a drink, soft or strong or the choice of either, and trays full of tiny cakes, flakes, nibbles and tidbits of every colour in the rainbow. Until mid-afternoon, you may be invited to partake of a meal, a table richly spread where each guest heaps a plate full of what he fancies and then rejoins the company in the sitting room.

Visiting is undertaken with much gusto. Parties meeting at friends' houses compare notes over the fried peanuts: "We've visited eight houses today, think we'll call it a day soon."

"Eight? Well, of course you are taking the kids...this is our 11th!"

Schoolboys visit all their teachers. Or nearly all—especially those who have pretty daughters!

HOW WILD IS THE WILD MAN OF BORNEO?

The wild man of Borneo is very, very tame. Visitors, from weekenders to two-year contract officers, say it again and again, "The people we meet are so friendly, so helpful." Maybe misguidedly so, as in the case of two lads on Sri Aman jetty, who helped a traveller put luggage into a bobbing dinghy while he was trying to take it out. This was during a howling thunderstorm which made communication difficult. In the end they managed, then adjourned to the nearby open market for coffee and a most interesting conversation for the foreigner, a forestry officer about to take on a posting in the district.

People who watch you go by as 'an expat' may stare, whistle or pass remarks. People you come into personal contact with are like long-lost brothers. Travellers who pass East Malaysia on world tours remark on the genuine friendliness of the bellhop in a Kota Kinabalu hotel, the room maid in Brunei, or the waiter in Kuching.

In shops, service may be slow, inefficient, disorganised but very seldom rude. The girls may not know their stock; you probably have to insist that you want to see a different size or colour, but they will remain pleasant throughout. They can be terribly determined to sell you something though!

Try to keep your temper in the face of what seems like provocation. It is not meant to be.

Face

Volumes have been written about the concept of 'face', an Eastern invention purportedly foreign to the Western sensitivity and temperament.

"The Chinese have a word for it…" sigh the pundits, happily, and leave us ordinary mortals to puzzle it out for ourselves.

'Face' is a person's self-esteem, as viewed by himself and society. Hermits, for instance, do not have 'face' problems. Within the group, each member has his own private sphere, his own dignity which he is prepared to defend.

This, surely, applies to all societies East or West? A knight of old, if we are to believe Sir Thomas Malory, would do battle if somebody had spoken slightingly of his lady's lute-playing.

The last Empress Dowager of China instructed her generals to take care of the 'pieces of colourful silk barbarian armies like to carry on long sticks, as they seem to attach extreme importance to them...', meaning among others the Union Jack. She did not say those red-haired devils' devotion to drapery was inscrutable, but that was probably what she thought.

All the best authorities agree that cowboys used to shoot each other dead by the dozen because somebody had uttered 'fighting words'. They did not use the term 'face', but that is what the sensitive soul with the itchy trigger-finger was defending.

We all have different ways of defining and keeping it; we all have 'face'.

In East Malaysia, a term often used in this connection is *malu*—shy, embarrassed, ashamed. If one in a group acts silly in public, the others will pull him back, "Hey, don't give us *malu*!" ("Don't embarrass us!")

Much distinction is made between feeling *malu* because of a mishap, or because of a person's action. If a girl's dress gets dirty on the way to a wedding, she will feel *malu* but her friends are prepared to laugh about it and help her make the best of it.

The best known modern cause of *malu* is a motor vehicle breaking down at an inopportune moment. Of course, that is annoying—it can make the driver feel ashamed if he misses an important event—but it is none of his fault. Nobody could possibly be blamed, so no personal 'face' is lost.

A nervous person who is given to starts, giggling and dropping things may admit that she is *malu* of her condition. But not to worry—"You're *latah*!" her friends tell her, "It's not your fault!" and then they tease her again so she dissolves into merry hysterics once more.

'Face' is only lost if somebody is personally blamed for something. The car gave up on us because Rahim had not filled the tank, so let us tell Rahim what we think of him!

No! Not if it can be at all avoided. There is a great difference between: "We shall be late for this dinner because Rahim forgot to fill the tank" and "We shall be late for this dinner because there was no petrol in the tank!"

If there is good reason to believe that Rahim, deliberately and with malice aforethought, omitted to fill the tank with the intention of embarrassing the whole party (for some wicked reason of his own), he has to take the consequences of a good ticking-off. But it should come from one of his own group, and it should be administered in private.

Having 'Face'

Even the worst of us have 'face'.

A kind-hearted Malay lady told me once that she felt extremely sorry for criminals. We had been discussing a sad case of robbery and murder, and I retorted that I felt a lot sorrier for the victim.

"Yes, of course, and his poor family too. But think of those felons having to stand up there with all the people looking at them while the judge tells everybody what they have done!"

I do not adopt her point of view, but I know what she means. Everybody, however bad, should be allowed to keep a minimum of 'face'.

None of my readers is going to have to deal with murderers and robbers, of course. But in the many frustrations and annoyances of daily life, try to avoid blaming one person, and above all avoid telling somebody off in front of others.

One of the reasons why household helpers leave a good job is because they are called 'names'.

"You stupid girl!" frequently repeated is enough for some. Do not permit a new helper to deal with valuable (breakable) equipment until you are satisfied she will handle it with care. You are quite likely to yell at her if she breaks it!

In some families, children are given to 'rubbing in' any admonition mother has given to the helper. "That was naughty of you to break the salad bowl, Ah Moi!" the little dears point out to her, and unless Ah Moi has very thick skin, she will leave that place.

The principle extends from the kitchen to the boardroom. Of course things do go wrong, and very often it is quite easy to pinpoint the culprit. He or she feels bad enough about having messed things up. Do not aggravate it by publicly chewing him or her out.

You are well within your rights if you insist that the problem must be solved, the mess cleared up.

"Ah Moi, pick up all the little pieces of broken glass very carefully and wipe up the spilt orange juice. Wash the floor afterwards or we'll get a lot of ants."

Ah Moi will not resent this. She would feel bad about:

"You silly girl, must you always break everything? The children will get glass splinters in their toes but you don't care..."

There is the occasional very timid, sensitive person who attempts suicide when he has been publicly scolded. Such cases are rare, but they have occurred.

Touching

An important rule in public behaviour is: never touch another person. Shaking hands is restricted to friends or properly introduced acquaintances, and even then it can be a pretty limp affair by Western standards.

It is impossible to get down a crowded street and into a packed market without touching people. The appearance of avoiding contact has to be preserved. If everybody is upright and moving, a very perfunctory show of holding in one's clothes is enough. One person walking past a group of others who are sitting or squatting (in the market, they may be scaling fish or trimming vegetables) has to hold her dress or his trousers in with a stiff hand; the idea is to prevent touching anybody's face or head with one's garments.

Even among close friends, a brief handshake is considered enough. Shoulder-slappings, back-pattings and the like are not appreciated.

Do not pat children on the head, pinch their cheeks, pretend to 'catch' them—though local women will do all that with your little blue-eyed blonds! This is a sore point for some foreign mothers. If it is considered so bad for us to touch local children, why can everybody else treat ours like rag dolls?

People only do it if the mother does not appear to object. Foreigners are considered to be outside the normal scheme of things; while nobody would want to deliberately hurt them, they are not thought to mind hands-on admiration of their offspring. As for all that golden hair, every granny in the market is tempted to check, once and for all, if it is not some dust that will come off with a good rub!

Some mothers may enjoy such publicity; few children do. There may come a day when the young child refuses point-blank to accompany his mother to the market or the mall.

Make it quite clear right from the start that you do not like anybody to touch your child. "Please don't! No!" and a firm negative gesture like pulling the little one towards yourself for protection will convey the message.

If the family's helper is allowed to take her young charges home to the *kampong* for a day, tell her that you do not want them touched beyond the polite handshaking that would be expected of anyone, nor fed sweets and biscuits other than what the rest of her family consumes.

Children may become very difficult at the very mention of upcountry trips if they associated them with unwelcome attention and limelight.

Public Affection

You will be surprised to see local twosomes of the same sex walking about hand in hand. It does not usually mean they are gay! Good friends, favourite cousins, brothers or sisters keep in touch this way. It is accepted behaviour, considered rather sweet by their elders.

A courting couple in the longhouse or *kampong* carefully avoid each other, anxious to escape teasing by the onlookers who are fully aware of what goes on. It is simply a matter of conforming to the social norm, though it looks all back-to-front to a foreigner.

At parties of the more conservative kind, men sit together in one place (verandah or front room), women in another, usually the kitchen.

Married couples may not even eat together in some places if they're at a public function. They walk a few steps apart. Among more conservative societies, they hardly even talk to each other in public.

No foreigner would be expected to conform to local mores to that extent, but they are well advised to keep visible displays of affection within doors. If a man finds it natural to kiss his wife before going out to work, he should do this out of his helper's view. The poor girl would be terribly embarrassed!

> Margaret Brooke, Ranee to Sarawak's second White Rajah, was admonished by one of the elder Malay ladies of the day that she must never, never be seen taking a man's hand in public! That was in the 19th century, but we are still pretty conservative in East Malaysia.

Many people are seriously upset by what is considered social kissing, 'pecking' in the West, though the practice is becoming acceptable between women and the younger set who have studied overseas. Granny still frowns, though!. Locals find it embarrassing to have to watch a foreign man swoop upon a lady of his acquaintance and kiss her right there in the open street. And she's not even his wife (and that would be bad enough)!

Some local men find it distinctly offensive if such attention is bestowed upon their own womenfolk. All rules of Eastern hospitality go overboard if the guest takes liberties with his hostess! "What does he take my wife for?" is the angry reaction of a husband, who will feel personally insulted by what was intended as a gesture of welcome.

Attracting Attention

Somerset Maugham notwithstanding, people do not clap their hands and shout 'Boy!' when they want something in the East. Most of the time an expat is only too noticed. Sneaking in unobserved, now that would be a feat!

But there are times, in a busy coffee shop maybe, when it is necessary to attract some attention to get service.

It is all right to wave a hand discreetly and call "Hello! Hello!" If the shop assistant is Chinese and female of any age, she can be called '*ah moi*' (girl). Ditto for a lad: '*ah meng*'. The owner answers to '*towkay*' and his wife to '*towkay neo*'. In this modern age, it is considered smart to use 'boss' for either.

To make the yell for help sound more like a friendly request, add '-ah' to the end of it. *Towkay*-ah! *Ah Moi*-ah! *Ah Meng*-ah!

A Malay shopkeeper may be called '*pakcik*' (uncle), his wife '*makcik*' (auntie), polite terms of the endearing kind.

'*Encik*' or '*puan*' (sir, madam) are more formal terms, and betoken serious intent. You would not make a complaint to '*pakcik*'; you would call him '*encik*' all right.

Young assistants in a Malay shop may be summoned more peremptorily than the older ones. 'Oh, *adek*!' (young brother for a lad or lass up to 15), 'Oh, *abang*!' (older brother, for any male older than yourself), 'Oh, *kakak*!' (elder sister, any youngish lady), will bring them in your direction. They will take their revenge by calling you uncle, auntie or sir, regardless of gender.

If you enter a shop where nobody seems to be in attendance, call out. A would-be customer standing silently in an empty shop is suspected of dishonest intent. 'Hello!' is appropriate; once you glimpse a sign of intelligent life, hail according to its presumptive age, 'Oooh, *pakcik*! Oooh *adek*!' etc. until you get a reaction.

Expats on Public Transport

Europeans are presumed to be rich and own flashy cars. You will be stared at and commented upon if you use a bus or boat; this is where even male foreigners get their share of attention!

East Malaysia is getting used to the foreign backpacker, though the female of the species never fails to fascinate the general public. Our own women carry loads almost bigger than their little bodies, and nobody thinks twice about it. On the other hand, it is a well-known fact that no European lady can lift anything heavier than a handbag, so the sight of a blonde girl bumping a frame rucksack is not one the loungers in a bazaar would want to miss.

The thing to do is grin and walk past. They do not mean any harm. Shopping housewives in a working-class part of Birmingham would comment on a Chinese gentleman lolling in the back seat of a Rolls too!

As you get further eastward, men tend to be overly appreciative of foreign women in buses, especially crowded ones. There, it may be best to avoid public transport during the rush hour. Pinchers and patters usually operate under cover of crowds.

BIRTHS, WEDDINGS AND DEATHS

Family occasions though these are, Borneans take an interest in the additions, subtractions and conjunctions of all their friends' households.

Births

The birth of a baby is announced informally. 'Births' columns are not common in local newspapers. Colleagues pass a hat around to send a card and/or a baby gift to a new mother or father on the staff; the expat will be asked to contribute.

Conservative families may invite guests to a welcome-the-baby party, especially if it is a first son. The correct gift for this occasion is gold—tiny finger rings are sold in goldsmiths' shops especially for this occasion. An ordinary 'baby present' is acceptable from an outsider.

If a close friend has had a baby, visit the house about a week after the happy event to bring your best wishes and a small gift. A phone call announcing the visit is appreciated. You would not want to be invaded without warning if you'd just had a baby!

You will meet more women around the place than ought to be there. These are the aunts, even unto the seventh generation, one or both grandmothers, a midwife or other wise women...it usually takes some careful search to locate the happy father.

As in other present-giving situations, you are expected to give a respectful gift to your social equal or superior, a useful one to your inferior. Bring flowers, sweets, a really pretty card or a pair of frilly pink bootees to the wife of your husband's staff member.

To your *amah*, whose position in your household makes her partly your responsibility, you may bring useful things

In Brunei, formal newspaper announcements inform the public of various rites of passage in the royal family: a baby's head-shaving (at one week of age), the first time its little feet touch the ground, ear-piercing or circumcision and engagements. Members of the diplomatic corps will be invited to attend parties connected with these joyous events, but never worry what to do when you get there—protocol will carefully guide your every step.

like a couple of chickens (the women may feed her chicken soup every day for a fortnight!), a bottle of tonic wine (unless she is Muslim!), baby clothes or money in an envelope.

Various communities have their own rituals for naming the baby and formally integrating it into the family; these are usually private affairs. Even a Muslim boy's circumcision, which used to call for a grand *kampong* celebration, is now more quietly managed.

Weddings
Chinese Wedding

Chinese wedding invitations come as glossy red cards printed in gold lettering. '*Ang samans*' the invited guests call them, sighing, "Red summons. Like a traffic summons. Costs RM 100 apiece!"

The grumbling uncle of many nieces is here referring to the fact that you cannot visit a wedding and not give an *ang pow* (red envelopes decorated with gold print) of about the size he just mumbled. Some people give RM 50, a new crisp banknote, but conservatives insist that everything for a wedding has to come in pairs.

'Even RM 60 is better than RM 70! RM 80 is fine, RM 100 is generous.' Nobody objects to RM 200 either, but they feel that the RM 50s and RM 70s are more appropriate for funeral donations (as of January 2006).

For relatives and good friends or business connections, this is really de rigueur. The gift may be enclosed in a wedding card; real *ang pows* are normally given by Chinese donors. The amount of RM 100 represents the socially acceptable amount a settled middle-class couple are expected to give as a wedding present.

Single expats, especially if they are not in the top income bracket, need not put more than RM 40 into the envelope.

Wedding guests who are not relatives, such as expat work-mates, may please themselves whether to send a gift of money, or some pretty crockery, household item or table linen.

The family will attend the actual wedding ceremony, at the registry office or in church, depending on the couple's religion. Traditional rites are held to lend dignity to the occasion and appease the grandmothers; legally they are not valid.

The tea-serving party which used to constitute the official wedding ceremony is now only held to permit the bride to collect dues from her new in-laws. She serves bowls of tea and bows low to her parents-in-law, grandparents-in-law, uncles- and aunts-in-law, and receives a gift of gold from each person so honoured. It is a purely family party; what expat friends will see is the banquet.

A Chinese wedding banquet is a rousing affair of ten or 12 courses. Both sets of parents give such a party, the bride's a day or so before the official wedding, the groom's on the same day or the day after. If you know both families, you may get invited twice to the same wedding, i.e., once to a daughter's farewell party and once to a daughter-in-law's welcome.

A wedding party looks like any other Chinese dinner, except that there is a rather long receiving line. As you make your way up the steps and shake hands with the happy parents, an elder uncle or two and a senior brother, discreetly pass your offering to one of them. There is probably a small table in a corner where gifts are piled, sometimes with an ornamental bowl for *ang pows*, but you do not put the thing there yourself. Discretion has its limits; slip the item to a family member. He will protest, loudly enough for the bystanders to hear, that it is far too big/good/precious, thank you very much, and deposit it with the others.

The idea of the *ang samans*, the red-wrapped gifts of money, is that they help finance the wedding dinner. Or more! Guests at a wedding banquet may while away their time between courses computing the probable cost of each dish, the estimated amount of *ang pow* received and then draw the balance. If you invite all the right people (i.e., those who can be relied upon to bring more than the average amount), you actually profit from the wedding dinner!

That may be so. By the time a daughter is equipped with her trousseau, dowry, a new car and a lavish honeymoon tour, the happy father will be only too glad of a windfall in the shape of wedding banquet *ang pows*!

Malay Wedding

There is a marked difference between a 'high-class' Malay wedding, a fairyland show immaculately stage-managed that would put Hollywood to shame, and a traditional Malay village wedding. Three or four parties are held for the former, with hundreds of guests including many invited from overseas, scores of uniformed attendants and maidens, peacock thrones for the young couple—you name it, they got it and more! Unlike at Arab weddings, the Malay bride is very much in evidence, decked in gold and diamonds, enthroned beside her brand-new husband to receive blessings and congratulations.

To the invited guest, a big-scale wedding looks and acts like a monster party. Food and service are of the finest, music and entertainment are choice; somewhere up in front, you see the couple among much glitter and shimmer. Some people are seen walking up the red carpet and ascending the dais, motioning about vaguely with silverware... But it is not until you have been to a *kampong* wedding that you discover what it is all about.

Kampong weddings are, as the word suggests, village affairs. If a friend or colleague gets married in the *kampong*, do accept the invitation!

There was an engagement some time earlier. Few childhood betrothals come to fruition nowadays, though some people still contract them. The official and religious ceremonies are normally held for family members and Muslim guests only, but you will be asked to witness the *bersanding*, the enthronement and blessing of the newly-married couple.

Come to the house, bring the kids! The thicker the crowd in the house, the happier the bride's parents will be. Coming from far away, you will be specially honoured. Just imagine, they have come all the way from Birmingham, Tokyo or Brussels to be here for our Soraya's wedding!

Greet your host at the door of the house, take off your shoes and walk in. Discreetly hand over your present, which may be a banknote tucked in a wedding card, or a 'useful' gift towards the new household. Take care not to choose an obviously 'Christian' card for a Muslim wedding.

It will be indicated where you are to sit. Women as a rule are taken to the inside room, men are considered hardy enough to brave the draughts on the verandah or front room. Soft drinks and small nibbles may be served, but save your appetite for the wedding dinner!

In country areas, the bridegroom is escorted to the bride's house with much pomp and circumstance and considerable noise. A horde of young boys beating tambourines and chanting songs is common, the *kampong* band if any, a trigger-happy uncle or cousin who fires his old fowling piece into the air from time to time. The bridegroom is decked out in a traditional silk suit, with a gold-brocade *sarong* artistically draped around his middle. Superior families have got a length of 'wedding cloth' specially woven to make both the bride and groom's outfits; this is, however, unusual and very expensive.

Some bridegrooms walk to their own wedding (it may be but a few houses from their own), others are carried in a beautifully decorated litter. If he is one of your household staff, he may ask permission to use your car, especially if it is a big and new Mercedes, Volvo or BMW. For once in his life he wants to shine! Do not worry that the vehicle will be used as a '*kampong* taxi' for the wedding. It will not! It will be polished to high gloss, hung about with colourful ribbons, used to drive the groom to the bride's house at walking pace so everybody can see what a noble conveyance he has, and then carefully guarded until it is returned.

Depending on local tradition, the bridegroom may be escorted up the steps and into the house, or he may be barred. The house door is locked in his face. A 'champion' defending the bride refuses him entry.

The well-provided bridegroom has brought his own retainer along, 'a man armed with iron' as tradition demands. The two champions engage in a mock fight, really a skilful *silat* (Malay self defence) duel not made any easier by its setting up and down a steep wooden staircase.

The old women of the household lean out of a window, commenting on the performance, urging on their favourite. Needless to say, the Best Man wins. The defender surrenders, the groom is led into the main room and seated beside the already waiting bride surrounded by her maidens, aunties and granny if extant.

The couple may be seated on two lavishly-decorated chairs, a divan or on the bridal bed. This differs from region to region. The assembled party feasts its eyes on the beautifully-dressed couple sitting bashfully side by side, eyes lowered, hands placed demurely on their thighs. Then elders step forward one by one to administer the traditional blessing.

An old person takes the lead. Conveniently placed on a tray are a gold ring on a stingray sting, a bowl of yellow rice grains, scented rice flour paste and a sprinkler of perfume or rose water. The elder touches the young man's forehead with the gold ring, takes a small pinch of paste and presses it on the same place. He dabs on a little perfume, then he repeats the same routine on the bride. Finally he tosses a few rice grains over their heads and hands. Having done this, he retires, to be followed by the person next in seniority.

Sometimes a foreigner is invited to bless the couple. If the bride was your *amah*, for instance, you would very likely be asked to 'perform the *tepong tawar* ceremony' as it is called.

Do not panic! Step forward slowly, knees slightly bent if you have to walk between seated persons. When you reach the dais, the old women surrounding the bride will be only too ready with advice and assistance. A questioning glance in their direction, a slight hesitation as your hand hovers over the tray of silver or brass implements, will prompt them to pass you the correct things in the right order. There is no need to say anything. Keep a grave demeanour throughout, walk back to your seat slowly. And do not forget—you bless the bridegroom first!

After sufficient blessings have been administered, the assembled company gets hungry. Food may be ready at tables, buffet-style, so men and women can eat together without embarrassment. In a really traditional *kampong*, the wedding dinner is served on the floor. In that case, stay exactly where you are, a woman among the women, a man among the men. You may be asked to eat with the *kampong* worthies, who are sometimes fed separately as a mark of respect. Continue to stick to your own gender.

Nobody will vociferously denounce a foreign woman who sits and eats with the menfolk. They will treat her with the same ceremonious politeness, but in that *kampong* she is quietly classified as *kurang ajar*—uncouth.

Each person is served a plate of rice; dishes of curry, soup, cut meats, vegetables and all sorts of condiments are put on the mat at regular intervals for people to help themselves. Never worry that you will go hungry! Everything will be assiduously pushed in your direction, they will ply you with food and more food!

The older ladies will take charge of a foreign woman or her small children, the men of a man and his big sons. 'Big' in this context means a lad old enough to behave and eat nicely in public. Little children need mummy's help at mealtimes; big girls are supposed to help her look after baby brothers and sisters. Big boys eat with papa and the men. Explain this to your Jimmy and enjoy his very best manners for once!

Do not touch any food until you are invited to start. An elder is likely to recite a prayer over it first; sometimes the young couple have to have their first conjugal bite before the guests may tuck in.

It is called *makan nasi temuan*—'the rice of first meeting', and can be quite amusing. Under the critical eye of the whole family and village, the bride and groom have to feed each other with sweetened rice. He puts morsels into her mouth, she into his. It nearly always does not work straight away, to the great hilarity of the assembly.

Borneo Wedding

The native weddings foreigners are likely to be invited to will follow either the Chinese style (big banquet in a restaurant) or the Malay (rousing party in the bride's home). Many indigenous Borneoans are Christians, and the invitation will specify the time and place of the church ceremony.

Upcountry weddings are likely to follow modified versions of the above. Longhouse brides are likely to be sweltering in a long-sleeved gown, veil and gloves; her father and the groom will appear in tailored suits.

Some Sabah and Sarawak native couples are going back to their roots: after the official church wedding, they have a second, traditional ceremony. The bridal party is dressed in beautiful ceremonial attire, beads, feathers and all. The young couple is seated on gongs while an elder waves a chicken over their heads, or they walk into and out of the house eight times, or whatever tradition dictates. Some weddings start with a formal party with lounge suits and long dresses and end up with a 'family bash' in traditional costumes the next day.

Do It Yourself

Foreigners intending to get married in Borneo have to conform to local law; they are advised to check with their own embassy or high commission about the details of having the marriage registered. Some prefer to be married by their own ambassador in Kuala Lumpur (for East Malaysia), or in Brunei.

Notice of the intended marriage has to be given on the prescribed forms to the local registrar. The forms are all in Bahasa Melayu; bring along a reliable interpreter so you know what you are signing!

Non-Muslim marriages are monogamous.

After the due time of notice, the marriage can be solemnised in the church of the couple's choice, or by the registrar. The local judge cannot marry you, and there are no J.P.s!

A Death in the Family

A death requires the immediate presence of all the family members who can possibly make it.

If your employee, domestic or otherwise, asks for leave because somebody has died, grant it at once. He will not say, "My aunt has died," by the way. The correct phrase is, "My aunt has passed away." East Malaysians are superstitious about the words they use, and they will feel easier if you too refer to auntie's passing rather than auntie's death. The deceased may have been of a relationship that does not seem to demand immediate attendance in your eyes. An aunt twice removed...thrice removed?

That's your point of view (and remember you do not even know all your own second cousins!) An East Malaysian would be gravely failing in duty if he stayed away. The bereaved household may live a long way from town; he may not even make it to the funeral. But please give him or her leave—the family would hold it against the defaulter for years and years and years if he failed to show up.

Most expats finish their tour of duty in East Malaysia without ever once seeing a funeral. You see them pass by in the street: a Chinese cortege is highly visible as well as audible, accompanied by religious chants blaring from loudspeakers, the friendly neighbourhood percussion ensemble, the local brass band if one is available for hire, and a string of lorries and buses carrying banners conveying the sympathy of associations of which the deceased was a member. The general public gives way to such processions. It is not good etiquette to overtake one or to cut across it.

But few expats have anything to do with these spectacles. That is why you cannot consult your friends about the proper conduct at a funeral, should you be required to attend one.

Whose Funeral to Attend?

The funeral of a senior staff member must be attended by fellow staff; depending on seniority, the boss may go in person. Flowers and a card should be sent for close family of a staff member. It is not customary to send flowers to a Muslim funeral; consult a Muslim on your staff about your firm's usual practice.

If a prominent business connection passes away, a representative of your firm will be expected to attend. Rather

At the demise of a prominent person of the state, business firms, government departments, etc, send representatives to the state funeral. A day of mourning may be declared. Keep tuned to the local radio station to get details of all the arrangements. If you are expected to walk in the head part of the procession, protocol will brief you on what to do, and also on what to wear.

than go yourself, you may prefer to send a senior staff member who is of the same religion as the deceased.

At the death of a business acquaintance's parent, wife, etc, send a card; flowers if the deceased was a Chinese or native Christian.

Workers 'on the same level', i.e., fellow teachers in a school, are expected to call at the house of mourning, to stay there for a while, to make themselves useful in catering for the many visitors and to attend the funeral. Follow your colleagues' example.

If a close member of your *amah's* family has passed away, it will be taken as an act of kindness if you take the girl home (assuming she lives within driving distance).

What to Wear

To 'society funerals', European men wear a suit, white shirt and dark tie. Ladies dress in sombre colours—grey, navy, dark green, etc. Do not wear full black, which is reserved for the bereaved family.

Wear plain, not very bright and fairly old clothes to an ordinary native, Christian or Muslim funeral. Red is out, as is glittery jewellery, new clothes and shoes—the latter for good reason if you are going to follow the coffin to the graveyard!

Pregnant women do not visit a house of mourning. Ring up to express your sympathy and explain that you will not be able to call in your delicate condition.

Chinese Funeral

You learn of deaths in the local newspapers. Pay a brief call at the house on the same day if you can. The place has been taken over by a gang of men dressed in strange clothing—T-shirts with a motto and rather shabby slacks. These are members of the local Benevolent Association, the Chinese version of the undertakers.

They usually serve tea to all comers. Take just a sip, go and shake hands silently with the chief mourner. Do not take children on condolence calls or to funerals.

Funeral visits are very brief, but it will be remembered carefully who came—and who did not!

Leave a card with the undertakers; it may include money. You would not give a donation in the case of a prominent businessman or a family generally known to be rich; send a wreath on the day of the funeral instead.

The cortege leaves the house at a set time, often 2:00 pm, for which reason some East Malaysians will never set out for a trip at exactly 2:00 pm!

If the bereaved family is conservative, its members will be swathed in unbleached calico on the day of the funeral, the grandchildren of the deceased in blue cotton, with pieces of the same cloth wound around their heads. The undertakers' men wear headgear ranging from straw hats to plastic solar topees. The outfits look comical to Western eyes—another good reason why you should never bring your children. You may find it hard to preserve proper dignity yourself!

The cortege proceeds on foot, headed by several lorries carrying bands, drums and amplified recordings of chanted prayers. In some cases the hearse is attached to long strips of unbleached calico and 'pulled' by the undertakers.

In most towns, there is a specific route funerals have to take. Traffic is blocked to allow the deceased a last chance to 'see' the familiar places of his life. Buses are stationed at a certain point and people with drivers have ordered their cars to wait for them there. Vehicles take the mourners to the cemetery.

People who drive their own cars follow the foot procession at a very slow pace. The undertakers paste yellow strips of paper on the windscreen as a sign that the cars belong to the funeral party.

At the burial ground, the immediate family assembles around the ready-dug grave, and the undertakers do their work. Outsiders stand back to show respect for the bereaved.

As the crowd gets ready to leave the cemetery, handkerchiefs with two red threads are distributed to all present. These should be waved over the left shoulder, tied to the wrist or fastened in a buttonhole while quitting this abode of ghosts to prevent any 'undesirables' from following you home!

Get out of your clothes as soon as you get home and take a bath. Some conservative families would feel upset if you attended a party in their house 'fresh from the graveyard'. Try not to schedule any social events on the day of a funeral.

Christian Funeral

Visit the house briefly when you hear of the death. Shake hands with the chief mourner and take a seat for a short while—men with men, women with women. The coffin may be right there on the floor, surrounded by candles or incense burners, covered with a pall.

Many families have a prayer group visiting the house; you could time your call to coincide with prayers. Ring up and ask.

Native Christians are likely to have a meal ready 24 hours a day of which all comers are invited to partake. Make an excuse if you do not want any and just accept a drink. Inquire during your visit when the funeral will be, and leave a condolence card with a donation (depending on the family's social and financial status).

Do not visit the house immediately before the funeral. You will find the wailing harrowing anyway, and it reaches a hysterical crescendo when the coffin is nailed shut prior to its transport to church.

Unless the deceased was a close friend, it is considered sufficient for a foreigner to attend the funeral service in church. Of course, the family will feel very honoured to have you in the house, but in some ways—among *kampong* folk especially—catering to what they imagine are your needs involves them in all sorts of extra trouble. At work, it is customary to collect money to send a wreath to a deceased staff member's funeral.

In some *kampongs*, every relative of the deceased, however remote, is garbed in formless black garments. Others use white or unbleached calico. This would not apply to a mere sympathiser, but you may possibly have a small patch of black cloth pinned to your left sleeve. If you object to this, just say so; in most communities, it is restricted to relatives anyway. You can take it off as soon as you get home.

After the church service, the whole congregation follows the coffin to the graveyard which is usually near the church. Most people hold umbrellas. In the bigger towns, the cemetery is reached by car; you may discreetly turn off the route and go home if you like. Attendance at the interment is not compulsory.

Prayers are read over the grave, the immediate family members lower the coffin and perform the last duties. Bottles or packets of soft drinks are passed around while the grave is being filled in. This is distasteful to many foreigners, whose ideas of funerary decorum are radically different from the East Malaysians'. Make an effort to at least pretend you are drinking; the mourning family would be failing in their duty and lose 'face' if they do not look after the deceased's friends.

At some traditional Dayak funerals, the burial party kill, cook and eat chickens before leaving the graveyard. Graveside refreshments are a non-Christian hangover that has been adapted to modern usage.

Muslim Funeral

Pay a call as soon as you hear of the death. A Muslim funeral is held as soon as possible, usually within 24 hours of the death, so do not delay. A condolence visit may be very brief, but it should be made while the body is still in the house.

Ask a Muslim friend's advice about a condolence card. They are mostly written in Arabic! Enclose a donation unless the family is very wealthy. Put a donation in a plain envelope with your name card if you cannot find an acceptable condolence card.

Shake hands with the chief mourner, saying the word of sympathy, '*Takziah*' (tuck-see-ah). No further speech is needed, nor any special action. On no account should you kiss the widow's cheek! This Western gesture of condolence is considered insulting. Sit with the other visitors for a short while. Conversation should be subdued and solemn; this is not the time for jokes and laughter.

It is not usual for non-Muslims to attend Muslim funerals. Women will not go to the cemetery but remain at home, consoling the widow.

Death Far From Home

It is very seldom that an expatriate dies in East Malaysia. For one thing, a person known to be suffering from a dangerous condition would not be sent to work in the tropics; for another, they are mostly young men and women in the pink of health.

But if it were to happen?

Immediately inform the person's employer, his embassy or high commission and the next of kin. Funeral or transport arrangements have to be made fast; the climate does not permit delay.

It is possible to get a body embalmed and flown home. This is very expensive but it can be done in the bigger centres of East Malaysia. Contact the local hospital or medical department for details.

If the deceased was at least nominally Christian, his remains may be buried in the cemetery of his denomination. East Malaysian churches are prepared to be charitable in such matters; a Baptist or Presbyterian will be granted a resting place in the local Anglican cemetery if there is no other.

There are no undertaker's firms as the West knows them in East Malaysia. The various churches have 'house groups' that assist their own members, but if the deceased was not a regular churchgoer, he or she is not likely to be connected with them. The local expatriate community might find itself in the place of the mourning family, especially if the deceased was unmarried.

If a person died in hospital, a local family would usually take the body home to their own house. With expatriates, this is hardly possible; bodies are kept cool in the hospital morgue until the day of the funeral.

Cremation facilities are found in a few East Malaysian towns. The Hindu and Sikh community sometimes dispose of their own dead in a funeral pyre. It is possible to have a body buried here, and order the remains to be exhumed and transferred to the home country a couple of years later.

GHOSTS AND COMPANY

Most Borneans have a certain belief in ghosts. Not many educated, town-bred folks will admit this, but the *bomoh*, the Malay medicine man, does good business, as does the resident medium in the Chinese temple. His ilk exists under various names up and down Borneo—*dukun, manang, sinseh* and medium.

A person needs protection against his enemies' nasty spells. Love is charmed from an unwilling maiden. The wandering spirit of a sick person is called back to his body. The *bomoh* deals with these and many other troubles. Chinese temples often have a fortune teller who also advises people about lucky and unlucky days. Any number of sophisticated, educated folk pay earnest heed to such warnings.

In everyday life, people take care not to point at things with a finger. Pointing at a person is rude; pointing at the moon or the rainbow is dangerous. If it cannot be avoided, gesture discreetly with the whole hand, or an index finger or thumb bent back. This looks like 'knuckling' rather than pointing, and is acceptable to both people and spirits.

Hunters, fishermen and collectors of jungle produce do not name the object of their quest. Golfers seem to have taken over this reticence of sympathetic magic, making use of all sorts of euphemisms rather than boldly proclaiming their outstanding skills.

Of course there are ghost stories. Few people admit to believing them; few people do not know at least a couple of real hair-raisers. Each government rest house up and down the country is said to have a haunted room. Drivers are warned not to give rides to a person sitting or walking by the roadside late at night, especially near a cemetery. It might be an old man or a young damsel, dimly perceived in the driving rain.

'...so you feel sorry for her and pick her up. But when you get to her house, she isn't in the car any more...' and if the hardy motorist goes to the house the next day, he will meet a weeping old woman who informs him that her daughter, answering exactly to the description of his vanished passenger, died three years ago on that day. She is buried in the cemetery near where he met her.

In the jungle, ghosts are numerous and dangerous. Some are after men's lives, or worse than death, their genital organs. Some ghosts fly through the air as disembodied heads, others look quite friendly and of course beautiful until one gets too close. One for the connoisseurs is a head that seems to be wearing a red scarf around its neck—but look again! It's a long, long tongue wrapped this way for convenient storage when not in use.

Worst of the lot is the *hantu buau*, a human body without a head, a not unnatural phenomenon in a region where headhunting was rife until the late 19th century. The warrior's conscience haunted him with the wraiths of his victims, lying unburied in the bloodstained undergrowth.

On a more harmless level, it is unlucky to comment on a pleasant smell while out in a boat or on a jungle trek, especially the scent of unseen flowers. Strong-smelling foods may not be brought into some parts of the jungle; a travelling party, however tired or hungry, will not stop to bivouac in areas considered 'unsafe' by the local guide.

A foreigner on a jungle tour need not take any unusual precautions. Simply follow the example of the old hands, refrain from making unnecessary noise and do not discuss the purpose of the party if the others do not.

It is easy to be educated and superior and declare superstitious beliefs to be silly. Few locals will enter into a dispute on the topic with a foreigner; neither will they think very highly of one who brashly ridicules what he does not understand.

'Things that Go Thump in the Night'

Ghosts in the jungle are one thing; you would not like them in your own house.

Young children who spend much time in the company of servants are likely to be entertained with ghost stories. For good reason—children are supposed to be more biddable,

and above all never stray out of sight of their adult protector, if they are terrified of every creaking floorboard!

No Western mother will approve of this kind of obedience training. She can forbid the servant to tell scary stories to the children, and she can make a point of always putting them to bed herself for it is at bedtime that ghoulies flourish.

Apart from what Timah comes up with, there may sometimes be strange noises in the night. If they are caused by ghosts, the judicious application of crucifixes, holy water, incense or charms are recommended. Your friendly neighbourhood *bomoh* will be only too pleased to advise you.

But you may not be so lucky. The disturbance may be due to Bad Hats, Oily Men, *kum-kum* or plain thieves.

Bad Hats
Professional thieves are said to have worn distinctive headgear in long-ago imperial China. This may be so; all that remains today is the expression 'bad hats' to describe the shady elements of town life.

There is a firm belief in South-east Asia that bad hats are part and parcel of life. One just has to put up with them.

Letters to the editor of a major Malaysian newspaper complained of a veritable epidemic of housebreaking and theft in one area of the capital a few years ago. Intruders were seen at dusk climbing about on the roofs of terrace houses, choosing their next 'job' at leisure. Did the victims report to the police before they wrote to the papers? No way—"We don't want to get into trouble with those bad hats!" is the standard answer.

The typical 'bad hat' is not a violent robber but a thief, who will usually flee if confronted. If strange noises are heard at night, ring the police, then turn on every light within reach. 'Bad hats' do not want to be recognised and later identified; shootouts between cops and robbers almost inevitably involve drugs. A man who knows he faces a certain death penalty if apprehended is less squeamish than one bent upon stealing a video recorder.

Oily Man (Orang Minyak)

If it isn't 'bad hats', it is an 'oily man'. He does his work under cover of semi-spiritual protection; opinion is sharply divided as to whether an *orang minyak* is actually a ghost, a man possessed or a straight-out thief. He is supposed to be naked and smeared with oil to evade the grasp of would-be captors.

The oily man's state of undress makes him a great favourite among women, of course. If there is a rumour of *orang minyak* around a neighbourhood, any unusual noise at night will reduce the entire female population to a state of shrieking hysteria. This makes work easy for the casual thief. He whacks a piece of wood against the side of a house, waits until the screaming volume has reached a satisfactory level, and then conducts a quick raid through an open window or verandah.

Kum-kum

The *hantu kum-kum* is a variation of the above, a ghost out to entice females for purposes of blood sucking. Not just any woman—a virgin.

Could an unmarried female of whatever age admit to not being terrified of the *kum-kum*? Obviously not. A few noises outside a house after dark are all that are needed to make it a very safe job for any thief with a little imagination and the musical talent to croon '*kum-kum, kum-kum*'! School boarding houses and nurses' homes are the *kum-kum's* favourite stomping grounds.

Headhunters

A real Borneo special is the headhunter. A rumour has to be started first, and here folklore can draw on the well-attested fact that in the old days, there were headhunters in Borneo, and a human head was needed to support the pillars of a new longhouse or a lofty burial pole.

When major public works are under way—a big bridge, a really tall building, a large dam—a headhunter scare may paralyse the entire area. Villages and bazaars are deserted before nightfall. Families bolt and barricade themselves indoors. Should there be an odd noise outside, nobody would dream of going out to investigate.

As for calling the police...

SETTLING DOWN

CHAPTER 5

'The Chinese houses of the Bazaar are decorated
with coloured porcelains; one sees green dragons,
pink lotuses, little gods and goddesses all along their fronts.
The roofs are of red tiles, some of these being higher
than the rest, reaking the line and making it
more picturesque. Behind the Bazaar rise a succession of
hills, on which are situated bungalows surrounded
by pleasant gardens of flowers and fruit.'
—Description of Kuching c.1880, by Ranee Margaret Brooke

WELL, HERE YOU ARE IN BORNEO! You have taken a few strolls to familiarise yourself with the sights and sounds of your new home town. You have buried yourself in books and enrolled for classes to learn the language which will enable you to make friends with the fascinating people you can so far only look at.

Now is the time for you to build your own base, your home for a few years. Maybe a house awaits you, furnished and staffed; maybe you will embark on an exciting round of house-hunting and house-choosing.

HOUSE-HUNTING

In the larger centres of East Malaysia and Brunei, housing is not a problem. Foreign professionals are usually quartered in accommodation provided by their employer, in anything from villas to superior bungalows. Next on the list are semi-detached houses, then terrace houses or link houses, four to six apartments built in a row. Apartments and flats in the Western sense of the term are becoming more common in the towns; young Malaysians are discovering the charm of a home that doesn't need lawn-cutting and hedge-trimming!

Some families have to look for their own accommodation. Do not be hasty and rush into the first set of walls with a roof that is on offer! Shop around and ask colleagues and friends about how much a house of this or that type would cost. 'The expat on his own' is a sitting duck for eager estate agents;

unlike another rash purchase, house rent is something you continue paying every month till your stay is up!

Most towns of East Malaysia are coastal or riverine. Low-lying areas may be subject to tidal or flash floods. Find out about such things, as well as the distance from the mosque (morning prayers are audibly chanted at the crack of dawn) and the nearest school (three traffic jams a day).

Single expatriates, especially if they are managers of large companies, may be amazed at the size of the house they are allotted and the lifestyle they are expected to keep. Company custom determines the amount of entertaining the man on the spot has to do. The company usually has a local officer whose duty is to advise his boss on such matters.

Flats

Bachelors of both genders often prefer to live in a flat. This is not necessarily cheaper, but many details of housekeeping and gardening will be taken care of by the management of the premises. Some, but not all, flats have servants' quarters attached. Depending on the rental agreement, there may be a washing machine, dishwasher etc; air-conditioning is standard in all new buildings. In the larger towns, laundromats are becoming increasingly popular.

Owners of luxury flats like foreign tenants because they are generally considered to be careful, and 'they help to keep the place looking nice!'

In most blocks of flats, there is a tenants' association that one is expected to join. This is in the occupant's own interest; it gives him an official say in problems like who cleans the staircases, plumbing, rubbish disposal and security arrangements. These necessities of life do not come by themselves!

House Size

Most foreigners find the houses in this part of the world large. Large, not necessarily commodious: the old Sarawak government bungalow is a charming, naturally-ventilated house set in spacious grounds, but it has only two bedrooms. Bedrooms big enough to hold parties in, each with a bathroom attached, perhaps even with dressing rooms. But still only two! These houses were built with the old-fashioned expatriate officer in mind, a crusty bachelor, or else Mr and Mrs, and room for a guest. The children would be in boarding school overseas.

A crop of new houses has sprung up within the last 30 years. Many of them are specifically built for rent: showy edifices, fully air-conditioned, pink marble bathrooms, the latest in artistic roof design and to hell with a tropical rainfall climate! Flat-top roofs start to let the moisture seep through. Acres of plate glass and gables at all angles trap the rain. And some of these architectural masterpieces are extremely difficult to keep clean!

Older houses, dating from between the wars or the 1950s, are of simpler design but usually solid and practical. They were built in the days before air-conditioning, when extra space meant extra coolness, ceiling fans whirred overhead in the main rooms, wide eaves shaded the outside walls and windows could be left open day and night.

Comfortable though they are, space and open windows have their drawbacks. If the house is anywhere near a road, there will be dust and traffic noise. If it is near trees, there will be insects. Older houses usually have all the windows screened to keep out mosquitoes. Swinging screens open like a set of windows; others slide on metal frames, but the odd mozzie still finds its way in!.

Bathrooms

The newcomer to Malaysia is struck by the number of bathrooms. Two are the minimum for a modern house, many have three or more. The master bedroom has its own en-suite bath, another serves the children's or guest rooms. There is always a bathroom near the kitchen; larger houses have an outside one for the 'outdoor staff'. In many houses, the downstairs bathroom was designed for washing clothes, by hand, by an *amah* who squatted before a running tap and scrubbed garments with a brush, one by one!

Washing machines are available, but in the older houses they may have to be put in strange places, including the back porch. Only the new houses have a laundry in the Western sense of the word.

It is specially mentioned in a house advertisement if there is a 'long bath' (bathtub). The common way to get clean and refreshed is by shower.

Traditional Baths

The shower is but a modern version of the old jar-and-dipper method, still seen in upcountry houses. Where piped water is not available, there is a *tankee* in the bathroom, a tile or cement tank or a huge ceramic vessel known as a 'Shanghai jar' or 'tong'. The *tankee* is often connected to the roof spout to collect rainwater.

There is a dipper near the water container, a coconut shell on a handle, or plastic ladle that looks like a small saucepan. Standing on the floor (sometimes on a wooden 'grille'), the bather pours water over himself till he is thoroughly cooled down. Next comes the soap, maybe a backbrush, then more cold water. There is a floor drain in a corner through which all the spilt water flows out.

Hot water is usually available in towns, seldom upcountry, though it is easy enough in this climate to manage without.

Conservative Chinese believe that health in the tropics depends on a prolonged cold sluicing in the early hours of the morning. Floods of water are required for this ritual followed by toothbrushing and gargling, accompanied by spitting, retching and coughing. If a traveller in an upcountry rest house is woken up by the sounds of a surfacing whale or a bathing buffalo at the crack of dawn, he can roll over and go back to sleep. That bathroom will not be free for a while yet!

The water tank in the bathroom is not for bathing in! There is a story of a travelling foreigner who arrived at the outstation rest house hot and dusty, was shown to his room and invited to have a bath. With a sigh of content did he lower himself into the *tankee*, quite prepared to 'rough it' in cold water. He soaped himself thoroughly and finally pulled the plug, letting the establishment's entire water supply gush down the drain!

This clumsy fellow has a twin in the Malaysian student in Australia who got off his plane late at night and was taken home by the local family he had been invited to stay with. He saw the long bath, but decided it was too late for anything but a quick wash—which he proceeded to take, right there on the floor, using the toothbrush cup to dip water from the tap all over himself...

Culture shock comes in many shapes and forms!

Kitchen

Older specimens of our abodes of gracious living have only a pantry in the house. The kitchen is 'below'—outside and linked to the main house by a covered passageway. Dishes have to be carried up to the house, and we still hear stories of cheeky monkeys or even birds that used to steal food *en passant*.

But this is the 21st century. The older houses have been adapted, and new ones inevitably have a proper kitchen on the ground floor. Electric and microwave cookers are available everywhere; gas stoves are fed with bottled gas except in places such as Miri where natural gas is tapped and piped throughout the town. Some cooks like to keep a couple of charcoal stoves handy for speciality dishes and in case of an emergency. They are useful to have on hand, but few people use them for everyday cooking.

When inspecting a house, turn on all switches, taps, etc. A tenant may find she has a shiny new stove in her kitchen but the oven does not work.

Servant Quarters

Behind or, if the site permitted, slightly below the older houses were the servants' quarters: three bedrooms, kitchen and bathroom. The ideal household staff consisted of a cook married to the driver, upper housemaid married to the gardener and a maid of all work who slept with the children in the third room.

Few modern houses have servants' quarters. If they do, it may just be one '*amah's* room' near the kitchen and the downstairs bathroom.

Nobody says you have to employ servants. They are available, however, and they can be a boon.

SERVANTS

Kuching housewives, foreign and local, agree that it is easy to find a servant, but very hard to find a good one. This is true for all parts of Borneo—for all parts of the world, I should say!

Today's 18 to 20-year-old girl has been to school. *Kampong* mothers complain that once a daughter has been educated, she will not do housework any more. She prefers to find a job less restrictive of personal freedom; something as low-status as farm work is out too. Factories are numerous in the main centres, and their preferred workforce is female. In Borneo, as elsewhere, girls are paid less than boys!

There are two ways of finding a servant:

- Contact one of the employment agencies in town (some are specially devoted to the recruitment of domestic help).
- Ask a friend's servant if she has a sister/cousin/friend who would like to work for you.

Domestic servants in East Malaysia are not the servile knee-crawling type, but they do regard their employers in *loco parentis*, as you will find out once she has begun confiding her problems to you.

Using an Employment Agency

The vast majority of domestic servants are recruited from other countries, particularly Indonesia and the Philippines. Depending on which part of the country they come from, such workers speak a fair amount of English. They are usually recruited on contracts of one or two years, so the problem of an unscheduled trip to the home *kampong* will not come up. If maid and mistress get on well, this is a wonderful arrangement; if they do not, well, there you are—stuck with a contract for two years!

The employment agency may have a small number of local girls on its books. Girls who register with general employment agencies, however, usually hope to find 'a job in an office'. The entire female population seems to have failed a typing examination or taken a computer course at one stage of their life! Failing an office job, they want to work in a factory or a 'food court' as the larger coffee shops are called. If they accept a household position, it is as a stopgap until something of higher prestige comes along. The girl is likely to spend a lot of time on the telephone, chatting with friends, looking for better employment.

This is not an absolute rule, of course. A girl can earn RM 400 working for a friendly mistress in a pleasant house, board and lodging provided free. In an office, she would get no more than that as a junior clerk, and still have to rent a room and pay for her food.

In some towns, employment agencies are listed in the phone book, elsewhere you have to find out through the morning coffee grapevine.

There is considerable red tape involved in getting a domestic servant if she is from outside the country. Work permit rules being what they are, it is almost impossible to import such a worker 'freelance'; the registered employment agencies do all the paperwork and the employer pays for the service. It is a good idea to shop around employment agencies a little and ask resident compatriots for advice. Some agencies allow for a 'trial period' of one or two months, at the end of which employer or employee can opt out if they find they don't get along with each other. The agency will then provide another worker, usually as part of the same package.

The Friend/Relative of a Friend's Helper
Finding a servant through a friend's helper is sometimes possible. The pitfall is that the girl may be eager to please her mistress and her mistress' friend, and press a basically unwilling cousin into presenting herself. On the other hand, a helper of long standing would be an excellent judge of her younger relatives' capacity in the field.

Trusty and True?
Are Borneo servants honest? It is impossible to answer yes or no. Certainly there are a few who steal things lying around the house, and some who have boyfriends in the shady parts of society. Some people in Sabah will not employ a Filipina because 'she is sure to be in cahoots with the illegal

immigrants' (a distressing number of 'illegals' are involved in violent crime), whether or not this is true!

What protection has the householder got?

Tell her at the first interview that you do not wish her to use the phone, or publicise your phone number—of course this is very hard to enforce!

If there is a constant succession of phone calls for the girl from different men, it might mean she is involved in something you would not like. It may also mean she has a very active social life. In either case, she is not the girl you should leave alone in charge of the home a lot.

If the girl was recruited through an agency, these rules can be discussed with the agent and the worker together.

Language in the Kitchen

The language problem creeps into most things in Borneo. It will certainly do so in domestic affairs. In Kalimantan, the employer must make every effort to learn Bahasa Indonesia. In Sabah, Brunei and Sarawak, girls who have been to school a few years know a certain amount of English. Even so, it prevents misunderstanding if the housewife knows enough Malay to make herself clearly understood.

Encourage the helper to use cookery books (in whichever language she can read), starting with very simple recipes where not much can go wrong. Read through the recipe with her first, and make sure she really understands and that all ingredients are ready at hand.

One of the basic sources of misunderstanding between expats and locals is just this: if a person does not understand what you say or write, she will not ask. This is from a sense of respect. In the case of a household helper, a friendly attitude on your part will encourage her to query things that are not clear. Recipe books are a good place to start, because they are impersonal. Nobody will lose face if something is a bit hazy—how many ounces to a gill?

West Malaysian ladies will discover fairly soon that Hokkien as spoken in Penang or Malacca is not the same as the Eastern variant. The finer points had better be settled in Malay. The names of foodstuffs, particularly fish, are different in East and West, too.

Japanese ladies, a close-knit group in most East Malaysian and Brunei places, usually help each other find domestic servants. A local girl who has been with a Japanese family for a few years has learned something of the ways, cooking and household routine of her employers. She will be a blessing to a newcomer; in families with children, the helper often picks up a smattering of Japanese.

Black-and-white *Amahs*

Black-and-whites, so called because they wore loose black trousers and white blouses, were women who migrated from China in search of work from 1900 until 1949. Many of them were married, and they sent most of their earnings home. Others, their single status displayed by a long plait hanging down their backs (instead of a married woman's chignon), preferred a career to marriage.

Liberated women before the word was invented! Tales about the fidelity, resources, ingenuity and untiring industry of the black-and-whites still abound, together with samples of their wit and sass. In a well-ordered household, the *amah* employed the lower servants, was trusted with the housekeeping money and kept the driver usefully employed when he was not actually driving. One driver was trained by the resident black-and-white to knead the dough for daily supplies of homemade bread!

The mistress could ring her home from an afternoon tea she was attending and inform the *amah* that there would be five guests for dinner, at eight o'clock. One question: "Can take pork?" The meal would be ready on the dot, beautifully served with silver and crystal in all the right places, neatly adapted to the guests' dietary and religious preferences.

Those were the black-and-whites, called *amahs* as a badge of distinction. The modern term for domestic servant is 'helper'.

GOD'S CREATURES, GREAT AND SMALL

A New Yorker quartered in a Sarawak longhouse for a few months marvelled that the cockroaches there were '*almost as big as the ones in my flat at home!*'

Foreign ladies with less nerve or humour go into hysterics over rats and mice, beetles, insects and reptiles of various kinds. While nobody recommends these as house pets, it is accepted that your house may have occupants that you know nothing of—and do not want to know.

Except for snakes, they are basically harmless. There are pest exterminators to call in if needed, but one soon develops a cool detachment about unscheduled housemates. You can ask your landlord to get rid of all or any of the creatures mentioned below. He will make soothing noises and not do anything much about them. There is one exception: termites.

Inside the rooms, termites appear as grey, dusty, flat, longish sort of hulls, not unlike sunflower seed husks, stuck to the wall here and there. If observed for a while, a yellowish head is seen emerging; at a sharp noise or vibration, it disappears.

Inform the landlord if any of these are seen around the place and you will be amazed at the speed with which he leaps into action. Termites can destroy his house!

Insects

Even in the most modern, up-to-date house, bugs and ants are found. A R Wallace, who travelled the region extensively in the 1850s, complains of 'four or five kinds of ants that attack everything not isolated by water, and one which will even swim'.

The good doctor was being conservative. In a house surrounded by fruit trees, you may meet 15 kinds, including one ant so tiny it will get into what you thought was an airtight biscuit tin.

Such pests are less numerous in fully air-conditioned houses. Seldom-worn clothing, the master's good suit for instance, is best put away with mothballs. The dangerous beast is not the moth, but the cockroach.

Wall-to-wall carpet, today's *non plus ultra* in tropical luxury, is the ideal breeding ground for bugs of all kinds. Lift a corner of the carpeting when inspecting a house! Some kitchens do not have cupboards under the sink to obviate another famous insect and mildew breeding place. Besides ants, beetles, and more harmless creepy-crawlies, there is the occasional centipede or scorpion.

Snakes, Scorpions and Centipedes

Yes there are snakes in Borneo, and yes they may be met with in town areas, but they are quite rare. One story of one snake can make the rounds long enough to give the appearance of a reptilian invasion!

Snakes, scorpions and centipedes, if they are found in the house, have usually gained access through the floor drains in the bathrooms. These drains have slatted metal covers to keep out such unwelcome intruders, but they do not always do their duty.

Confronted with a beast in the house, most women panic. For some reason, snakes always turn up when the husband is out of town! Servants may be of use, but are likely to do nothing more constructive than scream: '*Ular! Ular!*' (Snake! Snake!) A gardener or any man within shouting distance will usually come to the rescue if called in. He brings a stick, corners the offending beast and crushes it. In the case of a snake, he will pin it down by the neck just behind the head and break its top vertebra (this sounds easy, but it's not!). There is a slight possibility that the gardener, though willing, cannot kill a snake because his wife is pregnant and he is thus under a taboo. Ask him to get help elsewhere; it is unlikely that all the gardeners and drivers in the entire street are expectant fathers!

What if there is no man anywhere? The housewife will have to do the same thing herself. Here is a practical hint: most snakes dislike noise, and can be screamed and drummed out of the house. Just deploy your forces with some thought, leaving the exit route visible and open, or you will drive the reptile into a hiding place in the house!

It is not a good idea to spray insecticide on centipedes and scorpions. Of course it will kill them in due time, but their immediate reaction is to hide. They can hide in incredibly narrow cracks, and you will not know whether the crawly visitor has perished at last, or is still lurking.

Do not tackle snakes on your own unless you absolutely have to. Ring a neighbour, the local council, the police, and ask for help; the general emergency number is 991.

Some snakes are poisonous. Cobras are occasionally found in or around houses and they not only bite but also spit venom. This can blind a dog that barks at the intruder and gets too close! Cobras do have mates. If one has been killed near your house, watch out for a second one within a few days.

Bats in the Belfry

Many houses are inhabited in ways the occupant does not think of. There may be mice or rats, often not quartered aboard but climbing up water pipes at dusk to spend a merry evening above the ceiling boards. A cat in the house will keep them within bounds.

There are *cikcaks*, house lizards which make a funny clicking sound and catch insects. They also drop dry little pellets all over the place. Cicadas fly near the outside lamps once in a while. They are perfectly harmless, but look gruesome and make a shrieking noise. Naughty boys like to catch and squeeze them to scare their sisters.

Some houses have birds' nests under the eaves, some in the roof, and that is where bats may be found. They are not vampire bats! Fruit bats, apart from undisciplined digestive systems, are the quietest housemates you could wish for. A smaller, insectivorous kind should be encouraged to settle: each little bat eats about 3000 insects a night!

For those interested in mysterious Eastern medicine, bat steamed with seven herbs and Chinese wine is said to be good for asthma.

Dogs

Some foreign families 'inherit' a dog that goes with the house. If the animal seems in good health and is of acceptable temper, there is nothing wrong with that. A dog is very useful to give you notice of intruders and loiterers; small-time thieves are discouraged by canine attention.

Children are often offered puppies by a kind, well-meaning friend. Of course they do not say 'no', and the parents risk being regarded as monsters if they object to a cute, cuddly addition to the family.

Veterinary Service

The veterinary service of the Agriculture Department runs a pet clinic in most towns. If you keep pets, find out where the place is, and when it is open. It may be only a couple of hours daily.

There are private veterinary clinics in the main towns. These are more expensive, but their hours are much longer;

sophisticated medicine and equipment are available and the doctor has more specialised knowledge of small animals. The government vet's job is the protection of farm livestock; pussies and doggies are a frill!

Both private and government vets will neuter pets. Considering the gross dog and cat overpopulation of East Malaysian towns, and the difficulties encountered in disposing of even the sweetest kittens (your friends like a generous gift of kittens to their children about as much as you do!), householders are urged to have their pets spayed. When your stint here is up and the time comes to say goodbye to Rover and Kitty, a neutered pet is much easier to find a new home for than a happily reproducing one!

The government or private vet will put unwanted pets 'to sleep' at nominal charge.

Strays

Stray dogs in certain areas band together into howling packs. They are usually not dangerous, but unhygienic and noisy. Try sleeping with 30 dogs baying at the moon!

Local councils have dog catchers. They collect stray animals impounded by householders if the council (Public Health Department) is notified. They also go on raiding expeditions, though the dogs usually run a lot faster than the catchers. Sick or wounded animals should be caught and destroyed. If one is lingering around your area, inform the local council.

Few foreigners like the way animals are treated in Southeast Asia. It is not often outright cruelty, just indifference and negligence. To a suffering animal, it feels the same, of course.

There is an SPCA both in Sarawak and Sabah, and in Brunei. It is always short of volunteer helpers. Here is a challenge for a capable housewife with time on her hands to be involved in something meaningful!

WHAT TO BRING FROM HOME

"All essentials are easily available in East Malaysia," we say blithely, not always aware of who considers what essential.

Basic Electrical Items

Electrical household goods, radios, TV sets, CD and DVD players, still and video cameras, computers, digital equipment etc can be bought in any of the larger towns. People from New Zealand and Australia consider them cheap, especially in Labuan, which is a free port. Americans find them expensive. The current here is 210–240V, which means electrical equipment from the United States or Canada cannot be used unless a transformer is installed.

Hobby Paraphernalia

Camera buffs find that basic equipment is sold everywhere, but accessories may be hard to find.

Hobby photographers used to processing their own films are advised to stock up on chemicals and paper to keep them going for a few months. Since the takeover of digital photography, the stuff is getting hard to find! Photo shops will order things for customers from Singapore or Kuala Lumpur, but that takes time. If you intend to rig up a darkroom in the spare bathroom, give careful thought to the climate. Water comes out of the tap at over 20°C, which will affect development times. (I measured it for Kuching: 26°C at 9:00 am in July.)

Within a small, tightly enclosed space, the air will become incredibly hot in a very short time. Can you afford to install air-conditioning or another effective form of ventilation that will not let in light? Working on negatives with sweaty hands is difficult, loading a film into a developer tank is impossible!

Other hobbyists do well to bring along a few months' supply of what they need, be it a particular kind of super glue, spare parts for miniature engines or special lacquer paints. You will eventually ferret out where in East Malaysia these can be bought, but do not drop a favourite hobby because you ran out of some essential ingredient. Find the local association that unites fellow enthusiasts, and you will be let into the secret of where to get what.

Needlework enthusiasts will find embroidery circles, quilting bees and a wide selection of fabrics, threads, notions and other paraphernalia. Only dress patterns are in short supply, probably because there are so many good dressmakers around.

Furniture

Transporting furniture is expensive and slow, though some people coming on long-term contracts prefer to bring their own.

Consider that insects, mildew and climatic influences may spoil your heirloom pieces; perfectly adequate furniture is available in East Malaysia. The latest style is rattan cane, often fancifully plaited and moulded, and elegantly styled rubberwood furniture.. Many foreigners take home a set when they return to their own countries, convinced that they would never get it so cheap there.

The everyday stuff available in the local shops is not of top quality workmanship or design. It is serviceable, meant for use more than beauty. If you move into furnished quarters, you may find the furniture and fittings beautiful or awful—there is no accounting for tastes! But it is not generally considered economical to import such large articles from overseas.

PHONE BOOK

Spend half an hour with the phone book and an English-Malay dictionary sometime early in your stay.

The East Malaysian telephone directories, one for Sabah and one for Sarawak, share a few peculiarities. Each is divided into government departments and private subscribers. It is with the former that newcomers have their little troubles—as indeed do most locals.

For instance, where would you look for The Sarawak Hospital? Under H in the English index? It's under Health Department, pages 5–6, in the separate 'Government Departments and Statutory Bodies Sarawak' index. This index is quite useful if you have time in your hands. For instance, why has Kuching got two city councils, of which one is listed under 'Local Authorities', and the other is not? If you've got a serious problem like a landslide in your backyard, you might need a relevant emergency services number fast!

Compile a Phone List

This is why we recommend that a newcomer spends a couple of hours—better still an afternoon—with this absorbing book, a dictionary, a notepad and a pencil. Search for the numbers you are likely to need and note them down.

In the main towns of East Malaysia, the emergency call for Police and Ambulance is 999, for Fire Brigade 994, and general emergency 991. Ring the number and request the service you need. Have your best Malay ready for making a brief report; the person at the other end may or may not understand English. Do not forget to give your exact address, directions to your house if necessary and your phone number.

One useful number to know is 103 (9103 in upcountry areas) in both Sabah and Sarawak. This is the Directory Inquiry. The telephone system is being improved all the time, which means wholesale changing of numbers up and down the country. If you have trouble getting a number, ring 103 and ask, "Has 72463 been changed?" and they will tell you the new number if it has. They will also give you listed numbers if you know the correct name of the subscriber. 103 will give you the other service numbers, such as Telegram, Fault Repair, Overseas Calls etc. (See the Resource Guide at the back of this book for more useful telephone numbers.)

A word of warning. It is pointless to ask 103 for the number of Mrs Tan. There are pages of Tans in the book! 'Bill Tan' will not get you much further; you have got to know his full Chinese name, William Tan Chung Ek.

DRIVING

The drivers' licences of most Commonwealth countries are valid in Malaysia. An International Drivers' Licence is acceptable. Anyone over 18 in possession of a valid licence may drive a car.

Cars do not need a warrant of fitness. They must have their road tax paid up to date (a disc, which must be visibly displayed in the windscreen) and third-party insurance. Road tax is paid at the Road Transport Department.

There are traffic lights and zebra crossings which suggest the drivers should stop...maybe. The rule of thumb is that after the lights turn red, three more cars can whizz through. There are white lines on the road, broken, single and double; there are yellow lines along the sides, yellow grids in intersections. These add colour and beauty to the East Malaysian landscape, and that is all they do. One seldom sees yellow lines along the roads in the congested inner-town areas. It is not because they are not there, but because they are solidly parked over with stationary vehicles.

Driving in Malaysia

There is a story about a taxi driver in Manila who drove through every red light, ignoring his foreign passenger's anxious protests. But when the cab came to a green light—slam!—on went the brakes, sending the passenger hurtling forward.

"What did you do that for?" the shaken tourist asked.

Answered the cabbie, "You think I want to be hit by some idiot running the red light from the other side?"

Nobody in East Malaysia drives like this of course...for all we know the story is told in Manila about a Kota Kinabalu taxi. But the general Malaysian standard of driving, if not murderous, is not very high.

A foreign driver out for the first time should not try to cruise at his customary speed unless he is alone on the road. An East Malaysian is not sissy enough to blink indicator lights. He will turn left or right or change lanes any time of the day without any sign of any kind. The circular traffic carousels, useful enough if everybody enters and exits in the correct lane, are a constant snarl of left-turning drivers on the right side and right-turning drivers on the left.

What all this means in practical terms is:

'Give way even if you do not have to according to the Highway Code. You may be in the right, but court cases take an awfully long time around here!'

Drivers involved in collisions may get abusive, in some cases violent. Insist that the police be called, and make a proper report. Small damages are often settled 'out of court'; cases which have to be tried are likely to be lengthy affairs.

PUBLIC TRANSPORT

There are buses in all the towns of Borneo. They are divided into 'urban buses' in the towns, and 'upcountry buses' serving the rural areas as far as the roads reach.

With a certain amount of research and cunning, it is possible for the non-resident to find out which bus to take. They are usually numbered; what is missing is information about which bus goes where, how and when.

Before entering a bus, ask the driver or conductor, "Does this bus go to Piasau?" If the reply is negative, ask, "Which number goes to Piasau?" If they understand, they will tell you. Fees are not very high so you would not be badly out of pocket if you got into the wrong bus and landed at the other end of town. On the other hand, you may have wasted a few hours waiting for the next bus to take you back to the starting point.

In most town buses, there is a conductor who sells tickets once the bus is in motion. Toddlers ride free, while children and students in uniform pay less. In case of a dispute, there is a measuring gauge near the steps. If the youngster stands taller than the 'free' mark, he pays half; if he exceeds the 'half-price', he pays a full fare.

It has been rumoured that there are timetables governing the urban buses, but, like all rumours, this one is difficult to verify. Bus drivers have their own, very individualistic ideas on the topic.

Vans are used as buses in most parts of East Malaysia; some of these are registered and licensed as can be seen by their white number plates and yellow roofs, others are not. The general public doesn't seem to mind whether it is a lawful van or a 'pirate bus', as long as it gets them home in time.

River and Rural Travel

Towns on a river usually have *sampans* to take passengers across the water. Even if there is a motor bridge, pedestrians like to cross from *kampong* to *kampong*. River ferries may be motorised or rowed. The fare is paid upon alighting; in Kuching, 30 cents are discreetly deposited on the miniature foredeck. These *sampans* may be hired for private river cruises at RM 30–50 per hour (as of January 2006), upon mutual agreement.

Rural or 'upcountry' buses depart from a bus station somewhat out of town, known locally as the 'midnight bus stop' because many overland buses travel at night. It is a good idea to ask a day or so beforehand which bus will leave when, and reserve a seat if possible. They are usually very crowded, not just with passengers but with their movable property and livestock. Do not ever sit on a fighting cock!

The overland or express bus is air-conditioned, and will run more or less to schedule. It is likely to have in-trip entertainment in the form of taped music, played at top volume. A trip can take 12–14 hours, an endurance test for those without the foresight to bring ear plugs or cotton wool.

The rural passenger bus stops where there is anybody standing by the roadside, or when somebody wishes to alight. The rolling stock is in less than pristine condition. The seats may be wooden boards laid across metal supports—for good reason. If a passenger brings a few sacks of *padi*, a generator, or a man-sized basket full of durian, how could he stow them if the seats did not conveniently lift up?

Passenger buses provide the foreign traveller with a real 'slice of local life' experience, and possibly lumbago or sciatica the next day. Some of Borneo's rural roads aren't up to much, though the trunk road is generally in good condition.

SERVICES

Water and electricity are available in all East Malaysian and Bruneian towns. Find out on which day the meter reader is likely to turn up, and chain your dogs if they are playful. The man may be Muslim and consider the touch of a canine defiling; regardless of religion, he won't like to be bitten!

Urban households are supplied with a green 'wheely-bin' for rubbish. Ask the neighbours on which days rubbish is collected, and have your bin ready. Because of stray dogs, it is a good idea to keep it inside your gate, and put it outside only when the collectors approach.

If there is no rubbish collection in your road, ring up the health department of the local council and find out why. It is listed under Majlis Perbandaran for Kuching, Sibu, Miri, Labuan, Tawau and Kota Kinabalu; Majlis Daerah or

Majlis Daerah Luar Bandar for the district towns of Sabah and Sarawak.

BILLS

Water, power and phone bills can be paid at their respective offices, or at the post office. If the last is chosen (it is usually the easiest to find), look for the SBBS counter; the queue is likely to be long. If you pay at the post office, the cheque must be made out to the Director of Posts; cash is acceptable and probably easier. Some banks accept payments for utility bills, or have arrangements for paying them online.

BANKS

Cheques have not quite caught on yet in East Malaysia. Many shops will not accept one unless the shopkeeper personally knows the person who signs it.

Some expatriates have found it difficult to start cheque accounts. They are asked to furnish references, guarantors and the like, not to ask for an overdraft, only to open a humble account with unimpeachable traveller's cheques and bank drafts!

There have been some sinister rumblings in Malaysian banking circles a few years ago; it is possible that some of the more conservative local banks are determined not to lose a penny through trusting anyone too much! Be aware that names used in banking transactions must correspond with names on the person's passport or identity card; an Elizabeth Smith may have trouble with a cheque made out to Betty Smith!

The Post Office Savings Bank is open to depositors of all nationalities. It certainly is the bank with the most branches throughout Malaysia. Credit cards are commonly accepted in the hotels and shops of the larger towns.

There are ATMs in the larger shopping centres and in all banks. Most of these can be used to withdraw money from bank accounts overseas.

MAIL

There is mail delivery to most urban areas. Houses are required to have a mailbox that can be reached from outside

the gate or fence. Ask your landlord to attend to this if it is not in order.

When informing friends and relatives overseas of your address, give the post code. It is there for speedier delivery of mail. How long do letters take? Unfortunately, this can be unpredictable. Mail is usually sorted quickly and despatched to the airport; there it ought to go off with the next plane. It probably does, but an unfortunate missive to Kuala Lumpur, under two hours' flying time, can take ten days or it might be there the next day—you cannot be sure.

CLOTHES

East Malaysia's temperatures range between 22–33°C at sea level. It is a little cooler at higher altitudes, where a light blanket is needed at night. In the coastal plains, no more than a cotton sheet is required. Many houses are air-conditioned, a luxury one gets speedily used to, but watch out for an unpleasant climate shock each time there is a power cut!

For everyday wear, light comfortable clothing is recommended. Blouses and skirts, slacks and dresses are fine for ladies. Do not bring too many from overseas as they can be made quite economically here.

Tailor-made

There is an excellent choice of cloth available in the towns: pure cotton and silk, linen, every kind of man-made fibre, the lot. The home dressmaker is advised to bring her own patterns, as none are available here. Many foreign ladies enjoy the service of local dressmakers.

These skilled and versatile craftswomen can turn out any style, from an illustration in a fashion magazine or a sketch. Some work faster than others. The really popular ones may be booked out for some time ahead. All dressmakers have more orders than they can handle in the weeks before Chinese New Year (January/February) or Hari Raya (movable). Some charge more during these festive seasons, so plan your wardrobe replenishments for the slack times.

Men's clothes are made by tailors, most of them very competent workmen. Find one you really get on with, and stick to him!

Off-the-rack

Ready-made clothing is available in shops; so are shoes. The problem here is that many Europeans are larger than the standard Asian sizes, and find it difficult to buy 'off the rack'.

The consensus among Kuching ladies is that you do not need to bring along many clothes from your own country, but you must bring shoes if you take anything larger than a size 6 or 7.

Ladies' foundation garments are not available in sizes bigger than D-cups; DD-cups may be found in Singapore and sometimes in Kuala Lumpur, but it can take some looking around to find the items.

A man will need a suit for formal occasions and dinner parties (most restaurants are air-conditioned to sub-arctic temperatures), and ladies are expected to wear formal gowns, not bare-backed or hanging free, please! The sight of too much female skin does offend some people, and

is considered rude if the governor or any other dignitary is present.

It would be perfectly possible for children to run around naked all day, but this is inadvisable for two reasons:

- Nudity in all but the very smallest children gives offence. Not even *kampong* boys bathe without clothes on any more, and they play in the river wearing shorts, even T-shirts. Visitors and household staff would be upset at the sight of young children playing about naked in an expatriate's house.
- There are some stinging insects around, notably the Painted Fly, which can inflict a very painful and lingering bite. Sloppy overalls and a T-shirt limit the areas where insects may attack, and make them more visible to the child himself.

HEALTH IN THE TROPICS

East Malaysia is not one of the tropical danger zones. With due attention to hygiene and diet, a person may be as healthy here as anywhere on earth.

The common travellers' 'shots' have been suspended for Malaysia. Smallpox is practically eradicated; cholera does break out sporadically but it can be prevented by strict food hygiene. Where this is lacking, no amount of vaccination will help.

Dr E V Haller, one of Germany's foremost specialists in the field of tropical medicine, listed the most common causes of ill health in the tropics as follows: fevers, enteric infections, parasites, skin infections, venereal disease, poisonous bites and stings. He also pointed out that the most common causes of death among Europeans in the tropics are traffic and flying accidents.

Fever

There is no need to take malaria prophylactics in East Malaysia for anyone living in the urban centres.

The medical department carries out regular insect-spraying exercises in areas described as 'hilly, remote and forested, timber camps, recently developed land and plantations'. Any foreigner whose work will take him to such places, especially near the Indonesian border, should take precautions. The prophylactic pills are available from any private doctor or the medical department. Like other preventatives, they must be taken to be of any use. Malaria is much easier to prevent than to cure!

Another mosquito-borne disease does occur in East Malaysia: dengue haemorrhagic fever, carried by a vector that breeds in building sites and badly maintained urban properties. Periodic fogging with insecticide is carried out by the health authorities in affected areas.

If a person suffers from what looks like particularly virulent measles, get a doctor's opinion; it might be dengue.

Vector-borne diseases can be prevented by the use of insect screens on houses, mosquito nets on beds and the use of mosquito repellant on skin and clothing when walking in the jungle. Mosquitoes breed in water, so be sure there are no puddles or water containers anywhere near your house. Larvicide must be sprinkled in water tanks or rainwater barrels.

Mosquito sprays and coils, while beyond a doubt effective, should not be used indiscriminately.

"Of course the stuff kills mosquitoes," a Kuching doctor says. "But it will kill you in the long run, too!" He warns particularly about the poisons' cumulative effects on the liver and kidneys.

Common Cold

To everyone's chagrin, it is perfectly possible to catch a common cold in this part of the world. Treatment is the same as elsewhere, an aspirin or something like it and plenty to drink. A cold is particularly unpleasant in the tropics because it makes one feel even hotter. Resist the temptation to loll in air-conditioned rooms or under a fan! If a cold persists for more than a few days, consult a doctor.

At the time of writing, there are sporadic outbreaks of bird flu in several parts of South-east Asia.

Enteric Infections

Vulgarly known as the gripes, enteric infections are common and preventable. Mothers must insist even more fiercely than in cool climates that children wash their hands thoroughly after visiting the toilet, and before eating. In towns, there is no need to boil drinking water at ordinary times. If there is a cholera scare on, this simple operation will help to preserve peace of mind if nothing else.

Kitchen hygiene must never be relaxed. This applies to the thorough washing of vegetables and fish as well as the prompt and sanitary disposal of refuse. Flies carry germs! Shellfish and crustaceans caught in coastal or brackish waters are best avoided if there is any danger of enteric fevers.

The old-time method of washing vegetables in a weak solution of potassium permanganate has proven inefficient. If there is a serious threat of infection, it is safer not to eat any raw vegetables and fruit except those that can be peeled. A few days' shortage of Vitamin C is preferable to a few weeks of cholera!

There is one use for potassium permanganate: a very weak solution is the ideal cool bath for a person with heat rash. Let a small child splash in it for five minutes, pour it over yourself dipper by dipper-ful, slowly. 'Weak solution' means about five to seven crystals in a baby bath, to tint the water barely pink—unless you want a purple baby!

Parasites

Everybody gets parasites from time to time; there is no shame attached to such infestations. If one of the family has worms, it is a good idea to de-worm the whole lot, servants and all. While you are at it, get the appropriate doses for the cats and dogs from the vet and make a party of it. Vermifuges come in various forms; a pharmacist or doctor may be consulted. Syrups are available for small children.

Contrary to common belief, men are not exempt from intestinal parasites. Bachelors need to pay attention to this aspect of their health, and take a dose if they need one. Fathers of families should set a shining example by taking the bitter pill in front of their (admiring) children!

Skin Infections

The most common skin troubles suffered by expatriates are prickly heat and fungal infections.

These are much more likely on sweaty, poorly-ventilated skin. Cotton or linen clothes should be worn in preference to synthetic fabrics, and sandals instead of shoes wherever permissible. The daily bath may be multiplied. On a hot day, there is nothing wrong with two or three or four showers!

The frequent use of strong soap can destroy some of the skin's protective bacteria, and actually encourage skin fungi. Lather up once a day, in the evening, and use tiny amounts of baby soap for the other baths. Nobody gets really dirty in the tropics, all you have to wash off is sweat.

Sexually Transmitted Diseases (STD)

STD are 100 per cent preventable. The careless are advised to seek medical advice at once if they have contracted one of these infections.

Prostitution is outside the law in Malaysia and Brunei. VD clinics do exist, but there is no compulsion for prostitutes to go for check-ups.

Variously known as 'hostess, bar girl, dancing girl, model, singer, masseuse or barber girl', they ply their trade under no hygienic restraint, though many are 'protected' by small-time criminals and gangsters. Brothels are set up under various respectable fronts; bona fide entertainers, models, hairdressers, waitresses, etc. suffer from the reflected ill fame.

East Malaysia is only just queueing into the international tourist traffic. The untreatable types of STD found in Thailand are not common here, but they do exist, as does AIDS.

Unprotected sex with a strange partner may have fatal results, here as elsewhere. *Caveat emptor*!

Bites and Stings

Snakes have been dealt with in the previous pages. If anybody has been bitten, do not stop to find out the name and address of the reptile, including its markings and the shape of its eyeballs—rush the patient to hospital at once, and leave directions for somebody else to catch and identify the attacker. The doctor treating the patient will want to know what kind of snake it was, but get the victim to hospital first.

Scorpion and centipede stings are best attended to by a doctor too. They are not fatal except in small children, but competent medical attention can prevent a lot of suffering. Stings get inflamed, black and blue, and are very painful.

There are some stinging insects around. One encountered even in well-maintained gardens is the Painted Fly.

The Painted Fly looks like a small moth, grey with bars of bright yellow and black on its wings. The sting gives a burning sensation; eventually it will come up in a nasty boil. After this has been dealt with in the traditional manner (magnesium sulphate ointment hastens 'heading') it will subside, and come up a second time a few weeks later! Regular spraying under shrubs and bushes keeps the Painted Fly at bay.

Medical Services

There are large hospitals in the East Malaysia and Brunei capitals, and district hospitals in each district. In more outlying areas, there are clinics manned by a 'dresser'—as the male hospital assistant, nurse or sister is still called. A Flying Doctor serves the really remote parts.

There is a Mother and Child Health Service with clinics throughout the states, providing health care from prenatal to pre-school. Immunisation given by the MCH and government hospitals is free; private clinics charge moderate rates.

Few foreigners make use of the Government Health Services, except the occasional unscheduled stay in hospital where they would normally be warded as paying first-class patients.

In towns, there are any number of excellent private doctors and dentists. Employers, fellow workers or friends will introduce newcomers to their favourite physician. Doctors are also listed in the *Yellow Pages* under 'Medical Practitioners—Registered'; acupuncturists and Chinese physicians are listed separately.

Many foreigners go to Singapore for regular medical check-ups. There is a Japanese hospital there too.

Home Remedies

Not everything needs emergency surgery, of course. Mothers have their own household remedies for scratches and sore throats; if you are addicted to one particular brand, stock up before leaving home.

There is no shortage of patent medicines in Brunei and East Malaysia. The products of Lever Brothers and other Western pharmaceutical firms are well known here.

Local housewives have their own panaceas. Two readily adopted by newcomers are *minyak angin* and Tiger Balm (consistently called 'Tiger Bum' by my family). The first is a distillation of eucalyptus, the second an ointment containing a strong decoction of camphor. The two are considered to cure all ills, from insect bites to broken hearts—almost.

Minyak angin comes under various brand names. One with an axe on the bottle is called *minyak kapak*, another sports a goldfish and is therefore called *minyak ikan mas*. The stuff is available in tiny bottles which ladies carry in their handbags, schoolboys in their pencil boxes, businessmen in their briefcases, grandmothers in their shopping baskets and soldiers in their rucksacks.

All insect bites call for the application of *minyak angin* or Tiger Balm. For headaches, the stuff is rubbed on forehead and temples. A sore stomach is anointed with the goo, and three drops of *minyak angin* in a glass of hot water are taken to relieve indigestion. Sprains, bruises, anything that does not bleed, may be liberally rubbed with oil or balm. A person who has fainted or vomited is made to smell it, toothache is soothed by rubbing *minyak* or balm on the cheek and even the gum.

The use of either *minyak angin* or Tiger Balm is quite harmless. It will not interfere with other medicines, it is soothing to both patient and amateur nurse, and in many cases it really helps.

One word of caution: it stings like fury if applied to the eyes or sensitive skin areas like mucous membranes!

Keeping Fit

In the tropics and everywhere else, regular exercise of a type suited to the individual is essential for preserving good health. In East Malaysia's towns, there are sports clubs, fitness centres and golf clubs. Even in the most remote *ulu* area, a fellow can go jogging three evenings a week.

Do not overdo it, and do not take violent exercise at midday. Nothing and nobody rushes around in the noonday

heat—the buffalo is in a mud wallow, the dog is under the house and the farmer is in it. No, 'these locals' are not lazy! They have been working since dawn. From 6:00–10:00 am, and again after 3:00 pm, hard physical effort is comfortably possible. Around noon, it is very exhausting.

Exercise at noonday is possible, but not advisable— remember that only 'mad dogs and Englishmen go out in the midday sun'!

A newly arrived foreigner has to be extra careful. Do not start your exercise programme by playing rugby with those who have been acclimatised for a couple of years. You can kill yourself that way!

EDUCATION

The official language of Malaysia is Bahasa Malaysia, now the medium of instruction in all schools; Science and Mathematics are taught in English. A formalised version of Malay, it is generally understood in Indonesia and Brunei, too. Newcomers are advised to learn it.

Evening classes in Bahasa Melayu are generally available, and private tutors can be engaged to coach groups of learners. That is fine for mum and dad. What about the children?

Private Schools

There are English-medium primary schools in Kuching, Brunei, Kota Kinabalu and Miri, some catering exclusively for expatriate children or the staff of specified companies. Such institutions are designated 'private schools' and are supposed to cater for foreign children only. The Lodge Preparatory School in Kuching admits locals, providing an approved course in Bahasa Melayu for them.

Such schools, not receiving any government subsidies, have to be self-supporting and are quite expensive. They charge RM 2000 or more per term (as of january 2006), plus various entry fees, levies and deposits.

Teaching Young Children Their Mother Tongue

Private schools in East Malaysia teach in English. A number of students may be German, French or other Continentals,

Japanese or Korean. How do these children maintain contact with their mother tongue?

Through, as the term implies, the mother. Ladies equip themselves with books appropriate to their children's ages, and teach them at home. This is hard going for both mother and offspring, but "What can we do? These children would never keep up with the Japanese (or Korean, or German, or any other) education system if they had no correct grounding!" as the mother of a pre-schooler and an eight-year-old explains. She spends three to four hours every afternoon teaching her children. The family uses only Japanese for everyday conversation.

Japanese and Korean families sometimes leave primary-age children at home with relatives, to make sure they will not miss out on their education.

Older Children

Private schools usually employ trained and experienced staff; most go up to Form III or V (Year 9 or 11). Parents of older children have to make a difficult decision: do we leave the youngsters in boarding school, or teach them at home?

The full weight of this problem usually rests on the mother. She is the one who will miss a child 'abandoned' thousands of miles off; she is the one whose nerves will be worn to a frazzle by a home-taught teenager who snubs his mother as 'teacher'. If he is taking science subjects, chances are he really does know more about the whole business than she does!

It is impossible to state which is the correct alternative. What suits one teenager is wrong for another; separation that binds one family closer breaks up another. The advice given here is meant as a guideline to help a family make this difficult choice. It is not intended to make it for them.

- Talk it over with the child first.
  He will not appreciate being haggled over by all his relations before he himself is consulted, or worse still, informed about his fate.
- Discover if the child has special attachments.
  Are any brothers or sisters or good friends in boarding school in their own country? Has the child got any

preference in this direction? Would he like to join a favourite cousin at school?

- Avoid giving the impression it is a punishment.
  If either alternative is publicised as punishment for the child, you may be sure he will hate it at sight! "Just wait till you get to boarding school—they'll make you toe the line!" is as bad as, "With manners (exam results, a hairstyle, etc.) like yours, I'd be ashamed to send you to boarding school!" or, "He's so much trouble, I'd better keep an eye on him myself!"

- What about leaving the child with a close relative?
  In some families, a child can be left with a close relative. This is often a good solution, provided host and guest get on really well with each other, and the child is not made to feel a 'poor relation' after his parents have winged off to Malaysia. It is in most cases inadvisable to leave a 16-year-old with a septuagenarian granny.

- Consider boarding schools in the region.
  There are a number of boarding schools in West Malaysia and Singapore, some of them teaching English, French, German or Japanese. Contact your embassy to find out more about such establishments before your departure. For one thing, there may be lengthy admission formalities or no immediate vacancies, for another your child will resent it if his education is treated as an afterthought of the 'we'll just wait and see' kind.

- Correspondence or online distance learning courses are ideal for some.
  Some countries, Australia, New Zealand and Canada in particular, provide excellent correspondence courses for their secondary school students. A child of average intelligence can practically teach himself, with very little help from mum.

  The problem is that some students, free of the restraints of formal school, think they are on an endless holiday with the occasional half-hour spent throwing together a few assignments. Mother dear has the unenviable task of making sure the boy is at his books, actually working, during what has been agreed are the school hours.

Some parents pay a local tutor to supervise their children's correspondence lessons; with youngsters below Form 5 (year 11), this may be a good idea.

FOOD AND ENTERTAINING

CHAPTER 6

'In some coasts, one tree yields them coco-nuts,
meat and drink, fire, fuel, apparel with its leaves, oil,
vinegar, cover for houses etc, and yet these men,
going naked and feeding coarse, live commonly
an hundred years and are seldom or never sick.'
—Robert Burton, *The Anatomy of Melancholy*, Oxford 1624

THE STANDARD CUISINE IN EAST MALAYSIA is Chinese/Malay. There are many differences between the two, but they share the basic staple, rice, which is considered food per se in these parts. Meat and vegetable dishes are served to give flavour to the rice.

This applies to down-to-earth home cooking. A big wedding dinner may consist of 12 courses without one grain of rice. Still, for every one banquet, there are 30,000 nourishing meals cooked by frugal housewives, and the foreign resident will do her shopping and marketing with them!

Groceries are available in local shops and supermarkets. Milk powder, butter and fresh milk in cartons are sold in most places. East Malaysia is not the spot for a variety of cheese and fine wine. Brunei is better stocked in this respect than Sabah and Sarawak.

Housewives establish a grapevine among themselves to combat inexplicable shortages. One year, no greaseproof paper was available in town, another there was the Great Peppermint Essence Drought. News that such-and-such shop has skimmed milk powder, cream in cartons, bitter chocolate squares, cloudy ammonia, or that bran is available at—guess where—the pharmacy, spreads around the morning coffees and afternoon teas. A friend taking a short trip to Singapore or Kuala Lumpur is asked to bring back bits and pieces for her circle. One learns to share, borrow and substitute.

Japanese residents have a special problem when it comes to food supplies. They do not care for Malaysian rice, which does not cook to the correct consistency for their favourite dishes. They get together and arrange for rice supplies to be shipped in. Spices, sauces, pickled and preserved foodstuffs essential to a standard Japanese diet are sometimes available in Singapore or Kuala Lumpur. One Japanese lady from Kota Kinabalu will do the shopping for her friends if she's going on home leave. Every traveller to Tokyo is given long shopping lists for supplies.

It is perfectly possible to maintain a foreign lifestyle in Borneo, but it is not cheap. The housewife who can feed her family on local rice, vegetables, fruit, fish, chicken and meat will have noticeably lower food bills than the one who buys only imported produce.

MARKETS

Towns have large 'wet markets' where fish, meat, fresh vegetables and fruits are sold. Fish can be fresh, salted or smoked. Vegetables include preserves and pickles, salted eggs, beche-de-mer, sea slugs and any number of objects that seem to prompt the old animal-mineral-vegetable question. A couple of stalls sell tinned goods, cakes and ready-cooked foods as well. Pork is sold in a separate section of the market, usually behind a partition. Beef and mutton or goat may be fresh or frozen. Poultry is guaranteed fresh, still cackling.

Some local housekeepers go shopping every morning. This explains the small amounts that may be bought—50 cents' worth of onion leaf, three chilli peppers or half a fish. This leisurely habit dates to the pre-refrigerator days; it is much more common, and indeed practical, to buy a week's supplies of meat and fish and store them in the freezer.

In the open markets, bargaining is the order of the day. The seller demands RM 18 dollars for a chicken, the shopper immediately offers RM 10. The fowl will eventually change hands at RM 15 or thereabouts. Nobody says you have to bargain, but your household budget will stretch further if you do. And if you do not, well, that is why locals are convinced that all expats are *rich*!

The bean sprout and soy cake seller in a wet market.

There are supermarkets in all the towns and larger villages of East Malaysia. Sometimes, old shops are re-arranged 'supermarket style' and sell groceries as well as a limited amount of fresh produce.

Supermarkets make fresh-food shopping very much quicker, if slightly more expensive. Everything is in one place, meat and vegetables are ready-packed. Some local housewives still prefer the wet market for farm produce because it is fresh, "How do I know how long this cucumber has been lying here, wrapped in plastic film?"

Other household supplies, like cleaning materials, are cheaper in the big supermarkets than in the 'village shops'.

MAJOR FOODSTUFFS
Rice, Potatoes
Rice is available in every bazaar, potatoes in most. There is a selection of different kinds of rice. In towns, there may be various types of potatoes but do not count on it. Do not plan a dinner around a huge dish of fluffy mash until you

A roadside stall provides convenient and affordable access to fresh fruits.

have scouted the market, because on that day all you may get are the yellow Chinese 'curry spuds', good for keeping their shapes but too gluey to mash!

Rice, in plastic packs of 10 kg, is sold at a government-controlled price. Special kinds, such as glutinous rice, fresh farm rice, new harvest and Bario rice, are sometimes sold open by the kilo. The old measure, the *gantang* (about 4 kg) is seldom used nowadays.

Flour, Bread

Wheat flour is sold by the kilo at grocers' shops. It is advisable to spread flour on a flat basket and put it in the sun to air for a few hours before use. Self-raising flour in packets and cake mixes can be bought in some supermarkets. Study the expiry date carefully, and take a calculated risk. Climate and transport can ruin some of the raising agents used.

A number of specialty flours are available: rice, corn, mung bean, soy and sago. These cannot be used to substitute for wheat flour.

Bread is sold in all bazaars. It is of varying quality; a lot of bread and pastry shops have sprung up in the last five or ten years, and some of them are excellent. Once you have found a good baker, stick to him!

If you like to bake your own, dried yeast is available at grocers' shops. See the section on vegetarian food at the end of this chapter.

Pasta

A variety of Chinese pasta under the generic term '*mee*' (broad white noodles or yellow spaghetti) is available at all bazaars. There is the freshly made, still soft *mee*, which is cooked on the same day it is bought. Dried *mee* comes as broad yellow wheat noodles, white rice noodles, thin white rice vermicelli and very thin transparent bean flour vermicelli, appropriately called 'cellophane noodles' as that is how they look when cooked. Though they are all pasta, they are best used in local recipes.

Italian-style pasta is available in supermarkets and good groceries, some of it imported from Italy. Check the expiry

date and scrutinise the clear plastic packets for beetles or weevils before buying.

Fish

Fish is sold in wet markets, at kerbside markets and in grocers' shops. A number of markets still offer fish for sale in the late afternoon, but by that time, it includes free smells!

During the months of the winter monsoon (November–February), the South China Sea is rough, and not many fishing boats dare put out to sea. What fish is available during that period has been kept on ice and may not be fresh. The owner of a big freezer may like to stock up on fish in September. Properly cleaned and packed, it should be good for several months.

Salted fish is available all year round, smoked fish on and off, but it is worth waiting for. River fish is usually not sold in town markets, though it may be available in upriver bazaars. During the monsoon, pond fish are often offered for sale.

Poultry

Poultry is sometimes sold live in the fresh market. The shopper buys a fowl and takes it home for her cook to deal with, or she pays the poultryman extra to kill, pluck and draw

it. An experienced hand will finish a fowl in 7 minutes flat! Geese and ducks are bought in the same manner.

In towns, Muslims can buy ample supplies of ritually-pure, *halal* meat.

Ready-dressed chickens are offered for sale; there are a number of chain stores specialising in poultry. Half- and quarter-chickens are available at most poultry stalls, useful for the single householder or small family. In supermarkets, frozen chicken pieces are sold. Some housewives still prefer to buy a live chicken to slaughter at home, but the bulk of poultry arrives in the market-place minus feathers.

Pork

Pork is sold in a separate section in the market, in deference to religious sensibilities. Chinese butchers have an exuberant method of hacking meat and bone into strips and chunks; the housewife who wants pork chops will have to go to the market very early in the morning when the carcasses have not been mutilated yet. Some supermarkets sell pork in Western-style cuts.

Beef, Mutton

These meats are mostly imported, on the hoof or frozen. They are available in most large towns. Local beef may include buffalo, and is only suitable for cooking in the traditional style.

The beef butchers are Malays, but their style of dissection resembles their Chinese friends'. The inexperienced buyer is offered 'beefsteak' from any part of the cow at all, including the tail!

Lamb or mutton is only available frozen. At certain times of the year, local goat meat is offered for sale, but it needs special cooking.

Soy Products

Bean curd cakes of various kinds are sold in the wet markets. The same stall also stocks bean sprouts and soy milk.

Bean curd is a cheap protein. This comes as a pleasant surprise to foreign housewives who are used to buying soy products as 'health foods' very expensively.

Vegetables

Vegetables are available fresh all year round. People in Sabah are fortunate to be able to buy locally-grown cool-climate produce like cabbage, asparagus, broccoli, celery, etc. In Sarawak and Brunei, these are imported and somewhat more expensive.

Ordinary vegetables are beans, leaf greens, cucumbers and various kinds of gourds, garden leaves and roots.

Chinese Herbs

In the wet market, there is usually a stall selling plastic packets of Chinese herbs. Do not let appearances fool you—they are roots, bark, berries, seeds, aromatic wood shavings, fungi or bird's nests. Even flat dried frogs and sea horses go under the name of 'herbs'!

Herbs are for cooking in chicken soup, basically harmless combinations guaranteed to make a schoolboy pass exams, keep a young lady cool or an old lady warm, and generally maintain the health of the family. Consult a Chinese friend about which mixture to try. Some add a pleasant taste to chicken broth, but be warned: ginseng may be the miracle wort of all times, but it is horribly bitter if used in generous quantities!

Stronger Chinese medicines are sold at the pharmacy. Among *materia medica* including Elixir Os Draconicus (dragon bone elixir), you may find a product that is reported to be a herb at one season and a worm at another...some herbs!

WHO COOKS WHAT?

Home from the market, plop the shopping basket down on the kitchen table and go have a shower. You probably need it. Your helper will put things away, clean the fish and chicken and wash and cut the vegetables.

Who cooks what? In some households, the everyday cooking is done by the helper. Special dishes are prepared by the housewife, who may teach the girl her own preferred methods.

It is a good idea to take the cook shopping from time to time. Let her buy what she thinks will make a good meal, and let her prepare it. It will most likely be rice, curry or soup, one of the 1001 local fish dishes, or green vegetables cooked with small shreds of meat or dried fish.

Some foreign families have one 'local food day' per week. Children either just love such treats or consider anything outside the sphere of bangers and mash or pizzas as 'yuck!'

Make it clear from the start whether the family can tolerate foods like chilli peppers, curry (hot) and prawn paste in its many guises (pungent). Do not tell the girl to 'cook it just as you like' and then scold her because it is hot, sour or pungent or whatever! How was she to know the master does not like sago grub in black sauce?

Doing It Alone

The household helper is regarded as a basic fact of life in middle-class East Malaysia and Brunei; it is in fact possible to do without one.

Managing a household for two is well within the capacity of a healthy woman who is not holding down a job of her own. Washing machines or the laundrette have replaced the wash *amah*; vacuum cleaners and the universal shoes-off custom cut down on house-cleaning time. There are window washing firms in the larger towns.

Cooking for only a couple is not very time consuming. With a little planning, marketing can be done once a week. Many local housewives subscribe to a catering service that brings cooked meals to the house on a contract basis.

EATING OUT

East Malaysia shares with the rest of South-east Asia a tradition of readily available, reasonably-priced cooked food.

Itinerant food hawkers start their rounds at dawn, and the coffee shops have a good array of breakfast take-aways or eat-ins. Some families like the delicious *seo bee* (meat dumplings) or *pau* (steamed buns) for breakfast, others prefer *moi* (rice gruel) with an assortment of tidbits on the side. The frugal housewife will fry up last night's cold rice with some onion and small salted fish. Bread is also quite commonly eaten at breakfast.

Mid-morning, the *kwe tiau* (rice noodles) man cries his wares up and down the kitchen lanes of the new housing schemes; mobile grocery shops in vans stop at their regular spots and are quickly surrounded by women with baskets—self-conscious little smiles on their faces, for the good housewife has been to the wet market at dawn!

You could have sworn you had seen one, but there is no such thing as a steam bicycle in Borneo. That was the *satay* man. He sells skewers of spicy chicken or beef strips grilled over a small charcoal fire. *Satay* is cooked on demand, so he has a charcoal grill ready lit and gently smoking, mounted on the back of his bike.

Towards dusk, mobile *mee* stalls take up their pitch at every street corner in the residential parts of town. Some of these are mounted on trishaws (three-wheeled bicycles), others are carried on a yoke; the with-it *mee* man operates from the back of a van.

What does a *mee* stall stock? Oodles of noodles—long spaghetti, short spaghetti, broad noodles, thin noodles, fine

A hawker selling *satay*, grilled meat on skewers, in front of a coffee shop.

vermicelli, transparently fine vermicelli, puckered ravioli, and a rice flour concoction my teenage sons used to call, tersely, 'grubs'.

These are served in tasty chicken stock as variants of *mee* soup; fried *mee goreng* comes 'wet' with sauce or 'dry', fried crisp. Each vendor has his own specialties. It is a lengthy but worthwhile task to test all the *mee* in one's neighbourhood.

The local councils license and supervise food hawkers. Dishes and utensils are clean...sort of. Many buyers from the immediate vicinity bring their own containers in which to carry food home.

Coffee Shop / Food Centre

One step up on the social scale is the coffee shop, or its maxi-version, the food centre. These establishments are owned by the person who provides the drinks; a number of food stalls are set up near the entrance, serving snacks at the tables.

The patron inspects various foodstalls, orders what he likes and sits down. A waiter, elegantly attired in a white singlet and long shorts, takes orders for the drinks. These he bellows down to the back of the shop, where the drinks vendor is at work beside his shiny copper.

Way back in the 1960s, a couple of Peace Corps girls are said to have ordered coffee at such a shop. The waiter nodded, then yelled down to the kitchen, *"Noh kopi!"* (two coffees). The girls, sorry to hear there was no coffee, got up and walked out.

To avert further international incidents of the kind, remember the following:

If you want...	You order...
coffee with condensed milk	*kopi* or *kopi-susu*
black coffee with sugar	*kopi-o*
extra strong coffee	*kopi-kau*
black coffee without sugar	*kopi-o kosong*
coffee with unsweetened milk	*kopi-si*
coffee, unsweetened milk, no sugar	*kopi-si kosong*
iced coffee (condensed milk)	*kopi-peng*
black iced coffee	*kopi-o peng*

Tea is ordered in similar fashion, as *teh*, *teh-o*, *teh-kau*, etc. The best known chocolate drink, Milo, follows the same rules.

In many coffee shops, there may be a small jar of salt with a tiny spoon on the table. Malaysians like to sprinkle a few grains of salt in their Coke, lemonade or other fizzy drinks 'to take out the gas'. Fresh lime drinks are often served with salt already in the glass; be sure to order this delicious thirst-quencher 'without salt, please!' unless you want it spiked!

If a female is on her own, she should melt unobtrusively into a corner. Near the counter is fine if the shopkeeper is a woman. Old-fashioned places have some of the tables arranged railway-compartment style, with tall backs or little curtains to provide discreet seclusion. The typical middle-aged housewife on her way home from the market only patronised coffee shops with this essential installation!

Love in a Coffee Shop

In Sibu, wealthy district town of the lower Rejang, 'modern' parents used to permit their daughters to meet approved suitors in a coffee shop. There, the bashful twosome sat in a curtained cubicle, nervously blushing over their *kopi-peng*—and the matchmaker was stationed in the seat immediately behind them, ear-to-curtain to make quite sure the bounds of decency were not overstepped. Judging by the steady increase in Sibu's population, the system worked well in its day.

Coffee shops have one or several *mee* cooks on the doorstep, and a *satay* man. Food centres may sport up to a hundred food stalls offering a huge variety of edibles. At breakfast time, there may be dumplings and buns for sale; where a rice cauldron is espied, you may be sure of a tasty lunch.

The chicken-rice man sells plates of rice with cut, steamed or roasted chicken, slices or long strips of red pork, half a boiled egg and braised innards. You order *nasi ayam* for chicken-rice and *nasi campur* for samples of everything. If you like some but not all of the ingredients, point out which ones you prefer. *Nasi campur* or *nasi ayam* comes with a bowl of clear soup and a spoonful of cucumber pickle and chilli sauce or fresh cut chilies in a separate little dish.

A word of caution: in South-east Asia, meat carving is not the elegant art it is in Western Europe. If it is an art at all, it is martial. The chicken is split in half with one spectacular blow, each part is flattened with a couple of resounding whacks of the cleaver's broadside and then hacked into sections at right angles to the backbone. Splintered ribs and all! The drumstick is sliced bone-in. So a certain amount of care is advised when eating. A hearty bite on a bit of chicken bone could crack a tooth!

If you do not like poultry skin, ask the cook to remove it before he starts hacking.

Haute cuisine of yesteryear—suckling pigs fit for an emperor's feast were roasted outside the shophouse. Modern restaurants have grilling facilities indoors.

Fast Food

The more with-it coffee shops have 'fast food counters'. Shiny stainless steel containers hold braised, roasted, stewed or curried chicken, fish, pork, mixed vegetables, steamed greens, brinjal or jungle ferns fried with chilli and prawn paste. You pick and choose two or more of the dishes, the stall keeper ladles a portion of each onto your plate of rice, and there you have it—a nourishing, nutritionally balanced, extremely tasty lunch for three or four dollars. Any of the above can be eaten on the premises or taken home.

Take-home food is wrapped in plastic sheets and boxes. Specify when ordering whether you want to eat it there, *makan sini*, or take it away, *bungkus*. Two *mee goreng*, one chicken-rice and three *nasi campur* will satisfy six healthy appetites.

East Malaysian-style fast food is not junk food! There is nothing wrong with a take-home lunch of fried fish, brinjal curry with lentil sauce, steamed silver beet and chopped chicken. No housewife need feel guilty about bringing her family packed lunches from her morning's outing.

Is a woman's place in the home, slaving over the hot stove? For that matter, does the family want a square meal at lunchtime? Many prefer a sandwich and a cold drink!

Fasting Market

During the month of Ramadhan, when pious Muslims fast from dawn to dusk, a special 'fasting market' is held in most towns and bazaars. In the bigger centres, this amounts to a food carnival of the most delightful sort.

Families stroll among the many stalls and select enough food for their sundowner breakfast. Here are prawns or chicken wings grilled on skewers and fish grilled in bamboo clamps (top quality fish would disintegrate if it were spitted). Here is every variety of *satay* with rice steamed in little square baskets and every colour and shape of steamed, fried or baked cake. Here is the special dish for breaking the fast, a combination of sweet jellies, corn grains, raisins and fruit slivers served over a mound of shaved ice flavoured with multi-coloured syrups and condensed milk.

Foods at the fasting market are sold in plastic bags to take home. The housewife will set them out on dishes, and the family has to wait until the melodious chant of prayer from the mosque announces the end of the day, and permission to eat.

Non-Muslims are welcome at the fasting market. It is a marvellous place to take a camera too. Out of respect for those still fasting, do not buy food and eat there before sunset. Have it wrapped and taken home, or sit down at a little table and wait for the right time to 'break fast'.

EATING OUT IN STYLE

Between coffee shop and air-conditioned restaurant, there is the open market, an establishment much patronised after dusk. Here, friends and family groups gather for a comfortable tuck-in. It is the ideal place to take an elderly aunt who does not like air-conditioning.

The invitation is, "Let's go and have a *makan* (meal)!" Dress is informal, as befits the cool but by no means cold evening air. Food is acceptable to excellent and prices are reasonable.

An open market consists of a number of cookshops, usually housed in premises provided by the local council, which surround an open square set with tables and chairs. Flowery signs proclaim: 'AH MENG, To Prepare Feasts for Customers', 'AH HONG, The Home of Good Food', or simply 'Where All the Good Food Come Together'. They are not exaggerating!

A newly-arrived family in East Malaysia keen to test local conditions will get a good deal at the open market. The food is visible right there, displayed in glass cases in the shops. There may be a tank full of live prawns—you cannot get them fresher! The cook is on show too, skilfully wielding his huge chopper, ladles and spatulae over an enormous *wok* (a bowl-shaped frying pan), called *kwali* in most of East Malaysia, surrounded by sauce bottles.

As customers draw near, they are ambushed by boys from the various stalls, yelling out their establishment's name, speciality of the day, or simply "Here! Here!", indicating where they would like you to sit, namely at their tables.

It is wise to smile and ignore the eager lads. Stroll past the shops first and see what is offered. Some specialise in seafood, others in meat dishes. There is the occasional Buddhist-vegetarian stall serving many varieties of soy and mushroom products. At a safe distance from the Chinese cooks, there are some Malays selling *satay*, grilled cuttlefish, chicken wings or whole meals of curried meat, fish and vegetables.

Make your selection after a leisurely tour; it is all right to order a few dishes from several stalls.

One place sells drinks. If you are really lucky, a shapely girl draped with a satin sash tries to interest you in buying the brand of beer she is promoting. Chinese tea is usually served free with a whole meal; with snacks it has to be ordered separately.

'Modern style', the server demands payment as he brings the food, especially snacks. If a whole meal of several courses was ordered, payment is usually made at the end. Customers may settle with each stall they ordered from, or ask their 'main supplier' for one bill for the whole meal, including all extras. He will inquire from the other stalls what is owing to them and pay them their share. This system works well and saves the customer the bother of having to pay for the *satay* here, the drinks there and the main meal somewhere else.

As the night progresses, the open market gets noisier, happier, but alas no cleaner. By about midnight, a considerable amount of debris has accumulated around the tables. Some guests are not fussy about flinging paper serviettes, chicken bones, clam shells and other inedibles to the ground. Stray dogs nose around for such cast-offs; there is the occasional yowling fight settled with a swift kick by one of the waiters.

Unless your nerves and your general resistance can tolerate this sort of squalor, go to the open market between 7:00 –9:00 at night when it is still reasonably pristine. It will all be cleaned up by the council men with pressure hoses the morning after, but to enjoy a meal al fresco after midnight, a fellow needs to be very hungry indeed, or slightly sozzled.

IN MORE AND MORE STYLE

Most business and some private entertaining is done in restaurants. A newcomer is likely to be invited out a lot by the people he will be working with, a convivial meal being considered a good way of introducing a new chap and showing him around.

Dinner invitations may be issued by telephone or card a couple of days ahead. Same-day invitations are usually for all-male dinners; it is recognised that the missus cannot be expected to have her hair and wardrobe in dining-out trim at 2 hours' notice!

If the card says RSVP, do respond! It makes life so much easier for the person who is planning the entertainment. Sad to say, many local people do not reply, so you never quite know who will turn up at your parties!

It is all right to ask 'Mr and Mrs?' when the invitation is received. A new arrival's marital status may not be known, so his wife is omitted from the invitation through ignorance. The rule is that if the host brings his lady, the guests follow suit.

Invitations often specify dress. 'Batik' or 'batik long sleeves' applies to men, who are invited to wear these long-sleeved colourful shirts without tie. Otherwise, dress is semi-formal, a long-sleeved shirt and tie for men, a smart dress for women. This is the time to wear polyester, tricel, dacron, all the man-made fibres that are too hot for the daytime.

Avoid skimpy outfits with no visible means of support. For one thing, you will embarrass your host; for another, you will provoke leers. Furthermore, you may freeze! Restaurants are air-conditioned, from cool to cold to arctic.

> Batik shirts are acceptable wear for men on all but state occasions with the governor or royalty present. Then, the invitation will prescribe 'National dress (for locals)/Lounge suits'. The white linen cutaways have gone the way of white plumes and poms. Bum-freezers are seen only on armed forces personnel in mess kit nowadays.

Bill of Fare

Many restaurants serve regional varieties of Chinese cuisine. Teochew, Hokkien and Hakka are considered 'home-style' fare; Foochow, with its famous glutinous rice dishes, caters for the hearty appetite. Cantonese is what a foreigner may have tasted in Chinese restaurants in his own country. Szechuan, with its lavish use of chilli and hot spices, is a favourite with Malaysians brought up on curry and *sambals* (spicy prawn paste).

There are Malay and Indian restaurants in all the main towns of East Malaysia. In Sabah, excellent Filipino cooking can be tasted. The dining rooms of the big hotels serve mainly Western, though they have local dishes on the menu, and there are continental or fusion restaurants in all East Malaysian towns..

And So To Table

Invitations to a Chinese dinner are early, usually 7:30 pm. One is expected to be there more or less on time, and the food should be on the table by 7:45 pm. The host or his representative stands at the entrance to greet his guests. If he is not there, one of the staff will direct new arrivals to 'Mr Tan's dinner'.

The table is round, set with bowls, chopsticks and glasses. Guests are seated according to the host's ideas of what is proper. A middle-aged hostess will have the ladies around one half of the table, the men opposite. If the sexes are mixed, married couples will probably be seated next to each other. Unmatched mixing is still considered a little fast!

You will be offered a drink as soon as you arrive. All that is best and most expensive is available and eagerly pressed on you by host and hostess. Feel free to opt for Chinese tea or soft drinks. The days of obligatory tumbler after tumbler full of fine French cognac are mercifully past.

A Chinese meal is served in separate courses. The wise diner looks around among the greenery decorating the table for a menu to ascertain how many dishes there will be. Six are adequate for a friendly dinner, eight to impress a business client. Ten will clinch a really big deal. A wedding banquet designed to put all future in-laws firmly in their place can run to 12!

You probably cannot read the menu, but the number of lines tell you how many courses to expect and ration your appetite for. It is acceptable pre-dinner conversation to ask a table neighbour for a translation of the menu, and take the occasion to compliment the host, "Wow—*eight* dishes! You really spoil us, Mr Tan!"

Make appreciative little murmurs at the mention of expensive dishes (bird's nest soup, jellyfish and other marine freaks). Your host will feel obliged to disparage the luxury, "This one not really first-class, they couldn't find it all over town!" But he will purr inwardly that the good stuff will not be wasted on culinary ignoramuses. And you may be sure that it is first-class!

Do not feel embarrassed if the price of ingredients is blatantly discussed. This is not common among the younger set, but it can still happen, "Wah, these mushrooms are really excellent! Bet they cost RM 80 a *tahil* (a little more than an ounce)!" Followed by a modest disclaimer, "These are the RM 55 ones, the others were out of stock. Now, Datuk X, he orders his supplies direct from China..." and so it goes, where the most pricey bird's nests may be got, horror stories of bleaching the cheaper 'black' nests with sodium hypochloride to make them 'white', or how one entire dinner party died after eating blowfish at the wrong stage of maturity.

Dinner conversation can be immensely educational. The foreign lady will be surprised that men are usually very knowledgeable about the preparation of speciality dishes. Ask, admire, ask more! Everyone likes to show off his expertise, and you stand to learn a lot about the strange things you have been eyeing doubtfully in the wet market.

And so to table. Flowers are removed before the first course is served. This may be the 'cold dish': sliced cold meats, hundred-year-old eggs with ginger, lumps and balls and finely-sliced cakes of fish, squid, soy, anything at all. Everybody picks favourite morsels out of the serving platter with his own chopsticks; the host may help specially-honoured or obviously inept guests to choice tidbits.

Spoons and forks are always available for anybody who is not at ease with chopsticks. Do not feel shy to ask for them. On the other hand, every one of your fellow guests will be only too delighted to give you chopsticks tuition.

There is no such thing as the wrong fork at a Chinese dinner! Chopsticks, spoons and fingers may be employed ad lib. Bones can be deposited on the tablecloth. Toothpicks are used (behind a discreetly sheltering hand) right there at the table.

"Here I can do everything my mother would kill me for doing at home!" an English teenager gleefully commented.

The dishes are served in succession. At the better restaurants, bowls and plates are changed after a particularly messy course.

Conversation is unceasing and noisy, tending to get more so towards the end of the meal when the spirit flows freely—take this in any sense you like. A loudspeaker adds the latest in sentimental pop music to the din. The merry roar of '*yam-seng*' demands instant bottoms-up of all guests at the table. There are places for a quiet meal in East Malaysia, but Chinese restaurants are not among them.

A Chinese dinner ends after the last course of sweet pancake, preserved or fresh fruit. The host gives the general exit signal and rises, all file past him with many thanks and leave the restaurant. Lingering over coffee is not done for the simple reason that no coffee is served. You would not know where to put it anyway!

Often, Chinese dinners are but the beginning of the rest of the evening. Some of the party proceed to a nightclub, a karaoke lounge, or to a quiet game of *mahjong* somewhere. A plea of work tomorrow or children at home is accepted as an excuse if you want to sneak out. The dinner itself takes about one and a half hours.

Wedding Feasts

At a wedding feast, the bride and groom make the rounds of all tables in the room, followed by the best man and a couple of lads carrying bottles of cognac. They thank each guest individually for his or her presence; the lucky guest is then obliged to drink their health in a bumper poured by the bride's own fair hands. A plea for 'just a little!' is usually respected, especially if you assure them that you have already been well and truly looked after. This is a little pat on the back for the kinsman who plays host at your table, and whose duty it is to see that nobody walks out totally sober.

A little survival tip for wedding feasts: unless you are specially invited to sit at the head table, come early enough to be able to choose your place with a few people you know. It is not fun to sit for 12 courses among a crowd who spends the whole evening yelling happily at each other in a language you do not understand.

Not expats only! A local Hokkien lady remarked that when she is invited to a wedding, she asks to be seated with friends, not 'people who say good evening to me and then talk in Foochow all evening, as if I were a ghost (i.e., invisible)!'

YOU AS HOST

If hospitality is due and you do not feel up to entertaining at home, it is in order for a foreigner to invite friends or business associates to a restaurant meal. At the better establishments, it is a good idea to reserve a table. If you like to hear at least part of what your guests are saying, you can book a separate chamber in which you order the loudspeakers with the music turned off.

Order the meal itself in advance. If even one of your guests is Muslim, do not go to a Chinese restaurant unless you know it is officially certified as *halal*. Most restaurants will produce pork-free meals, but *halal* involves more than that. It shows delicacy on your part to choose a Malay, Indian or Indonesian establishment.

How to order a meal for ten in a completely foreign environment? Choose a restaurant where you have been as a guest. Tell the manager the number of people you are entertaining and how many courses you would like to offer. The standard table is ten; eight to 12 can be catered for comfortably. For larger parties take two tables, with the wife as hostess at one and the husband as host at the other.

If you particularly liked one dish on your last visit, mention this. A dinner of five courses should include one soup, one dish of fish, one of chicken or pork, one vegetable with some meat or seafood, one fried course and finally a (supernumerary) sweet dish. Fresh fruit is a great favourite to conclude a rich repast. Some people eat white rice with their meals, others have fried rice or fried noodles as the last course.

The manager of the restaurant is the right man to advise you about the choice of food and the correct serving sequence. For instance, you do not start a Chinese meal with soup! Tell him in advance how much you are prepared to spend. RM 600 for six courses? Very well, and throw in fresh fruit as an extra. A certain amount of bargaining is expected; you may telephone two or three restaurants for quotes before making up your mind where to go.

The common expat fear that one will be 'had' is probably exaggerated. The restaurateur is keen to retain customers, especially if they are likely to turn up with a tableful of guests a couple of times a month!

Invite your friends with cards or phone calls, making it clear whether it is Mr and Mrs, or stag. Ten minutes before the time specified, settle your wife at the table and take up your position at the door to greet guests as they arrive. Your wife will receive them, seat them and order drinks. The most senior lady among them expects to be seated by the hostess, but there are no hard-and-fast rules. Just avoid putting an attractive young wife next to the town Casanova if you intend to do any further business with her husband.

The meal itself proceeds smoothly. The host sees to it that conversation never flags and glasses are kept filled. Towards the end of the sweet course, he discreetly goes to settle the bill at the counter; soon after this, general departure is in order.

MR & MRS TAN AT HOME

A few East Malaysians and Bruneians are immensely rich and own palatial homes that make one think of soap opera sets. Expect a luxurious setting, servants at every corner and a gourmet meal either cooked by the resident chef or catered by the local four-star hotel.

But these families are exceptions. The majority of people you come into contact with live in plain housing, are paying off a mortgage, and by carefully nursing a middle-aged car, manage to make ends meet. A modest bungalow on a fifth of an acre is the aspiration, a terrace (link) house the norm for the urban wage-earner.

Invitations to the home are an honour and a privilege that the foreigner should not take lightly. This modest terrace house with three bedrooms shelters your friend, his wife and three children, the resident grandmother, two nephews who go to school in town, a niece who figures as baby nurse, housemaid and cook.

An invitation to dinner at a private house is for about 8:00 pm. Guests may be up to half an hour late. Take off your shoes at the door unless the hostess is wearing hers (some people do this to make foreign guests feel at ease).

A guest may bring a little present: flowers, attractively wrapped chocolates or a souvenir from his own country. Such a thing is not expected of him, but it is a delicate matter much appreciated and long remembered.

Guests sit in the lounge, sipping drinks, nibbling nuts and making small talk until the meal is ready. The men will be in one bunch, often on the verandah, the women huddle in the parlour. Move from time to time to say at least 'good evening' to everyone there. Make a point of paying your respects to the host's parents if they are present.

Meals 'at home' are often buffet style as it makes serving easier. For guests not used to local food, there is the added advantage that they can pick and choose without inviting comment from others.

The senior lady is usually called to start the meal. A certain amount of compliment ensues between the hostess and guest; eventually they descend upon the table together and get started. Be lavish with praise for a home-cooked meal. Hostess and cook

It is a delightful surprise, luckily not too rare in East Malaysia, to find an elderly person who speaks excellent, slightly old-fashioned English. He or she may have been to a mission school in the 1950s, and worked for the colonial government or one of the foreign business companies. Properly approached, such an old gentleman may be the source of fascinating tales about the Old Days. Even if there are language struggles, make the proper remarks about family, children and grandchildren. Discreet praise is acceptable, "Your son has a nice house here, Mr Tan." Inquiries about a grandson who is studying overseas are always welcome.

will start to apologise for the 'poor fare', but both enjoy your appreciation of their labours.

There are always mounds of rice, white or saffron-flavoured. Help yourself to this first, then pick from the other dishes. Some are curries, stews and vegetables. Ask the hostess about unfamiliar things—who can blame you for not recognising tree-heart braised in coconut cream, dark hunks of grilled wild pork, an assortment of sambals with bunches of blanched wild vegetables, or green mango cut into matchsticks and served up as a spicy salad. An Iban family right in Kuching is likely to serve all these for a celebration dinner. They may be jungle foods, but we have our connections...

After dinner, coffee will be served. The guests stay on chatting for at least an hour after dessert. A family dinner fills an evening, usually ending at about 11:00 pm.

DROP IN ANY TIME!

When East Malaysians are invited to a meal at a friend's house, they inevitably ask, "What's the occasion?"

Conviviality for its own sake is held at a restaurant; there must be a reason for an invitation to the house.

This does not apply to casual dropping-in in the daytime or evening. People like to call on each other for little half-hour chats. They would avoid mealtimes and busy times, and quietly excuse themselves if they see that their host is occupied.

Casual callers are offered a drink; it is obligatory to accept it. You may confuse local friends by asking, "What would you like?" or, worst of all, "Would you like a drink?" They will certainly say 'No' to the second question, and put you down as extremely stingy!

But there are times when the portals have to be flung wide. The safe return of a family member from overseas calls for a *makan selamat* (festive meal), so does recovery from a serious illness, the engagement of a son or daughter, or an elder's birthday. That is when you will be invited to a meal at home, be it ever so humble.

This is not a matter of law, of course. Foreigners may invite a few local friends to their house 'just to meet you all'.

It is common to give a dinner, tea or lunch for visitors from overseas. 'Mr and Mrs Smith invite...to meet Mrs Smith senior!' Now this is something East Malaysians will understand, and as it involves honouring an elder relative, they will make every effort to turn up in droves.

If your household staff is up to it, by all means give a formal sit-down dinner. A buffet is easier, for all the reasons outlined earlier. A very popular version is the barbecue-buffet. This permits the master of the house to display some measure of domestic usefulness without losing face before his Malaysian friends, and much of the preparation can be done beforehand.

Whichever mode you choose, remember the first consideration is your guests' comfort, not the display of your gastronomic resource. A battery of glasses and cutlery at their plate intimidates local people who have never been overseas. The rigeur of a sit-down meal makes it impossible for somebody to pass up a course he does not like.

Besides aversions and fads, there are some foods certain East Malaysians cannot eat. Not 'don't like' but '*can't eat!*'

FOOD RESTRICTIONS

Muslims are strictly forbidden to drink alcohol or eat pork. They do not usually mind if their fellow guests have a quiet beer, but it is distasteful to them to be in a place where pork is served. Have nothing with pork, lard or bacon if you are entertaining Muslims. You may know that a certain kind of sausage is certified pork-free; a less knowledgeable Malay lady, your workmate's wife perhaps, might feel dubious and upset about it.

Beef and poultry fit for Muslim consumption is called *halal*, ritually pure. This means it has been slaughtered according to the proper ritual. Ask for *halal* meat when shopping for a dinner party. It is available everywhere in the markets and cold storage shops. It tastes the same, costs no more, and you can serve it to your Muslim friends with a clear conscience.

If you like buying live poultry at the market, ask a Muslim to slaughter it. The driver or gardener is usually quite happy to do the job for a small tip.

Just to be on the safe side, ask if your guests take cheese before building a meal around a huge fondue. Some like it, some eat it under duress, others cannot swallow it. Some will not even try. "No wonder Europeans are so white," my late brother-in-law muttered once when offered a slice of cheese, "eating soap the way they do!"

Hindus and Sikhs are forbidden to eat beef. There are not many Hindus in East Malaysia, but if you are inviting an Indian, ask him, "Do you take beef?" It is a question he is used to. There are a few Chinese Buddhists of a particular sect who will not touch beef either.

Ask your guests, when you invite them, if there are any foods they do not take. Many of the Ibans in the Kuching area, for instance, belong to the Sebuyau tribe and do not eat venison; Melanaus or Sabah natives may be Muslim, but have seemingly non-Muslim names. There are a few strictly vegetarian Buddhists around, but they are less likely to accept dinner invitations.

There is good reason why fish is so popular in East Malaysia. For one thing, people like it; for another, it is the one food everybody (except vegetarians) can eat.

Never urge a person to drink against his will. Have a variety of soft drinks ready for those who prefer them. It is not false modesty that makes people decline. Encouraging a Muslim with, "Oh, go on, Encik A, have a beer! Encik Z (another Malay) can take it!" is about the worst thing you could say to and of the two persons involved.

Vegetarians

All the above have been written for people eating a standard type of diet including everything. You may be vegetarian.

You will not find it easy.

There are actually some Buddhist and a very few Hindu vegetarians around, but they live within their own families, their routines carefully geared towards producing acceptable food.

Buddhist monasteries and convents are always vegetarian, as are the *chai tung* homes housing elderly Chinese women; unfortunately, an outsider cannot share their resources!

Eating out is a problem. Most local dishes are prepared for the whole table-round; obviously one person cannot order 'without meat' just for himself. If all the other guests are prepared to abstain, order vegetable dishes with mushrooms, bean curd (in many forms) or egg. Even then, you cannot be sure they have not been fried in lard, or seasoned with a handful of dried prawns or anchovies, or oyster sauce.

One person ordering for himself can insist, "*Jangan campur daging, jangan campur ikan!*" (Do not add meat or fish.) To really impress the cook, tell him, "*Doktor kata saya tak boleh makan daging/ikan!*" (I cannot eat meat or fish by doctor's orders.) That is something that is understood and respected.

There are a number of vegetarian restaurants in East Malaysia. Anything called 'health food' is worth investigating; if the menu features 'vegetarian pork, vegetarian fish'; that means textured soy protein cunningly assembled to resemble the meat in question. While the ethics of this approach may be questionable, you can get 100 per cent vegetarian fare in such places.

Some Chinese vegetarians eat egg, others do not. Certainly none of them makes use of the milk products much employed in vegetarian Hindu cuisine. A veteran Kuching doctor recommends vegetarians to eat either eggs or milk products; he does not think soy proteins can sustain a person who has to do a day's work.

Make it clear that you are vegetarian if you are invited out, and be prepared for a startled gasp from your would-be hostess. It may be kinder to offer to turn up late, 'in time for the fruit and coffee', pleading some other appointment.

Cooking at home is easier, as there are always plenty of vegetables available. It will take you a while to find acceptable proteins.

In the wet market, the bean sprout seller also stocks a variety of fresh soybean curd. There is the 'dry' yellow, the firm white and the very soft white, all of which can be cooked in a variety of delicious ways. Western taste will get used to soft curd à la bolognaise, in omelettes or in sweetcorn soup.

A number of dry soy products are sold in all grocers' shops, as are soy, mung, black and red beans, lentils, split peas, salted and preserved beans. Legumes with a cereal (rice is the most obvious), mixed with sesame seeds—also available everywhere—makes a delicious dish.

Gluten is sold fresh in some wet markets, or tinned (usually fried). Chinese vegetarian cuisine makes use of mushrooms, soy products and a lot of gluten. A number of Chinese vegetarian cookbooks are printed 'dual-language' (Mandarin and English), and are well worth studying. Make friends with a reliable grocer and bring along the recipe book to buy unfamiliar ingredients.

Milk products are harder to find. Away from the larger towns, we rely on milk powder; unflavoured yoghurt and cottage cheese may or may not always be available even in Kuching or Kota Kinabalu! Cheese is usually to be had, at any rate cheddar and some kinds of processed stuff. People who really depend on these foods for their general diet should learn how to prepare them (the good news is that you do not need an electric heater to keep your yoghurt at the right temperature) and bring along sufficient supplies of dried bacillus bulgaricus, rennet tablets, etc. This applies to wholemeal bread too. You can often buy wholemeal at the better grocers.

Where there is a Sikh temple, *atta* (wholemeal) flour will be available, and if you ask nicely, they do not mind selling you a few pounds every now and then. A number of 'bake shops' in the larger East Malaysian towns are producing a variety of breads: wholemeal, rye, French, and some delicious pastries. These bakeries may be quite small, but they're well worth searching for!

Kosher Food

There is never any problem about kosher (food prepared according to Jewish law) meat. Every Malay or Muslim Indian restaurant is kosher, as are the beef and chicken markets. Local cuisine does not use dairy products, so the vexing question of contaminating *milchiges* with *fleischiges* does not arise!

ENJOYING YOUR STAY

CHAPTER 7

'All travel has its advantages. If the passenger visits better
countries, he may learn to improve his own, and if fortune
carries him to worse, he may learn to enjoy it.'
—Dr Samuel Johnson, lexicographer, author and critic

TRANSLATING NEEDS INTO ACTION

Here you are, living in a comfortable house, the children in school, life starting to assume a routine. Get the inside of the house and the family life safely settled first, then it is time to look outwards to see what the rest of Borneo is doing—and join them at anything that looks like fun!

You may be a quiet family that prefers reading, watching films, music and sedate sports. The necessary facilities are right around you. You may be avid hikers and trampers, intrepid travellers or adventurers. What better place than Borneo?

The following pages are full of suggestions and hints on how to find what you are looking for to make your stay here happy, lively and unforgettable.

TO MAKE A HOUSE A HOME
What About the Children?

Children are in many ways more susceptible to change than their parents. Papa sees the move to East Malaysia as a step up in his career. Mama sees it as an exciting adventure. Both parents had the choice to make this move, or stay at home. Bobby sees it as a break from all his friends at kindie, his grandparents, everything that made up his world.

A toddler eventually learns to settle in, but familiar objects such as small items of furniture and books (even if slightly tattered) will help. Bring whatever the youngsters need to feel at home. A move overseas is not really the right time to dump that old teddy, that ridiculous favourite pillow, blanket or whatever 'fetish' a child has been nursing as a bedtime comforter.

Bring about as much clothing as you will need for a month, then buy or replenish according to what the other fellows at school or kindie wear. A new child in an established crowd has some adjustment problems anyway; do not aggravate them by clothes that give their peers an opening for comment and teasing.

Conspicuously 'healthy' is as bad as conspicuously fashionable! Even if the father's terms of contract allow a chauffeur-driven car, one parent should accompany a young child to school for the first week at least, and after that, once in a while. Keep an eye open for what other children are wearing, what type of drink bottles they carry, and what sort of tuckboxes and schoolbags they have. These are the kind your child will want, though maybe not immediately. Let him take his old favourites along, but be responsive to his requests for new ones.

"Why a new schoolbag? This is the one your nana gave you!" is a crushing answer to a six-year-old who has been teased about the swag he carries to school.

Children Have Culture Shock Too!

Parents, especially mother, will find that their sheer physical presence is needed more than it should be according to Dr Spock.

"It's a drag!" said a young Australian woman in her second month in Bintulu.

"Roy and I are invited out almost every evening. I'm asked to all these supper functions and teas and sports mornings (she is a keen sportswoman), and here is our Mavis hanging on to my skirts and being ever so difficult each time I leave the house!"

Mavis was four. She had gone to kindie quite happily back home. Now she refused to go, spent the morning snivelling if she was taken anyway, and 'simply won't play with the other kids!'

Mavis is suffering from culture shock.

Not all children have serious problems, but they must not be ignored. Take the child along to your functions if that is feasible, and try to spend evenings at home with her even though you could be painting the town red at that very moment.

The child feels disjointed and lost; her parents are her only security. However kind the helper or baby *amah* may be, she speaks differently. She has different ideas from those the child is used to. She is a stranger. It takes time for strangers to become friends, as any grown-up in a foreign environment knows perfectly well.

A young child's reluctance to go to kindergarten or school must be handled with care. Five-year-old Bobby is a shy little fellow who is overwhelmed by numbers: so many strange kids, and he on his own! He had a little trouble settling into kindie when he first started in his home country too.

Mother-to-mother action is likely to be successful here. Invite a couple of ladies with one or two children about Bobby's age; have plenty of toys about so the owner need not worry about his particular favourites.

Small though he is, and new though he is in this place, a child has strong territorial feelings. In school, Bobby knows he is the intruder; here in his home, he is the owner, the defender, or (this his mother would like him to be) the host.

The mothers drink tea and chat, not paying much overt attention to the children. If Bobby clings to his mother and climbs on her lap, she keeps him there for a wee cuddle and then puts him down again.

"See, here's Jason feeling all lonely without anybody to play with!" stressing to Bobby that he is the resident here and Jason is on strange turf.

This way the child is allowed to meet strangers on his own terms. This house is still very new and unfamiliar to him, but it is his. Here he is surrounded by the security of his own toys, his own mother and his own world.

Getting mail and email from home is exciting and comforting for everyone. For a literate child, a letter addressed to him by name, a private missive, is a very different thing from 'love to Bobby and Mavis' at the end of an epistle from granny! Thoughtful grandparents, with a little bit of prodding from mum maybe, write individual little notes to their grandchildren in East Malaysia rather than include them in the family letter as afterthoughts

Children must be encouraged to write to their relatives, to help make up a cassette or video recording which will be handed around back home. These recordings are a delightful improvement on the art of letter writing. Quite a small child can send messages, the sound of familiar voices is reassuring to all. Some families turn out veritable masterpieces of speech, music and carefully-orchestrated background noises like the *kwe tiau* man singing out his wares, the call to prayer from the mosque and Timah pounding spices in the kitchen.

Older children, preteens and teenagers suffer the trauma of loss too; separation from good friends can be very painful. Usually, they are more articulate than their younger brothers about wanting things like clothes to help them conform outwardly to the new environment, but they miss their 'gang' silently. They were more dependent on the peer group back home than little brother, whose chief security still comes from mummy.

Do not reprove a lad for 'carrying on' about his old cobbers. Encourage him to write letters, send photos and postcards, and have his own email address, and let him keep his correspondence private. Just keep an eye on their net-surfing. There's some pretty objectionable stuff out there!

A growing lad (or girl) needs his own life, his own contacts. Transplanted into a foreign environment, where he is known mostly as 'Mr Smith's boy', the individual ego needs fostering. Some youngsters will be secretive about such matters, and in most cases it is best to let them be. Once they have made new friends in the new country, the red-hot urgency will go out of the home correspondence; it will subside into normal, healthy pen and online friendships.

What About Us All?

Don't many grown-ups go through just the same development? In the first few weeks here, there is simply no time to write. Slight indignation is felt if letters from home do not arrive regularly, friends don't phone—but as for me to write or call back is just impossible! I'm in a whirl of activity.

Then the move is complete. The household is arranged. Now I have time to write. Glowing accounts of a tropical paradise at first, toned down as the weeks proceed and reality seeps through.

This is when the friends and relatives at home simply do not write enough! The mailman is watched for with eagerness and the computer is left on all day to catch any 'incoming mail' promptly. The postman's unconcerned passing on the other side of the road hurts (we ring up the post office to complain). What can be the matter with mother, sister, all those who promised so faithfully 'keep in touch'? Or is the net down?

Then comes the telephoning stage. Long-distance calls are made, not to relay important news, just to find out what went wrong. Have you forgotten us so soon? Do you realise how hot and uncomfortable and mosquito-bitten we are here?

'My family ran up a phone bill of nearly RM 1000 in our second month here!' says a Canadian engineer in Miri, grinning.

They got over it; maybe the phone bill helped. By the time anxious enquiries dropped in from Aunt Mabel, who heard from dear Winnie that Nellie and the kids are having such a dreadful time in East Malaysia, the Nellie in question will send back glowing accounts.

Bobby and Mavis are in school and love every day of it. Roy's work is absorbing and challenging and he gets to travel to all these out-of-the-way places. Nellie herself plays squash two mornings a week, takes lessons in Chinese painting and works three afternoons at the local School for the Blind. Couldn't enjoy life more!

The Equal Partner

Malaysian labour laws are designed to protect the interest of the local workforce. A foreign woman who has been pursuing her own career cannot simply go and look for a job unless her prospective employer can prove to the relevant authorities that there is no citizen available who could do the same work. If there is a vacancy at the local 'international school', a properly qualified foreign teacher whose husband is working here may get the job, or his company may offer her employment. In all such cases, a work permit is needed, with all the bureaucratic hassles and red tape the term implies.

This will not come as a surprise to new arrivals. The condition is always very clearly spelled out when a prospective employee is interviewed. Yet living here as a lady of leisure can result in secondary shock to a woman who has been gainfully employed and simply cannot get much fun out of sitting on a cushion sewing a fine seam. For a few weeks, yes, it is as good as a holiday. But for two years?

Some ladies do volunteer work in charitable institutions. Places like the Cheshire Home, the Blind Centre and the orphanage are often short-staffed and accept volunteers gratefully. A special skill may be put to good use at the School for the Blind, the Deaf, the Handicapped.

Occupational therapists, physiotherapists, speech therapists and special teachers of handicapped children may be sorely needed but beyond the organisations' means. Much satisfaction can be derived from doing a really good job, but there will be no monetary rewards.

Some enterprising ladies run courses in their own homes. If the teacher is skilled and expert, she may charge small tuition fees. A trained pastry cook, for instance, could reasonably expect to be paid for giving cake-making lessons. Many foreign women are sought to give language lessons to their local friends' children (particularly Japanese and English, occasionally French); this can be a welcome source of extra income to a woman used to earning her own. A travel agency may ask an expatriate lady to act as interpreter; it's one way of travelling to the country's beauty spots and getting paid for it!

Strictly speaking, such classes should be registered, a work permit applied for and the teacher should pay taxes. In fact, they are tolerated as long as they do not mushroom into full-blown schools. Discretion is the watchword here.

GETTING INTO THE SWIM

All old hands agree that a newcomer should 'join anything at all and any number of things which will force him to go out and mix with people!' The unfortunate initial impression that East Malaysians don't like strangers melts away if one meets them at the library, in running shoes, around a tea table, or over a welfare project.

What's On?

There are English-language newspapers in all East Malaysia and Brunei towns. Read them.

Magazines and weeklies from overseas will keep you in touch with your home country; the *New Straits Times* gives you world news from a Malaysian viewpoint. But it is in the local daily that you find out which roads will be closed for the Vesak Day procession, where this year's Harvest Festival will be celebrated, when the Tamu Besar will be held, fixtures for outdoor sports from football to kite fighting, or what films are on at the local cinema.

The local daily is an interesting source of 'background' as well as news. Where but in Sarawak would you read a public apology, from Mdm X (address and identity card number supplied) to Miss Z, 'for having used a broomstick upon her in an uncalled-for manner'? Thank-you notes to St Jude for prayers answered? Flowery wedding congratulations to the parents of the bride?

Condolence notes are signed with not just the name but also the business address of the advertiser. Obituaries list the deceased's sons, daughters, sons-in-law, daughters-in-law, adopted sons, adopted daughters, adopted daughters-in-law and adopted grandchildren. Even step-grandchildren and foster-grandchildren are meticulously classified, though most advertisers lose heart at the fourth generation and simply lump them in as 'many great-grandchildren'. In Sabah papers, the bereaved family expresses its gratitude for funeral visits and gifts under the heading 'Return Thanks'. In Sarawak, it is simply 'Acknowledgements'.

A thick black rim around an advertisement does not mean it is an obituary, it means it is important (expensive).

Congratulations may be thus framed, or with a more appropriate border of hearts and roses.

Congratulations are serious business in East Malaysia. The more enterprising newspapers canvass for ads among the friends of anybody who has anything to celebrate: mother's 80th birthday, receipt of an award, daughter's wedding or son's graduation. You are offered 'part-share', less prestigious as your name will appear with another dozen or so fellow congratulationists, or 'single', one name only on a quarter- or half-page.

It is from the local newspaper that you find out what's on. Make use of the information, get out and about and have a look.

Libraries

There are public libraries in all the major towns of East Malaysia. In line with national policy, they stock more and more books in Bahasa Malaysia, but their English sections are in most cases still varied and interesting. Look for the 'Borneo Collection', books on the history, geography and anthropology of the region.

The museums have good libraries. People engaged in bona fide research may get permission to use these.

Consular Visits

The British Council maintains a limited presence in Kuching and Kota Kinabalu. A representative from the British High Commission in Kuala Lumpur visits the East Malaysian offices at regular intervals, mostly for passport and visa matters; he also stops in Bintulu, Miri, Labuan, Sendakan and Tawau. Brunei has its own British High Commission; the manager of the Chartered Bank in Kuching is an Honorary British Consul.

There is a Chinese Consulate in Kuching; several countries maintain the services of an Honorary Consul in Sarawak, Sabah or Brunei. Find out from your embassy or High Commission in Kuala Lumpur.

Brunei has accredited high commissioners and ambassadors from many countries.

Films

There are film shows at the various clubs, but these are for members only. Public theatres are wilting from the onslaught of the video tape player: two-thirds of Kuching's cinemas have closed down in the last five years. What film shows there are left may be classified under the headings BLOOD, SWEAT and TEARS.

Films are censored according to an unfathomable principle which leaves horror, gore and violence intact but slashes 15 minutes of rampant indecency out of *South Pacific*.

Entertainment in the SWEAT category is interesting in a way the producer never intended. East Malaysian viewers try to piece together what could have been the plot from the fragments spared by the censors. In movies with really screaming headlines, these may be very scanty! The *Rambo* and kung fu movies have so little plot that it doesn't matter anyway.

TEARS are Indonesian and Malay productions called *A Mother's Love* or *Sweet Maiden Innocence*. They are epics of honest poverty versus wicked affluence, richly laced with ghosts and howling thunderstorms out of which the heroine emerges with her poor but honest designer rags and hairstyle (and everything else!) immaculate. The set is a wild mountainous landscape and a Rolls Royce. The villain either falls to his death off a lofty crag during the thunderstorm, or he hath repented him of his wickedness and is ready to throw self and heroine at his mother's feet for the required blessing. The Rolls is somehow worked into the last scene to show the girl's made it.

P Ramlee films deserve special mention—old black-and-white strips with an undying appeal to all Malaysians and many foreigners. The late P Ramlee, acting in most of his own productions, had a unique talent for mixing sentiment and humour in exactly palatable proportions. Even people who do not understand the lingo (vernacular Malay) can follow the plot from the actions. Many P Ramlee films have subtitles too.

In Sabah, a considerable number of Indonesian and Tagalog films are shown to cater to immigrants from the neighbouring countries. International 'blockbuster' films tend to reach East Malaysia within a weeks of their debut in Kuala Lumpur.

Music

Music can be a wonderful medium for meeting people and making friends with local amateurs. It is an international language. There are good music teachers in the main centres, specialising in the more common keyboard and string instruments. Royal School, Trinity and Australian Board examinations are taken in East Malaysia and Brunei.

Friends meet informally for an evening's music. There are no large orchestras, but the keen amateur will soon find somebody to play duets with. If you are prepared to give recorder lessons to children, you will soon have all the mothers flocking to you! A query pinned to the notice board of the local club will bring some response.

One enterprising foreign cellist contacted a local music teacher with a request, not for lessons, but for two violins and a viola. The result was a string quartet that lasted his two-year stint here and survived as a string trio after his departure.

Television

Those who do not like films can always watch TV. Rather more than half the air time is taken up by Bahasa Melayu programmes; the rest is divided into Chinese, Indian and English. The occasional good film is strewn in among stuff of soap opera kind, and drowsy afternoons of cartoon strips. Satellite channels can be subscribed to in most locations.

TV Brunei airs a number of BBC programmes; residents in the adjacent parts of Sarawak and Sabah like to tune in to the sultanate's programmes.

The foreigner longing for culture has a bit of a problem on his hands. Some go to Singapore or Kuala Lumpur regularly to hear concerts, see ballets and stage shows. For most people, such jaunts are limited by financial constraints.

Many foreigners bring their own video tapes, CDs and DVDs. Much exchange takes place among like-minded enthusiasts. Some lament that there is no choir, no orchestra and no dramatic group to join; others simply form their own.

Drama

There are often amateur dramatic circles centred on the clubs, teachers' training colleges and the local radio station. This is a fine way to meet local folk. You do not need to be a tragic genius to take on the Second Gravedigger in Hamlet or help with the costumes!

Sports

If it is neither music nor drama, sport may be your cup of tea. There are sports clubs in every town and bazaar of East Malaysia. No school, however remote, is without a football field which often doubles as the only helipad in the region. Basketball courts of varying degrees of excellence are attached to nearly every Chung Hua (Chinese-medium) school. Recreational clubs in the larger centres have tennis and squash courts, swimming pools and golf courses.

There are packs of Hash House Harriers all over Malaysia. Those who thought a 'harrier' was a small hunting dog are misinformed: it is an otherwise reasonable, well brought-up fellow who delights in crashing through the undergrowth at twilight in the company of like-minded persons. 'Hashing' is a form of paper chase. The 'hare' sets a trail and the 'harriers' follow. Held weekly in many East Malaysian towns, 'hashing' is taken very seriously by all its practitioners, the after-hash refreshments being one of the most rigidly kept traditions.

Expats and locals 'hash' happily side by side. Once they all emerge at the end point, sweaty and thorn-scratched, with a pack of mangy farm dogs yapping at their heels, they are in precisely the right frame of mind for forming friendships, and drinking lots of beer.

On a moral note, let me hasten to point out that in some places the 'hashettes' run separately, chastely segregated from the fellows.

Clubs

There are clubs in most main towns of East Malaysia and Brunei, over 20 are listed in the *Yellow Pages* of the phone books. While the Rajang River Motor Launches Crew Club or the Ying Chuan Chin Clan Association may be considered special-interest groups, others are of the familiar sports/golf/country club type; many have reciprocal arrangements among each other which is an added bonus to the frequent traveller.

Entry to these clubs is by invitation. In practice, every newcomer is asked by his local business or social acquaintances if he would like to be 'put up' for election. No properly seconded applications are blackballed. For that matter, the polling device of white and black balls has gone the way of solar topees and button-up boots!

Memberships cost RM 15,000, or more! Flying and yachting clubs are more expensive because of the equipment and facilities they provide.

To join or not to join? This is a financial question for many people. Can we afford the entry fee, the monthly subscriptions, the danger of signing chits merrily until the monthly bill whams in? In most clubs, one cannot purchase anything for cash, only by signing a 'chit'. Children have been known to run up remarkable amounts in chips, ice cream and coke to which they generously treated all their friends each time mother parked them at the club while she went out shopping. There usually are rules against unsupervised

Idyll off Sabah's east coast.

children roaming the premises, but these are not enforced with equal strictness at every club.

Consider that much of expat social activity does take place at the club. Christmas carol singing and the pantomime, swimming competitions, fancy dress parties and many of the things 'all the kids at school' are involved in may be held at the club for want of a better venue.

Many expats in East Malaysia have never joined the club and still manage to live happy and useful lives. There is no compulsion. The club is no longer the only place where one can entertain, play tennis or go for a swim. It certainly is not, as it was in British India, the place for Westerners to be among themselves! Membership of East Malaysian clubs is overwhelmingly local.

Informal Groups

The club is not the only thing that may be joined. Women with young children have semi-formal associations for mutual company, baby-sitting and general chit-chat, which usually meet by rotation in members' houses and can give much help and reassurance to the newcomer.

Foreign wives are going to find it difficult to get around if they do not drive. There are buses, but your house may be a long walk to the nearest stop. Why not pick up your courage and learn to drive in East Malaysia?

For the handicraft-inclined ladies, there are sewing circles. A few local dressmakers run sewing and pattern-drafting classes. There is always something going on at the local women's institute. The artistic may get together and persuade one of East Malaysia's excellent artists to give private lessons in batik, Chinese ink or copper tooling.

Join a photography club, join a nature club, learn tai-chi, take up tae-kwon-do or boxing. There is even an Adventurers' Club in East Malaysia, for the sportsman who wants something wilder than rugby. Try sailing, scuba diving, model aeroplane construction and flying. The shops selling relevant equipment will be able to put a newcomer in contact with a club or association that fosters the sport or hobby of his or her choice.

All the Fun at the Fair

Apart from the wet market, many towns have a jungle produce market variously styled Sunday Market, Native Market or Tamu.

Here, jungle produce, handicrafts, vegetables, antiques and 'antiques' (be sure of your Ming before you buy—there is a whole cottage industry devoted to the production of fake antiques!), household goods, clothing and all sorts of stuff are offered for sale. There are also food stalls, to be patronised with care if you are a new arrival. Keep a sharp eye on your purse or handbag, too!

In Sabah, the major rural centres have what is called a Tamu Besar, a Great Tamu, once a year. These are folk festivals well worth visiting! They are distributed throughout the year so one will not take the glory from another.

The first Tamu Besar is held in Sipitang, about 50 km inland from Beaufort, in early May. This is Murut territory; apart from a big market of traditional produce and handicrafts, there are blowpipe-shooting contests and a ladies' football match. People dress up in their colourful costumes for this event, and there are beauty contests for traditionally dressed ladies at most Tamu Besar.

The Tamu Besar in Kota Belud, 80 km north of Kota Kinabalu, features a parade and equestrian events by Bajau horsemen, an agricultural exhibition, legal cockfighting—the works!

Keningau Tamu Besar, inland from Tenom, is usually held in late June. It is famous for pony and buffalo races and a cross-country race for all comers.

Buffalo races sound exotic and hilarious. They are both, but apart from that, the buffalo is still the accepted mount and beast of burden in Sabah's rural areas.

Kudat at the northern tip of Sabah gets its turn in early July. Home district of the Kadazan Rungus, this Tamu Besar features the best and most varied dancing and costumes besides the usual attractions.

> Buffaloes make characteristic paths, a deep mudhole for each step. Travellers are advised to hoist their feet up in front of them when fording a shallow river, as there may be a 'buffalo ditch' under water that could pin the rider's legs between the side of the ditch and the animal's leathern flank!

The Tuaran Tamu Besar in late July features water sports, including boat racing. Here too the Bajaus add their colourfully-mounted antics to the fun.

Beaufort, 100 km south of Kota Kinabalu and accessible by train, has its tamu in early August. There is a night procession of illuminated vehicles, a best-decorated shophouse competition that guarantees the town well dressed, if nothing else!

Semporna, situated in the 'wild east' of Sabah, holds a Tamu Besar for the east coast in early September. The special attraction here is a boat beauty competition, native craft fancifully decorated vying for a prize. Those who like their Sabah 'unspoilt' may brave the rigours of a trip to Semporna—half an hour's flight, or a long day's drive—tourism has barely touched this region. There is not even an expat community here!

The weekly Tamu are very interesting too. The Gaya Street tamu in Kota Kinabalu stops the traffic in a very literal sense, but it's well worth strolling into.

There are smaller festival days, sports days and school picnics which involve the whole township in many East Malaysian and Bruneian centres. You find out about them from the local newspaper or radio station.

The clear waters off Miri, Labuan, Kota Kinabalu and the East Coast of Sabah offer many wonderful scuba-diving sites. Participants in an overnight dive trip, especially to the off Sabah islands, are strongly advised to inform friends and the local police station of their plans...just in case! If there have been reports of unsavoury characters lurking in the area, it may be better to put off the island-hopping trip and go climb Mount Kinabalu instead.

East Malaysians celebrate National Day on 31 August with fun and gusto. In addition, Sabah has the Harvest Festival on 13 May, and Sarawak the Gawai Dayak on 1 June. Both festivals are based on traditional thanksgiving rites for good harvest.

Brunei National Day is on 23 February and the Sultan's birthday on 15 July. Both events are celebrated with parades, fireworks and public entertainment.

Outings

The bad news first: Wherever you are planning to go in East Malaysia, it is a long, long way and the road may be bad.

Then the good news: Once you get there, you will love it.

The sheer size of the East Malaysian states startles people again and again. Sarawak by itself is as large as the whole Malay Peninsula, though it has about a tenth of the population. You can drive upcountry or sail upriver for hours without meeting a sizeable township. Kuching's nearest picnic spot is about 50 km off; a 'quick drive' to Mount Kinabalu National Park takes two hours from Kota Kinabalu.

And when visitors get there, they may find the place pretty basic, and well decorated with the rubbish of previous picnic parties. This is a sore point with visitors and locals alike—apart from setting a good example and 'hoping the authorities will do something about it', we cannot really offer a good solution to this vexing problem.

If the organised and recognised recreations are not too numerous, enterprising people find their own.

Seaside

Much of Borneo's population live along the coastline. Chances are you are less than 80 km from the sea. Boating, sailing and windsurfing are the obvious pastimes for the well-heeled. There are a few luxurious 'beach hotels' in both Sarawak and Sabah.

Many people like exploring the beach, fishing and collecting crabs and shellfish (be careful to do this far away from any *kampong*, as the villagers may have traditional rights to the local oyster-bed!). At the right seasons, you may watch the villagers catch and prepare *ikan pusu*, the small anchovies used in almost every traditional dish.

The seaside and beach are fun, but the sun is not. The light breeze might deceive the unwary: fair skins need strong sun protection, hats and loose voluminous clothing. Bikinis may indeed annoy the local population (most seaside-dwellers are Malays and other Muslims, who have strict views on female dress), but a bikini-sized sunburn can make you very ill. Many locals of both genders enjoy their briny dip dressed in jeans and T-shirts. Modesty is its own reward in this case!

Many would-be picnickers are put off by the miles and miles of mangrove swamp that cover parts of the Borneo coast. Bathing is not much fun here as the mangroves grow in mud, but it is an interesting area for exploring animal, plant and human life. Be careful, however, not to venture into the mangroves without a reliable local boatman or guide. It is easy to get lost among the myriad diverging channels, many of which dry up during low tide. On the positive side, mangrove stands protect the shoreline from marine disturbances like heavy storms or tidal waves.

What is there to see among mangroves, apart from mosquitoes? An incredibly complex eco-system, for one thing. And a few unexpected signs of human activity. A light smoke above the dense green plumes suggests the presence of a sugar tapper. The apong palm's flower stems can be tapped for a sweet juice, which is boiled in huge cauldrons to make a thick syrup or hard brown sugar. The tapper makes his sure way in the thick, sticky mud, kindly pointing out what resembles a path to unexpected visitors. His is a lonely and boring occupation. He usually welcomes an excuse to pause for a while, offer a sip of sugar sap to his guests. Even here, halfway between the tides, the law of hospitality is respected.

On slightly firmer land, a thick billow of smoke indicates a charcoal kiln. Charcoal is used for cooking in the more old-fashioned households; speciality restaurants keep charcoal pots or ovens ready for fancy dishes.

If you meet a boat laden high with mangrove sticks, follow it. It is probably on the way to a kiln. The green mangrove wood is fired for 14–27 days in a brick kiln daubed airtight with mud; no shortage of that essential commodity here! The finished product is taken to the market by boat. In fact, everything in the coastal plains moves by boat.

In Praise of Mangroves

A village elder in the Nonok peninsula north of Kuching recalls how, during the time of the Japanese occupation, his people hid all their food grain in huts built up small creeks and inlets among the nipah and mangrove swamps.

'The Japanese soldiers kept on demanding so many sacks of rice per family, and we kept on showing them the empty storage bins in our houses. Sometimes we gave them a few bushels of maize, but they never found our rice. They would not have dared venture into the small sidestreams off the main rivers, it's just too easy to lose your way!'

National Parks

Brunei, Sabah and Sarawak have many national parks among them, well within reach of the state capitals and farther afield. There is a large orang-utan sanctuary at Sepilok near Sendakan, the old capital of Sabah.

Cockfights

Cockfighting is a favourite pastime much practised by East Malaysian men. As it inevitably involves gambling, it is subject to licensing and restriction. This means, in plain language, that most of the cockfights you hear about are likely to be 'secret', unlicensed events.

For obvious reasons, cockfights are not advertised as tourist entertainment. You will not be invited until you have been here for a while, and your friends think they can trust you not to blab.

Illegal cockfights are periodically raided by the police. Owners of fighting birds are arrested, as are bookmakers. General bystanders are fairly safe, though a foreigner may prove too much of a temptation for an eager cop. As there is nothing they can charge him with, he will be taken along to the police station and then ceremoniously released. He

Spectators enjoying an exciting cockfight.

is luckier than the fighting cocks, which will end up in the curry pots of various charitable institutions.

Women do not attend cockfights. There is no law banning them from the cockpit. Their presence there would simply be unpopular. Nobody says anything, but the over-curious lady is firmly indexed an overaged tomboy from that day on!

The cocks are armed with steel spurs fitted over their own; a fight is a quick flurry of feathers and a spurt of blood. The loser is either killed on the spot, or runs out of the 'ring'.

Having said this much, do we advise foreign men to visit cockfights? Well...if only to be able to say afterwards how awful it all was. But do not be caught betting!

TANGIBLE MEMORIES

Nobody lives in East Malaysia for a tour of duty and forgets about it in a couple of years' time. Memories may be balmy dreams or nightmares, but some things you will remember forever. You may even join Mr and Mrs Whenwe who retired to Southampton in 1978; their every second sentence starts with, "When we were in Sabah...when we were in Brunei..."

Apart from what may be carried in the head and the heart, most sojourners want to take home a few tangibles. What things are suitable, available and unique to East Malaysia?

Give These a Miss

The days when a Rajah's servant took a tame orang-utan back home are over.

You may hear of somebody who 'picked up a genuine Ming jar for a song in Sabah', but that is a fairly old story. Old as well as story: I'd be more inclined to believe the one about the 'genuine antique plate—I knew the fellow who made it!'

East Malaysians would not do such a wicked illegal thing as faking antiques, of course. We blame the Indonesians. The Indonesians blame the Thais. Everybody blames Hongkong. Hongkong points an accusing finger at Taiwan... which suggests that 'bargain antiques' are seldom or never genuine.

Borneo people fully know the value of a T'ang jar, a celadon plate, and treasure it as an heirloom. In the villages and longhouses, many families own such pieces, but they are extremely unlikely to sell them.

Do not ever try bartering cigarettes for such a piece with its simple-minded native owner! You will provide him with a really good story about this simple-minded European who offered him a carton of fags and a Mickey Mouse watch for his heirloom 16th century Swankhalok dish!

Antiques are sold in reputable shops in most of East Malaysia's main centres. In upcountry towns, a few good pieces are sometimes found gathering dust on a shelf in the general goods store. But none of them are cheap.

If a departing resident should not cast a beady eye upon East Malaysia's antiques, what memorabilia can he take home?

Handicrafts

Borneo handicrafts are world famous for fine workmanship and endless variety. Sabah, Brunei and Sarawak have a pool of craftsmen and craftswomen who carve, weave, plait, forge, cast and chase metal, throw and glaze clay, print fabric and paint in oils, Chinese ink, water colours or *batik*.

There are active Handicraft Promotion Boards both in Malaysia and Brunei. Their projects and workshops are well publicised. Spend the occasional afternoon watching the trainees even if you are not planning to buy anything just then. There is always something new and interesting to see—and you will probably end up buying something anyway!

At the various Kraftangan centres, handwoven and screen-printed textiles may be bought. They come in full lengths, or made up into scarves, pillows, table mats, bags of many kinds, tablecloths and serviettes—all ideal Borneo souvenirs. Reed and cane crafts are regularly offered for sale, colourful beadwork catches the eye. These make ideal presents or home-bringsels, being light to transport and fairly unbreakable.

The latest development in this direction are the Common Facilities Centres, workshops in rural areas where young people are taught the traditional crafts, with just a little

Interesting crafts for sale at a Tamu in Sabah.

help from Kraftangan. Machinery is used for the dull, mechanical jobs such as splicing and dressing basketry materials. Production of the lovely patterns is of course done by hand.

The purpose of the Facilities Centre is to keep the trainees in the village, among their traditional teachers (aunties, grannies) and near the raw materials. The atmosphere is informal, visitors are welcome because they provide a little diversion, if nothing else.

Frequent visitors may make friends with the instructor to the point where she permits them to try their hand at the simpler patterns. This, too, will create a diversion, if nothing else!

A centre has a showroom (it may be a shelf along one end of the building where finished products are sold). Surely the souvenir value of a bamboo basket is enhanced if you actually saw it taking shape!

Another good source of handicrafts is the waterfront or Sunday market. Upcountry people who come to town may have brought along a few carvings, baskets or leaf hats for sale to finance their shopping spree.

In Kota Kinabalu, the whole waterfront is one teeming market (the vegetable market is there too), partly in proper little stalls built for the purpose, partly on mats on the ground, along the overhead walkways that permit free pedestrian circulation. Besides Sabah handicrafts, Filipino basketry, shellwork and marine curios may be found there.

Every town has one or more such 'outlets', nearly always handy to the waterfront or the main upcountry bus station.

This is a good place to stroll around, test prices by a little desultory bargaining, mix with the upcountry folk and see the many strange things they offer for sale.

A 'modern' trend is the manufacture of multi-level coffee tables made of oddly-shaped pieces of driftwood or roots, with three or four slices of round timber as tables—*tapang* with its red heart for preference. If you are about to buy one of these, set it on a level surface and see how steady it is! The workman will make the necessary adjustments then and there.

There are two rules to observe for happy shopping:

- Keep a tight grip on your handbag.

  Carry only a small amount of money and NO irreplaceables such as identity card, passport, driver's licence, etc. Keep your car keys in a pocket. This is not to impeach the honesty of the market people, but wherever a crowd congregates, the good are mixed with the bad. Do not 'ask for it' by carrying or wearing valuables such as a thick gold chain visibly displayed, an expensive camera or audio equipment casually slung over one shoulder. Round the neck is safer and, in the case of cameras, looks more professional.

- Keep small children on a tight hand.

  You are not likely to lose them, but they might damage some of the fragile items offered for sale. If Jimmy somehow manages to smash an old woman's supply of shell craft, pay her for it. This is a time when you cannot very well bargain, and the old dear may sharply inflate the price of the goods. Better just keep Jimmy on a short leash from the start!

A full description of all our creative crafts ancient and modern would fill a book (see Further Reading at the back of the book). Look around your area, talk to your *amah* about what traditional handicrafts are made by her people and where they may be bought.

Art

Do not get carried away by Ye Olde Native Crafts to the point of ignoring Borneo's excellent artists.

The local press announces art exhibitions, solo or joint. Visit a few and keep track of the painters whose work appeals to you. The foreign resident has an advantage over the tourist here. He can 'discover' a few artists in his town, watch their development, and be there when one of them has produced a masterpiece.

Many artists are prepared to teach their skills to genuine learners. A few Japanese ladies took Chinese ink tuition in Sarawak and left the state as accomplished practitioners of this ancient art! Some tutors take in groups. This may be the ideal arrangement for your 'ladies' circle'; on the other hand, if you join an existing group, you will mix with local people who share your artistic interests, and whom you might not otherwise meet at all.

Art tuition for children is sometimes offered. Check first whether this is coaching for public examinations, or simply art for art's sake of the kind your young children would enjoy.

'Pavement artists' may occasionally be seen in the large shopping centres, drawing portraits from life or from photographs. The local secondary school probably has an art club which holds an annual exhibition; many an excellent piece of *batik* or water colour will be on show, and if the young artists do not mind selling their works, you may pick up a bargain.

Pottery

There are pottery workshops in all major East Malaysian towns. Nearly all the craftsmen are Chinese of Teochew extraction, descendants of many generations of potters.

Here, too, the long-term resident has the advantage of being able to make a leisurely selection. Potters are only too happy to produce to a customer's specifications—bowls or mugs with your initials, a favourite flower or your pet cat's portrait.

Clay may be obtained from the potteries. Depending on how chummy you have become with the foreman, you will get a sizeable lump free, or for 30 cents. Try your hand at modelling, and if you turn out something that is not too dreadful to be shown to an expert, ask if you could have it fired. The potter will not usually refuse, though he will decline to accept responsibility for mishaps.

Carvings, Knives

In Sabah and Brunei, many decorative items are carved out of buffalo horn: spoons, letter openers, small dishes and knife handles. Many knives are produced for sale, with decoratively-forged or inlaid blades and lavishly-crafted handles and scabbards. These are just as sharp as the utility ware. Due care is advised when testing a blade!

Bronze casting and silverwork were traditional Bruneian trades, recently rescued from near-oblivion by the efforts of the Handicrafts Board. Much of the antique silver jewellery seen in Sabah and Sarawak comes from the sultanate, including the spectacular silver-gilt cones worn by Tuaran Kadazandusun ladies with their antique bead necklaces.

Hats

One of the most striking souvenirs to take home is a hat. The styles and varieties are manifold: each district, each tribe and each village has its own. Most Borneo hats are large. Their main purpose is to keep out the sun and the rain.

A word of warning: What seems like a large colourfully-decorated conical hat could be a food cover, placed over ready-cooked food to keep the flies off. Ask the seller what 'this thing' is for. If he unhesitatingly puts it on his head, it's a hat. He would never do that with a food cover.

THE GREEN HELL OF BORNEO
Travelling

For those who cannot catch the next plane to get around in East Malaysia, travelling is not easy.

The old highways of Borneo, the rivers, are still used as major traffic routes. Longhouse and *kampong* boys learn to paddle little dugouts the way bazaar lads learn to ride bicycles. Farmers paddle to work and to market, though many now have outboard engines on their sturdy longboats.

Rivers of any size are plied by launches that serve as buses. Some of these are unique craft and would do any Museum of Transport proud. Others are the latest in air-conditioned speedboats. They are unpopular with riverside dwellers, undermining the support posts of longhouses and eroding the banks with their strong wash.

Goods and passengers are carried in coastal boats, the 'moto China'. Regular services run down one major river, along the coast and up the next. 'Regular' in this context means more or less when the boat is reasonably full, the tides and weather are fair and the skipper is in the right frame of mind. To travellers used to timetables and schedules, waterborne transport can be a sore trial.

Roads carry much of the traffic between towns and bazaars. Where the car fails, the battered rural bus may get through. Beyond reach of even the toughest four-wheel-drive, motorbikes and bicycles can sometimes be used. Borneans will not walk if it can be avoided, though they walk for hours and days if no choice is offered.

Tourists enjoying a slice of local life—a boat ride down a narrow river.

Coast-to-coast routes are usually river trips, one up towards the central mountains and one down away from them, and a gruelling walk or climb across the formidable barrier in between. If there is any option, people prefer a rough boat journey to any walk. They are prepared to push and shove their vessel up rapids and through shallows, putting up with a few spills and portaging a longboat across a watershed, rather than undertake a long trek which would involve hiring or borrowing river craft on the other side.

Interior people, the Penan for instance, are more comfortable on foot. Some positively dislike water; few can swim. They roam the savannah plains and jungles between the upper reaches of Borneo's major rivers. The journalist who dubbed them the 'lost tribes' was merely describing himself.

The Penan are not lost. They know exactly where they are coming from, where they are going and how to get there. An outsider who meets up with them is likely to be off his track. He certainly lacks their ability to melt unobtrusively into the Sarawak jungle and emerge, days or weeks later, at a trading place in Indonesian Borneo.

Have the Natives Been Spoilt?

Modern Borneo tourists frequently complain of two things: transport arrangements are very expensive and 'the natives have been spoilt'.

For the traveller who will not make use of public buses and river launches, the first is certainly true. He may arrive at a longhouse in the evening and see a dozen longboats with outboard engines tied up at the jetty. Next morning he finds that they are all going off to their farms or hunting grounds and not along his route at all. His offer to 'pay something towards the fuel' does not get him very far. He has to hire a boat and driver at considerable expense; come evening he may find that he is expected to pay for his stay in the longhouse too.

This sort of thing comes as a nasty shock to the readers of publications which advertise Borneo as a place where one can 'live off the land'. The disenchanted traveller abuses his hosts as 'spoilt' if they will not dispense largesse cheerfully to all comers.

The system of freely available longhouse hospitality is one that, like so many Dayak traditions, works well within its own framework. It just does not accommodate outsiders.

The traveller of old who made use of it one day was quite prepared to lodge and feed his present hosts when they came travelling to his region. The itinerant Chinese trader lodged in every longhouse he did business with; when his Dayak suppliers/ customers came for a visit to town, they slept in the loft above his shophouse. Every beneficiary was also a contributor.

Seasonal work and the physical difficulties of travel kept the numbers involved within manageable proportions.

The foreign tourist is never going to board and lodge his longhouse hosts on their travels. Along the more popular routes, they have started charging money for accommodation, entertainment and food. Endless streams of visitors put a sore strain on their material resources and interfere with their daily work; they have got to live on something.

Borneo people are polite, and usually feel ashamed if they cannot entertain all comers in style. No invited guest ever had anything but praise for longhouse hospitality! But the self-invited are beginning to feel uninvited. Longhouses near upriver bazaars, the most obvious targets for large numbers of tourists, may politely recommend visitors to seek accommodation in a Chinese hotel in the township.

"YES, WE ACCEPT VISA!"
Everybody who has ever hit Borneo within the last 150 years has felt obliged to visit a longhouse.

All the relevant literature enforces the belief that this is an island of hornbills, orang-utans, headhunters, Below the Wind and longhouses. Hornbills and orang-utans are protected species, all but invisible except in the National Parks. Headhunters are extinct. Below the Wind is not a place you could take a conducted tour to. That leaves the longhouses.

Not many prospective visitors stop to think that longhouses are private dwellings, just like their own flats, apartments, link-houses and semi-Ds back home in Britain, the United States or wherever. As the pace of tourism gears up, complaints are heard from longhouses in the more accessible areas.

Yes, we like visitors, but not six times a week. Our food resources, tempers and work schedules simply will not stand it.

Tourist Longhouse

The evolution of organised tourism was inevitable. For all the lure of an unspoilt jungle paradise, few visitors seriously want to risk leeches, open latrines, hepatitis, jaundice, malaria, sudden transport breakdown in the middle of nowhere (think of those onward bookings!)or a five-day jungle trek that ends at an empty longhouse because all the inhabitants have moved to their farm huts for the harvesting season.

There are any number of conducted tours, and the casual visitor is strongly advised to make use of them. He will be taken to a 'tourist longhouse' or 'tourist *kampong*', inhabited by a community of natives (Iban or Orang Ulu in Sarawak, Lun Dayeh, Murut, Kadazandusun or Bajau in Sabah) who expect guests at regular times, and have adapted routines to their reception and entertainment.

A traditionally-costumed welcoming party will be ready at the door, the obligatory drink of *tuak*, *borak* or *tapai* (rice wine) will be poured with a flourish. Guests are invited to sit down on the mats and take a rest.

The drumming and the dancing in the evening are laid on with a big smile; young people in their beautiful heirloom outfits are ready to pose for photos. Most tourist longhouses have a guesthouse attached where foreigners find simple sleeping accommodation of the kind they are used to, bathrooms with a door that can be shut and toilets that flush!

Compared to what a bus fare to the more accessible longhouse areas would cost, such trips are expensive. For one thing, the tour operator makes his living this way. For another, the longhouse folk are giving up their own work to be ever-ready for guests. This can severely interrupt farming and gardening, their traditional sources of income. And however quaint the natives, they have still got to eat!

An uninvited surprise visit to a longhouse disappoints many travellers because, first of all, there may be hardly anybody at home in the daytime. A couple of antique grannies will produce a drink and then go about their own housework. Such people who eventually turn up are dressed in their farm clothes.

The younger set will crowd around the visitor with questions about the health and well-being of the most up-to-date pop and film stars. If there is any music, it will be Michael Jackson or the Spice Girls from a CD player.

Many tourists feel let down by such a reception. But why?

Picture Mr and Mrs Jones of Iowa, suddenly confronted by a bunch of uninvited strangers on their doorstep. If they are let in at all, would they be treated to an impromptu six-course meal served on Mrs Jones's best china (unlike the longhouse wife, Mrs Jones has a freezer that could be full of precooked six-course meals!)? Would Miss Jones give a recital on the cottage piano for their entertainment? And would Mr Jones deck himself out in his dress suit so the strangers can take photos of the male American in his native costume?

The Joneses would do no such thing. Why should longhouse people?

Native Costumes

Borneo's native costumes are picturesque, artistically hand-crafted, dignified and valuable outfits, nowadays seldom worn.

Longhouse and *kampong* folk going about their everyday business are dressed in convenient modern style, with a few local variations. For purely practical reasons, a T-shirt is preferable to a handwoven silver-encrusted jacket most days of the week!

Elaborate costumes are kept for special occasions. Here and there, a few elderly people will wear 'something native'— most likely hats—for going to town, but no traveller should count on seeing the Malaysian travel posters come alive in the streets of Borneo towns and bazaars.

The best place to see costumes is at a *gawai* (harvest festival), in a tourist longhouse, or at any centre where tourists

In Sabah, some Rungus maidens wear old, valuable glass beads together with strings of plastic ones. No deception is intended: 'genuine antique beads' hand-melted out of, among other things, toothbrush handles, are made in the southern Philippines and sold in Sabah. They are not even cheap!

are regularly entertained. Here, it is in the interest of the organisers to put on a good show. In some places, visitors get a chance to put on modified native costumes to have their photos taken.

The original costumes are elaborate, usually quite old and valuable. Few tourists succeed in buying a 'genuine native outfit', though modern adaptations of certain parts may be offered for sale. There are antique shops in most large towns and bazaars where silver and brass belts, beads, old coin necklaces and the like may be bought. These are expensive, but modestly priced new replicas are generally available.

A dance or ceremony often repeated becomes streamlined; a cumbersome and elaborate dress often put on becomes simplified. Fashions creep into even the most determined efforts to remain traditional. To the dismay of some male travellers, Borneo maidens wear blouses. Those dancing for visitors cover their bosoms with stout cotton bras or more elegant sashes. Genuine 'topless Borneo beauties' are over 85!

The handwoven, handcrafted parts of traditional clothing are the most difficult to make and preserve. Shop-bought cloth is often used for costumes which are worn a lot.

No visitor should take offence at the obviously unauthentic pink and purple satins, the masses of sequins and tinsel that adorn 'modern traditional' costumes. They have been added in an attempt, misguided or otherwise, to make the dance look more colourful and attractive for our guests.

Upcountry Tour

An upcountry tour starts in one of the larger townships, usually with a road trip. The roads of East Malaysia are on the whole not very good though steps are taken to improve them. The prospective explorer should take comfort in the knowledge that what takes him six hours in a boneshaking bus took A R Wallace three days on foot in 1856.

The trip may continue by riverboat. The choice is between a simple longboat, a longboat with outboard engine, an open speedboat or a cabin speedboat. Travel by water is smoother than on a rough road, but the craft may be filled almost to the water-line. The passengers can hardly budge, wedged in on the floorboards between their own and everybody else's bags for the duration. Here again, a thought of Wallace and his three-week hand-paddled journeys may provide some relief. Energetic demands for more legroom will not.

Some Borneo river journeys are unforgettable experiences, but they all come to an end at the busy longhouse jetty.

Gawai

The guest sure of an excellent time in the longhouse is the invited one. At festival times, Borneans like to *balik kampong* (go home to the village) for the celebrations; a foreign workmate or friend may be invited along to share in the fun. This is the best way to truly enjoy Borneo hospitality!

The main festivals are the Harvest Festival in Sabah, Gawai Dayak in Sarawak and Hari Raya in both. A Borneo festival always includes an 'open house'. All guests are welcome and entertained to the full. In town areas, this may be a half-hour call, or an evening's party.

The visitor to an upcountry celebration is expected to stay at least overnight. Depending on the rite, some *gawai* last three days—spent in almost uninterrupted eating, drinking, dancing and general hilarity. Stealthy attempts at snatching a little sleep are usually thwarted by the longhouse girls, who will drag a guest to his feet for another dance, and yet another, or just one little drink, and then it is mealtime again. A *gawai* makes a good story after the event, but it takes stamina at the time!

Many native festivals end in a *pantang*, a taboo period during which nobody may enter or leave the *kampong* or longhouse. A foreigner who is invited to a *gawai* does well to enquire into the matter beforehand. In most cases, people may leave just at the end of the festivity, before the taboo has been officially declared. One who breaks the *pantang* endangers his own safety. Most foreigners would be prepared to risk this,

Gawai procession in an Iban longhouse.

but the safety of the community holding the festival may also be in jeopardy if even one person breaks out.

Members of commercial tour groups have 'mini-g*awai*' laid on for them, streamlined versions of the real thing. This is not quite so exhausting, and it does not involve a *pantang*.

RULES FOR LONGHOUSE VISITORS

The foreign visitor is forgiven many lapses in etiquette. 'He doesn't know any better' is the general attitude. A person with basic good manners is not likely to offend very severely.

The following tips will convince his hosts that the visitor is a cut above the ordinary tourist!

Shoes

Remember at all times that a longhouse is neither a zoo nor a museum; it is a private dwelling. Borneo people take off their shoes before entering a house in town or village. The same applies here. Follow the example of your guide.

In some places, shoes are left at the door entering the inside verandah, or by the wall of the family rooms. If the general populace walks around the verandah in shoes, visitors may do so; but never wear shoes to step on a mat.

Sitting Down

Mats will be spread on the verandah for visitors to sit on. Take off your shoes and sit down as gracefully as you can. Plumping down with a windy sigh and legs sprawling in all directions is considered a sure sign of weakness and degeneracy.

Women are expected to tuck their feet in decorously and pull their skirts down over their knees. Even if shorts or slacksare worn, the spreading of legs and knees is considered most unbecoming.

A Woman's Place

In a normal social context, women are invited to sit inside a room with the women of the *kampong* or longhouse, not on the verandah with the men. This can be a little trying, as foreign guests will be freely stared at and discussed. If ladies are invited into the rooms, they should sit near girls or young women, who are likely to know some English.

Family Rooms

Being invited into a family room is a privilege. Men in particular have no business inside the rooms unless they are specifically called in, usually for meals. The occupants of a tourist longhouse may be more tolerant of intrusion, but they do not like it either.

Among some remote Bidayuh, a stranger's eye on the cooking pots renders the food inedible; it will have to be thrown away. Thoughtless curiosity on the part of a well-fed foreigner could thus waste a poor family's daily meal!

The Walkway
Although the verandah of a longhouse looks like a wide open village street, the section opposite each family room is private property. The public thoroughfare is a path, about 5 ft wide, along the fronts of all the family room doors. There visitors may stroll up and down. If any interesting activity is going on, ask people's permission before leaving the 'path' and joining them to have a good look. They will seldom refuse; a mat maker, weaver, netter or carver likes an audience.

Photographs
Ask permission to take photographs. In some tourist longhouses, you are expected to pay a small fee, particularly to snap people dressed up in their traditional costumes.

Sleeping Arrangements
For staying overnight in a longhouse or *kampong*, it is a good idea to bring a mosquito net, a pillow and a light blanket. Sleeping mats are always available, other bedding usually is, but some travellers prefer to use their own. Men normally sleep on the verandah, women inside the room.

Toilets
In the old-fashioned, 'unspoilt' upriver longhouse, sanitary facilities are savage rather than noble. There may or may not be a place officially recognised as a toilet. The visitor should ask a resident of the same sex for directions to the *jamban*.

In primitive longhouses, women 'do their business' in the comparative shelter of a kitchen corner, over a section of slatted floor which ensures drainage. For a woman in a skirt or *sarong*, this is not too difficult; it is impossible to preserve decency if shorts or slacks are worn.

Sarongs are useful for this and other purposes of modesty. Borneo natives may appear to walk around 'half-naked', but they are very particular about exposure. Nobody stares at a person engaged in ablutions or elimination; still he is expected to preserve the decencies. Men 'step behind a bush' for their needs, but it is their business to find an unobserved bush!

Some longhouses have latrines in various states of hygiene and repair. Some of these have cess pits, others a little drain out the back. This may serve more than one purpose. A stranger to the system, perched high on the log of a drain latrine, probably finds the presence of a large, patiently waiting pig below a little unnerving.

Modern longhouses and *kampongs* have proper outhouses, often constructed thanks to the efforts of the state medical department. Even the staunchest admirer of primitive, unspoilt Borneo appreciates a little door between himself and the world at times.

There is, of course, no toilet paper in a *kampong* latrine; each user brings along his own supplies. A cigarette is also advisable, as smoke keeps the mosquitoes at bay. At night, a torchlight is added to the toilet requisites. If the facility is sited at any distance behind the main house, so is an umbrella or a large hat in case of rain.

Bathing

Bathing is done on the jetty, in the river, in full view of the public.

A minimum of clothing has to be worn by all except small boys; skinny-dipping is a grave offence to all East Malaysians. The ever-useful *sarong* can make an open-air bath possible within the confines of the strictest decorum.

Small children bathe with their mothers or big brothers and sisters, men on their own. The bather brings along a little bucket, soap, toothpaste and toothbrush, a towel, a dry *sarong* and proceeds to the lowest step of the jetty.

Women dressed in a *sarong* tied under the armpits step into the water and start soaping themselves. At waist deep, a perfectly thorough wash is possible. Then they rinse off by

Men and women bathe separately, usually in groups. The driver of an approaching longboat may linger offshore for a few minutes if he sees the jetty occupied by females. It is the height of bad manners for a man to stare at bathing girls and women.

pouring water over themselves with a little bucket or dipper. It is possible but not recommended to swim a few strokes in a *sarong*; unless it is properly tied, it may simply float off!

At the end of the bath, the dry *sarong* is pulled on over the head. To keep both hands free, it can be held with the teeth for a moment while the wet one is untucked. Then it is simply a question of wriggling the wet *sarong* down to one's feet and tucking the dry one properly. Proceed to the house, where women dress inside the room, facing a discreet corner.

Proper Deportment

There are chairs and tables in some houses, but much of the community's social life takes place on the floor. A person walking upright has to be conscious of those seated on mats, and take great care not to step on or near utensils. The usual way is to walk with knees slightly bent, holding both hands stiffly at the sides to avoid one's clothes touching other people. This is the polite thing to do even when walking among a chair-seated or standing crowd, particularly by women wearing full skirts.

To move forward in a crowd, put out both hands, palm to palm in a 'begging' attitude, and wedge yourself in. The occasional traveller from upriver is seen doing this in a well-mannered attempt to cross a busy road in town. (Note: It does not work!)

Food

Some native food may seem strange to one not used to it. There is always a big plate of freshly-cooked white rice for each person; fish, meat and vegetable dishes are served in bowls and platters and shared by everyone. There may or may not be spoons; savvy travellers bring their own.

Men and women often eat separately. If they share the same mat, they will sit segregated. Men usually sit cross-legged, women with their knees together and both feet tucked under to one side. It is rude to point one's feet towards the food.

Each eater is left to pick from the side dishes he fancies, adding relish to his rice. If he is specifically offered something, he should take a little.

Yes, some natives do eat snake, flying fox, bat, sago grubs, monkey, anteater, monitor lizard and other jungle delicacies. It is perfectly in order for the visitor to decline what he would rather not eat. Touching the edge of the dish with one finger of his right hand will convey the 'no, thank you' message.

Under no circumstances should you sniff unfamiliar food or drink. "Monkeys smell their food!" Displays of the 'yuk-yeech!' kind are also not appreciated.

Direct praise of tasty food is gauche. Say something like, "The women of this house are good cooks!" Everybody will immediately disclaim all credit, and be hugely pleased at the compliment.

If travellers decide to have a snack en route, in a boat maybe, they should offer something to those people sitting near them. Snacks will usually not be accepted unless they are biscuits, sweets or anything else small and easily shared. One person eating by himself is considered greedy!

Hygiene Tips

Borneo is by no means one of the unhealthy parts of the tropics. An early commentator, writing home about Kuching, mentions in his letter that while all household refuse is chucked into open drains, the twice-daily tide washes everything down the main river 'and the town is as sweet as you might wish'.

Municipal hygiene has progressed since those days; you certainly can drink the water in East Malaysia's towns. But once you proceed upcountry, a few basic health rules must be added to the information given in Chapter Five.

Drinking Water

In an upcountry coffee shop, order bottled drinks. Tea or coffee are always freshly prepared with water boiled as required, and thus quite safe. The drink usually offered in a longhouse is *tuak* (rice wine); cleanly prepared and stored, it is safe. When in doubt, plead an aversion to strong drink. Women get away with this more easily than men! If all else fails, say, "I'm taking medicine"; nobody would be urged to mix drink and medicine.

Ask for boiled water, usually stored in glass bottles in the kitchen. In Iban it is *ai mati*; in Malay it is *air sudah masak*.

In many longhouses or *kampongs*, sweetened tea or coffee is served. This has been boiled at the time of preparation, and is safe to drink. Cautious travellers carry their own flask of boiled water. Any hotel or restaurant will refill it on request.

Malaria and Others

Malaria does exist in East Malaysia. Travellers do not need to take prophylactics unless their journey will take them into the deep jungle, or near the Indonesian border. Parts of eastern Sabah have the occasional cholera outbreak, and a recent epidemic of measles was traced to illegal immigrants, so the standard traveller's vaccinations may be of use. Personal and food hygiene are usually sufficient protection.

Parasites

It is a good idea to wear rubber slippers when taking a bath on a jetty or in a communal bathing place, especially if it is near a primitive latrine, as protection against water-borne parasites. When bathing in the lower course of a river, it is advisable not to swallow water; clean water should be used to brush the teeth.

Infections

Small cuts, scratches, even mosquito bites are likely to become infected and heal slowly, due to the damp climate. Upcountry travellers are advised to carry disinfectant cream or lotion.

Sun Protection

Jungle trekkers will not have much trouble with the sun. They should take precautions against skin fungi.

In secondary jungles or by the seaside, normal sun protection is needed. The days of pith helmets are over, but a wide-brimmed hat and sun screen lotion can avert a nasty sunburn on an overcast day when many travellers think they should be safe. Take a cue from the locals who wear huge sun hats for any outdoor work!

Sexually Transmitted Diseases (STD)

Adventurous travellers are advised that there are STD in Borneo, just as anywhere else. Enterprising prostitutes are said to have set up shop in a few tourist longhouses, doing a doe-eyed native maiden act for the lecherous foreigner.

Great care is advised with obviously available 'longhouse girls'. STD clinics exist in upcountry hospitals but they are not widely used by those who need them most. So, buyer beware!

COST OF LONGHOUSE VISITS

The local currency is the Malaysian ringgit in Sarawak and Sabah, and the Brunei or Singapore dollar in the sultanate. Except in big hotels in the main centres, foreign money is not acceptable. Not even the US dollar!

The member of an organised tour should not need much money except for buying souvenirs. He will usually have paid his fee before even entering East Malaysia. In any case, it is wise to check that 'all meals' means all meals, not just breakfast and dinner.

Along the tourist trail, a number of shops dealing with souvenirs, books, antiques and curios accept credit cards. In most larger townships, there is a bank which will exchange travellers' cheques. So do hotels, but the rates are usually better at the bank. There are ATMs in banks and most larger shopping malls, but not in the upcountry bazaars. The solo traveller will need money for transport, accommodation and food.

Transport

Transport on public buses and boats is very reasonable; delays, breakdowns, overcrowding and unannounced route changes are included free of charge.

It is usually possible to hire a boat for a certain journey; agreements about the price for all parts of the journey should be made before embarkation. This is an expensive mode of travel. The fuel price multiplies in proportion to the distance from the main towns. The boat and driver have to be compensated for taking a day off farming duties.

Helicopters are available for private hire. This is a very expensive mode of travel, but it can cut a few days' travelling down to an hour's flight. Any travel bureau will be only too delighted to find a charter heli for the affluent tourist.

Accommodation

Accommodation may be found at local houses, rest houses or hotels.

People in the less accessible regions of East Malaysia will allot a traveller sleeping space in their verandah without questions asked; usually they will invite him to share their frugal fare. Decency requires that he contribute to the meal, most conveniently in the form of tinned food (these people may be very poor), but his hosts will not insist.

In many areas, especially at district headquarters, there are government resthouses. They are clean, simple bungalows, where two to four travellers can share one room and have the use of a bath and kitchen. Against an adequate tip, the resthouse keeper is usually prepared to cook food procured by the guest. Resthouses are not very expensive; there is, however, one snag. They provide accommodation for government officials travelling on duty. Casual lodgers may be turned out to make room for an official party.

Even the most upcountry bazaars have a Chinese hotel. They may consist of cubicles on the floor above a food shop, with shared bath facilities, or proper small rooms. Near the better-known tourist spots, there are small hotels with air-conditioned rooms, but the more economical 'local hotel' will also be found.

Food

Where there is even a vestige of a bazaar, there is a food shop. Very often, restaurant and hotel or primitive lodging are combined.

Food is neither fancy nor expensive at such places, there is always plenty of rice. Nobody with a moderate amount of money need go hungry.

Hawkers selling noodle dishes, cool drinks, buns and biscuits and the like are found near most boat jetties.

DO YOU SPEAK BAHASA?

CHAPTER 8

'"My gracious!" said Taffy, "now make another noise Daddy."
"Ssh!" said her Daddy, and frowned to himself,
but Taffy was too excited to notice.
"That's quite easy," she said, scratching on the bark.
"Eh, what?" said her Daddy.
"I meant I was thinking, and didn't want to be disturbed."
"It's a noise just the same. It's the noise a snake makes,
Daddy, when it is thinking and doesn't want
to be disturbed. Let's make the ssh-noise a snake.
Will this do?" And she drew this: S.'
—Rudyard Kipling, *How the Alphabet was Made*

Sᴀʀᴀᴡᴀᴋ, Sᴀʙᴀʜ ᴀɴᴅ Bʀᴜɴᴇɪ are inhabited by at least two dozen tribes, speaking about as many languages.

Purists distinguish between sub-tribes and sub-dialects; let a linguist loose among the morphemes and phonemes and lexical units of Borneo and he may well distinguish 50 to 60 languages.

No wonder there is no such thing as a 'Borneo Language'. If people of different groups want to communicate, they do so largely through the medium of a streamlined form of Malay.

ADVICE TO THE NEWCOMER: LEARN MALAY!

Malay has been the lingua franca of the archipelago for centuries. Modern efforts have standardised Indonesian, Malaysian and Bruneian Malay, and now the three versions are mutually intelligible.

The free-for-all version of town and village, river boat and upriver clinic is known as 'bazaar Malay'. Even among the most remote tribes, there are at least a few men who have a smattering of this useful dialect. Where there are schools, the children and teachers have a reasonable command of the official language besides the English which they learn in class but may be too shy to use in conversation with a stranger.

The traveller who plans to veer off the beaten path in Borneo does well to pack a Malay vocabulary book in his rucksack!

There is no substitute for it.

LOCAL DIALECTS

A foreign contract officer 'in the field' is well advised to learn the language of his region. If he is an agricultural teacher in Sabah, he may find a working knowledge of Kadazan of great advantage—but once out of Kadazan land, he is stuck unless he had the foresight to learn Murut, Bajau and Penan as well. Yet among each of these people, there are a few fellows who understand Malay of a sort.

Men who have served in the armed forces or the police, or worked as porters or guides with expeditions and government travelling parties, have picked up a few words.

The middle-aged staff in government offices speak good English, but the younger crowd is likely to be more fluent in Malay.

ENGLISH

A Frenchman may travel in England relying on the scanty French knowledge of the local population. They will be helpful, unless he roars with laughter each time they get a tense or gender wrong.

The good Bornean with a certain amount of English feels the same way. A traveller who expresses himself simply, clearly and makes an effort to understand what they tell him gets on fine. The smart aleck who mocks the local speaker's accent or faulty grammar is treated to elaborate courtesy in formal Malay and left standing.

The author of a book on Borneo who got a heat rash in the groin sent his local yokel to buy 'crotch creme', and he found it immensely funny that the ignorant bumpkin brought back clutch grease instead of prickly heat powder. Would anybody ask for 'crotch creme' at a chemist's in England? (And if 'yes', what would they get?)

Peculiarities

East Malaysia is persistently marketed as the world's last fortress of the wild and primitive. But it must not be forgotten that the oldest English school in Sarawak was founded in 1848! There are middle-aged people in Kuching whose parents and grandparents are literate in that language. The traveller should, however, be aware of a few improvements on the noble tongue of Shakespeare as it is used in East Malaysia.

Borneo English has its little peculiarities. Some are due to the source. A number of now middle-aged Ibans learned it from the British Army. If a boat driver struggling with his engine turns to a load of lady passengers and informs them, "This bugger won't start!", it may be inferred that he was a tracker during the Malayan Emergency in the mid-1950s, or a Sarawak Border Scout in the 1960s.

Like any living language, bazaar English is changing all the time, taking in new terms and dropping obsolete ones.

Abbreviation

Bazaar English goes in for extreme abbreviation.

"Hand me torchlight!"
"Torchlight where got!"
This means, "Where do you think I've got a torchlight?" i.e., there is none. This can be shortened even further to:
"Torchlight got?"
"Not got!"

"Lift up that plank!"
"Lift up how can!"
There is a reason why I can't lift it, or it simply cannot be lifted.

"On that light!"
"Off that light!"
Switch on (off) that light. If it is a question of potentially dangerous machinery, a misunderstanding could be fatal! Be alert for an agitated "Off it! Off it!" and quickly turn off whatever is running. You can always 'on it' again after he has his shirt tail out of the cog wheels.

"Go'head!"
"Go'sten!"
Directions to move a vehicle are given in naval fashion—"Go ahead!', 'Go astern!" In the heat of the action, somebody may

simply holler, "Hed-hed!" or "Sten-sten!" or the Esperanto, "Ooop-oop! Oi-Oi! Ooooo-ap!" When you feel a jarring impact, you have reversed too far in any language.

"Do you sell red cotton socks?"
"Not got!" ("No stock!")
This shop does not stock the article in question.

Tense
Tense is often expressed as 'last time' (past) or 'next time' (future), especially by those used to speaking Chinese.
"Do you sell green cotton socks?"
"Last time got!"
This means, "We normally stock them, but do not have any right now."

'Last time' means 'formerly'; 'next time' indicates the future, with no intention of expressing numerical order. 'Last time I go to Chung Hua Middle School' means the speaker used to attend that school.

"Next time I get rich I go to England" means 'I hope to go to England when (if) I get rich.' The speaker is not saying that he has been rich and poor in succession several times and is simply waiting for the next upswing!

Negative Questions
Avoid asking questions that demand an answer seemingly against the sense intended.

"Why don't you pick it up?" This cannot be answered by yes or no. A straightforward request is better, "Please pick it up!" The answer will be yes or no, plus an explanation.

"Do you mind eating pork?" requires a negative answer for the positive meaning.

"No I don't mind!" means 'Yes I eat it.' "Yes I mind!" means 'No I don't eat it.' Just ask, "Do you take pork?" and the answer may be yes or no according to the speaker's tastes.

The reproving "Do you mind!" is not generally understood. The lady of the house is getting changed when her helper comes into the bedroom, carrying an armful of linen to put away. An outraged "Do you MIND!" may be answered innocently with, "I don't mind—we both women!" while the girl starts to stack towels in their proper place. She is not being cheeky; she honestly does not mind, and that is what she was asked!

In a situation such as this, it is best to preserve a stiff upper lip, and tell the girl later on that you would rather she did not enter your bedroom when you are in it.

'Take Food'

'To take' is very generally used for 'to eat', as in, "Have you taken your rice?" The expression reminds the native English speaker of taking medicine three times a day, but it is the local norm.

To find out whether a person likes a certain dish, especially something he is not familiar with, the usual phrase is, "Do you know how to eat *sambal belacan*?" Resist the temptation to say, "Well, if I went to school and learned, I might manage it..." Your friend simply meant, 'do you like it?'

"*Belacan* smells bloody awful!" is not the right answer even if that is how you feel about the stuff. The difference between "I can't take it, it is too hot!" and "It's disgusting!" is clearly understood by all.

To Wish Somebody

This is used to describe greetings, giving the time of day. Polite people 'wish' their acquaintances when they meet them in the street; if wishing is omitted, the aunts will talk.

"Cousin George just walked past and didn't even wish us!" is a serious misdemeanour on George's part.

If a friend walks up to others seated at a foodstall, he may decline their invitation to join, "I just wanted to stop and wish you." And having wished them, he is on his way with a good conscience.

'Lah'

Malaysian English is freely laced with the particle 'lah'. It means nothing specific and is added for euphony, or to soften a seemingly bald statement.

"I've got to go home!" is considered more abrupt than "I've got to go home, lah!"

The 'lah' adds a note of lingering regret—wish I could stay, but what to do lah?

Direct Translation

Some oddities are the result of direct translation from the local language.

'Send', 'Follow' and 'Pick'

These refer to transporting a person by some means of conveyance, usually a car. If a gathering is likely to end late, arrangements have to be made to send (take) everybody home!

"Mr Smith, could you send Haji Ali home?" sounds like a preposterous request to the newly-arrived foreigner. How could he take it upon himself to send a venerable white-haired gentleman home like a schoolboy? ("Go on, Tuan Haji—off with you! At the double!")

What he is expected to do is 'take Haji Ali home' in his car.

If Haji Ali knows Mr Smith personally and they live very near each other, he would ask, "Say, Smith, can I follow you home?" This conjures up an image of Smith happily driving and Haji Ali jogging along behind. What is meant is, "Would you take me home?"

Neighbours who have a 'school taxi' arrangement with each other use the expression too. Foreigners may be startled to hear Mrs Tan proclaim happily that she can attend a luncheon today "because I don't have to pick my kids home. They follow Mrs Chong."

Are the poor wee things running along behind the Chongs' Volvo in the shimmering noonday heat? Not at all. The children of both families are in one of the two cars, driven by the respective owner; the two mothers take turns to drive.

'Picking' somebody 'up' is shortened to 'pick', as in, "I may be a few minutes late, I've got to pick Jane and Mary on the way."

The extension of this one is to 'pick somebody home': you pick him up and take him home: "My daughter's at school now. I'll have to pick her home at 1:00 pm" is clear to any East Malaysian.

The exercise is not without its own logic. You can only 'send' a person if you were in the same place together to start with; if you have got to make an extra trip to find him and then take him somewhere, you are clearly 'picking' him.

'Shameful' and 'Brave'

'Shameful' is used for shy, awkward, ashamed; it is a straight translation of the Malay *malu*.

Young girls are supposed to be modestly 'shameful'. If a girl refuses to come and shake hands with visitors, her mother explains, "Never mind Lily. She's very shameful!"

A schoolgirl may tell her mother that a new friend is 'not at all shameful', meaning the new friend is not shy. Such a girl is 'brave', not embarrassed or awkward. An aunt who disapprovingly describes a girl as 'too brave' is getting near the Western meaning of 'shameful'. The girl lacks maidenly modesty.

'Brave' usually refers to a person's social aptitude, not his physical courage. A brave warrior is 'very fierce', as is a fire-breathing chaperone!

'Friend'

This describes a fellow or comrade in the loosest sense. Most men would not hesitate to describe all their workmates as 'friends'. Schoolmates and classmates are always referred to thus.

Jimmy explains his dishevelled appearance with, "I had a fight with my friend!" Mama, apprehensive of the trauma the break-up of a lifelong friendship will plunge the lad into, advises him earnestly to 'shake hands and make up' the next day. "Why should I? I can't stand that friend—we fight every day!"

Expatriates will get used to hearing any compatriot, however unconnected and unknown, referred to as 'your friend'.

'My Special'

What would be described as a girlfriend or boyfriend elsewhere is 'my special' among the younger set. It means roughly 'going steady'; sometimes it is an affair of the heart as opposed to a family-sanctioned engagement.

The Agony Aunt in an East Malaysian newspaper has to occasionally advise a young man who asked a young lady to be his 'special', on how to tell her tactfully of a pre-existing fiancée.

'Rotten'

This unpleasant word is very freely used for anything that is worn out, broken, not working.

"Be careful on that staircase. It's rotten!"

"I must get a new pair of shoes, this pair all rotten."

"What's the time? I don't know, my watch is rotten."

'Disturb'

This expresses interference with something against the owner's wishes. The meaning is very loose, ranging from minor irritation to crime.

If a bad fellow 'disturbed' a girl, he could have pinched her arm or raped her. Further questioning will be needed!

Tommy has 'disturbed' Jimmy's sweets; he took some without asking. 'Disturbing' things often means 'converting to one's own use, not amounting to theft'.

The accusation "He stole my property!" is very serious indeed. If no proof is available, or the suspected thief is later found innocent, a charge of 'disturbing' will be more easily forgiven.

'Flower'

The design or profile. The pattern on cloth, wallpaper, tattoo—whether floral, straight lines or zigzag—is called the 'flower'. A tyre without 'flower' is bald.

Boys washing a tiled floor with buckets of water keep their rubber sandals on. Why? "Better like this, auntie. The flower on our slippers can eat the flower on the floor!", meaning that the rubber profile on the sole of the slipper can grip the rills between the floor tiles.

'Eat'

One common meaning of 'eat' is 'to engage, to get a purchase or grip'. Anybody who is likely to have anything to do with machinery had better learn this one!

If the brakes will not eat, a car is in trouble. More so if the gears do not eat either. You can tell by the squeaking noise that the fan belt is not eating.

This screwdriver is far too small to eat those big bolts. If a knife or saw will not eat, they are blunt. A slack bicycle chain needs adjustment to make it eat.

THE CHINESE HAVE A WORD FOR IT

There is a sizeable Chinese population in Borneo speaking... Chinese. It never fails to fascinate foreigners that their Chinese friends frequently talk to each other in English or Malay.

"I understand that they want to be polite when I'm there," an Australian teacher says, "and talk English so they don't seem to be talking about me—but even if I have nothing to do with the conversation, they talk Malay!"

Sure they do. One is Foochow, the other Henghua. Neither knows enough Mandarin to discuss the forthcoming examination schedules. The Chinese-educated group do speak Mandarin as a business language, but in Borneo, few people use it at home.

Depending on the source of the major migratory groups, the 'bazaar language' in Borneo may be Foochow, Cantonese, Hakka or Hokkien—and here West Malaysians are in for another shock. Hokkien as spoken in Penang is not the same as in, say, Kuching. The various Hokkiens can understand each other, but they get this mutual suspicion that the other fellow is an illiterate boor, and/or trying to make fun of them.

While Malay is more homogenous than the many Chinese dialects, it is quite possible for a West Malaysian with a strong regional accent to run into initial trouble in East Malaysia. In his early weeks here, he is constantly asked to 'repeat that, please' or 'speak slowly, please!'

The foreigner learning the tongue should model his pronunciation on what is heard on the radio. Basically, the dialect of Johore-Riau is evolving as the standard, just as the speech of southern England is nowadays accepted as standard English.

A TASTE OF BAHASA MELAYU

This is not the place to provide Teach-Yourself-Malay lessons. The following phrases and notes are a stopgap measure until you have learned the language. Remember, it is easiest and most enjoyable to learn with a class, harder but faster to read with a private tutor, hardest by far to study on your own!

Pronunciation Guide

The vowels in Malaysia are pronounced straight; diphthongs are spelt as two vowels:

- **a** as in *father*
- **e** as in *pet* in a stressed syllable, as in *matter* in an unstressed syllable
- **e** before a nasal is practically elided, but the nasal becomes voiced—*enam* (pronounced *nnam*) and *empat* (pronounced *mmpat*)
- **i** as in *tin*
- **o** as in *pot*
- **u** as in *put*
- **ai** as in *mice*
- **au** as in *house*
- **ya** as in *young*
- **ye** as in *yes*
- **yi** as in *yippee!*
- **yo** as in *yacht*
- **yu** as in *you*

A terminal *k* indicates that the preceding vowel is shortened, the *k* itself is not pronounced. *Makcik* is pronounced *ma'chi'*.

The consonants are almost the same as in English, with two notable exceptions that confuse people used to the English spelling system:

- **sy** as in *shoe*
- **c** as in *chap*

The first sight of a paint tin labelled 'CAT SEMEN' can be disconcerting, but let me reassure you that *cat*, pronounced *chat*, means 'paint', and *semen* is 'cement'. Cement paint. Simple. In the meantime, we have had another spelling revision to amend *semen* to *simen*.

Books

There are a number of excellent Bahasa Melayu books around. Buy one that is printed within the last five years. There have been many spelling revisions since 1963; the old books, however classic, are outdated.

To pick one word at random: *air* (water) used to be spelt *ayer*, only nobody ever really pronounced the unstressed 'e' in the second syllable. In the new spelling, it has been dropped.

So when you get an 'Air Bill' at the end of each month, it is simply the water bill! There is no charge for fresh air in East Malaysia.

I See You

You do not point at people, and you do not call them 'you'. Both are rude. So what do you call them?

If at all possible, address the person by his or her status. You will be called *tuan* or *mem* (sir, madam) left, right and centre. Return this with *encik* (Mr) and *cik* or *puan* (Miss, Mrs) whenever possible. Address your *amah* by name; instead of 'you', call her *makcik* if she is older than yourself, and *adik* if she is younger. Chinese household helpers are often called *che-cheh* (older sister). Following is a list of some other offices or distinctions. Use these instead of the second person pronoun within the sentence.

- *Cikgu* for a teacher
- *Doktor* for a doctor
- *Haji* (male) or *Hajjah* (female) for a Muslim who has been to Mecca
- *Kapitan* for a Chinese community leader
- *Ketua kampong* or *Penghulu* for a Malay community leader
- *Mandor* for a foreman
- *Towkay* for a shopkeeper

Having said all this about not calling people 'you', it must be admitted that the Malays have a word for it, two as a matter of fact, and they are both in common use.

Kau summons an inferior. Foreigners do not use this one. *Anda* or *kita* is used in polite conversation, for strangers of indeterminate status.

Royalty

There is a whole vocabulary specially for addressing royalty. If you are stationed in Brunei and have to communicate with the palace, you may have to learn it. Always rely on protocol for proper briefings—and never ever call His Majesty the Sultan 'Old Boy'!

Fleeting Meeting

- *"Mem dari mana?"* (Where do you come from, ma'am?)
- *"Saya dari Amerika."* (I'm from America.)
- *"Cik dari mana?"* (Where do you come from, Miss?)'
- *"Mana kampung Encik?"* (Where's your village sir?)
  This is often asked conversationally, "Where do you come from?" and leads to a discussion of hometown locations.
- *"Cikgu pandai cakap Inggeris?"* [Do you speak English, sir (teacher)?]
- *"Siapa nama cik?"* [What's your name, dear (to a girl or young lady)?]
- *"Nama saya* Mrs Smith." (My name is Mrs Smith.)
  It is accepted without question that a foreigner is called Mr or Mrs something. Do not start on the Jack-and-Ethel tack until you know each other a little better.

Do and Do Not

Two frequently used words are *ya* (yes) and *tidak* (no/not).
  "Tidak jauh" [Not far (from here)]
  "Saya tidak mengerti" (I don't understand)
  "Saya tidak tahu" (I don't know)

Sorry Lah!

This is understood almost everywhere: a rueful little grin and "sorry-lah!" But you can be more elegant.

- *"Maaf!"* (Sorry!—used in a general way)
- *"Maafkan!"* (I apologise!)
- *"Maafkan, salah saya!"* (Sorry, that was my fault!)
- *"Maaf saya tidak dapat menolong tuan!"* (Sorry, I can't help you sir!)
- *"Maaf, saya tidak dapat datang!"* (Sorry, I can't come! or I won't be able to come! The polite refusal to an invitation.)

Small Talk

You need proper starters for small talk, which is very popular in Borneo, as indeed anywhere else in South-east Asia.

"*Anda pandai cakap Inggeris?*" (Do you speak English?)
"*Anda boleh cakap Inggeris?*" means basically the same, but is more colloquial. *Boleh* means 'can' in terms of physical ability; *pandai* means 'know' in terms of acquired ability.

The answer would be:
"*Ya, pandai!*" (Yes, I do!)
"*Tidak berapa fasih!*" (Not very well!)
"*Maaf, tidak pandai!*" (Sorry, I don't!)

"*Siapa nama anda?*" (What's your name?)
"*Siapa nama encik/puan/cik?*" (What's the gentleman's/lady's/young lady's name?)

The second version is more polite because it avoids the direct you.

"*Siapa nama dia?*" (What's his/her name?) is asked of a third person well out of hearing, very discreetly. Indicate the object of your query with a glance, a small movement of the whole hand, bent thumb or bent forefinger. Pointing with an extended index finger is very rude, as is beckoning with one forefinger only. The correct way to ask somebody to 'come hither' is by beckoning with the whole hand, turned down.

You will constantly be asked, and you are expected to ask:
"*Berapa orang anak anda?*" or "*Berapa orang anak tuan/puan?*" (How many children have you got?)

The flowery term for children, *cahaya mata*, meaning 'the light of your eyes', is slightly formal and not used to describe one's own children.

"*Anak saya tiga orang.*" (I have three children.)
"*Saya belum kahwin.*" (I am not yet married.)

Never mind your age, if you are not married, it is considered a temporary state by your well-meaning Bornean friends.

If you are the host, compliment your guests up the stairs, through the door and onto their seats with:

"*Silakan naik!*" [Please come up (to my house)!]
"*Silakan masuk!*" (Please come in!)
"*Silakan duduk!*" (Please sit!)

Of course guests would come in and sit down anyway, but it is polite to urge them inch by inch.

When coming to a house uninvited, make sure of your welcome by asking:

"*Bolehkah saya masuk?*" (May I come in?)
"*Bolehkah saya duduk sini?*" [May I (can I) sit here?]

If, for some reason, you may not do what you requested, you will be told, "*Tidak boleh!*" (You cannot.)

'Traders busy themselves in arranging on their palm-roofed stalls a choice assortments of such articles as are likely to attract Dusun customers: cloth, matches, beads, gambier, buttons, tin lamps, tobacco-boxes, looking-glasses, knives and scissors, cotton-thread, needles, kerosene oil, cooking pots and other odds and ends, nearly all of which are cheap, nasty and made in Germany. The Chinese, Bajaus and Illanuns, being more sophisticated than the Dusuns, need to be kept strictly in order to prevent them from cheating the latter...'
—I H N Evans, *Among Primitive Peoples in Borneo*

A FOREIGNER IN EAST MALAYSIA most likely works in a company or office, a school or college, or a government department.

East Malaysian offices function like offices anywhere else on earth. There is the boss and the usual hierarchy, technical staff who think they know everything, the accounts department that thinks it knows more, the residential intellectual, the residential joker, the office flirt and the mother hen. It is a tightly-knit community and any newcomer would take a few weeks to fit in. A foreigner will take longer because he is conspicuous.

An expat will probably come in somewhere near the top of the structure. He should tread softly until he knows the way.

THE CONFIDANT(E)

There is one person whom the new arrival has more to do with than others. It may be his personal secretary or the chief clerk. Be sure to get notes from your predecessor as to whom you should listen to, whom you may trust and who usually deals with which aspect of the work.

People are not really frank until they know you. You meet a large expanse of ceremonially polite smiles. You need somebody who can cue you in on things such as which out of two concurrent invitations to accept (which is more important to our business?), whom to invite to these crucial first few business lunches and which politician you may praise in the hearing of which other politician.

There will be times when your confidant has a word with someone else's, and the two of them figure out what their bosses had better do.

THE RELAY SYSTEM

A request is often made from one private secretary to another, and then officially repeated when the answer is already known. This averts an unexpected refusal, and saves 'face' for both parties.

It is a common East Malaysian family practice transplanted to the office. A small boy wants something special from his papa. He asks granny to mention the matter to mama, who will then forward it to the higher authority. If either of the two intermediaries thinks the request is unreasonable, they will 'forget' to pass it on.

The same happens in an office. If one of your requests or instructions is 'forgotten' more than once, it may be worth your while to find out why.

PROPER CHANNELS OF COMMUNICATION

East Malaysians are on the whole polite people. They may be annoyed, but they will not show it. After arrangements have been made and orders given, the boss asks, "Is that all right then?" and all present will immediately assure him that it is. It may in fact be all wrong, as he will eventually discover.

It is better to spend a little time and have private talks with the key persons involved, "Say, Teo, about these deliveries ..." and let him know that you need his advice and opinion, based on his 20 years of experience in shipping. You give him 'face' by crediting his expertise, and he will tell you what he thinks is the best thing to do.

If you simply inform a meeting that the delivery time is to be X weeks, Teo will not disagree, though he knows that it's impossible. And you will know of this only when the stuff does not arrive month after month.

HOSPITALITY

Any but the briefest interview in an office is treated as a social call, with the obligatory drink. Do not ask, "Would you like a drink?" Offer the choice between tea or coffee, ask your client whether or not he takes sugar and instruct the tea girl accordingly.

When you call at somebody's office, he will give you a drink too. If you have a round of visits to make, you'll end up waterlogged if you attempt to finish each proffered refreshment! Just take a sip or two to show you do not disdain the offering. A brusque "No, I don't want a drink!" is taken badly.

LANGUAGE

Teo in the shipping department has studied commerce in England and has no trouble understanding you. More junior staff may not follow what you say. But when you ask, "Is this clear?", they nod eagerly, assuring you that it is. Then they go and do what they thought you said.

This happens everywhere, from the kitchen upwards. East Malaysians are too polite to ask, "What do you mean?", imagining that this would be criticism of the speaker's rhetoric ability. Neither do they like to admit, "Sorry, I don't understand!"

Try to modify a strong regional accent if providence has gifted you with one.

Speak very slowly when giving instructions to somebody who is not used to hearing your voice. Ask in a tactful way that they recapitulate what they are supposed to do.

This rule applies at every level of communication. A West Malaysian gives his instructions in clear Bahasa Melayu, but his Kadazan employee is more used to bazaar Malay. A Japanese speaks fluent but accented English, but his Iban clerk learned the same tongue from a Dutch missionary. A Hokkien from Malacca finds that East Malaysian Hokkiens pronounce a lot of words differently.

And so it goes. As you get more used to your staff, and as

An Australian teacher in Sarawak demanded why the date had not been written on the blackboard at the beginning of the lesson. Assuming the monitor did not know it, she asked him, "Don't you know what day it is today?" She pronounced this innocent question in true Aussie-style, "Don't you know what die it is to die?" to the great consternation of the lad, who thought she was threatening to murder him.

they find that you mean it when you say, "Ask me again if you don't understand", the problem will disappear. The first couple of months can be tricky.

ONCE AND FOR ALL!

Avoid saying 'yes' or 'no' at once if it can be avoided. Your East Malaysian friends often mean, "Yes, provided that ..." or, "No, unless ..." They are prepared to discuss the matter again after everybody has had time to think about it. Do not cut off communications by making, or demanding, an immediate decision.

STAFF

Office staff are on the whole very competent. Many East Malaysian girls who would have gone on to higher education in more affluent societies take a secretarial course and put their skills to good use.

For some odd reason, switchboard operator seems to be considered a low-status job, and is often given to an inarticulate person. Consider how very important her position is! The first contact a potential customer has with your firm is often by telephone. If an uncouth voice snarls, "Eh? Eh? What you say?" at him and then connects him wrongly three times in a row, he may decide to take his business elsewhere!

Newcomers are surprised to see that the office boy may have a venerable grey head, and is in some firms denoted 'peon'.

Sometimes, the office boy is the longest-serving staff member, and can be a good source of information about in-office politics. The young set are likely to make some affectionate fun of him, but treat him with the respect due his age.

Many offices have a watchman at the door. He may be employed by a security company, smartly uniformed and usually a retired policeman or soldier. Office staff are likely to call the guard 'uncle', which is a term of affectionate respect; he isn't related to everybody!

Senior staff may be overseas trained or graduates of local universities or technical colleges. If you work in a government

department, local graduates will be the majority. There is a certain amount of rivalry, in terms of status and snobbery, between local and overseas graduates.

Do not get mixed up in this. One East Malaysian can make a disparaging remark about a local diploma to another. You do it at your peril!

OFFICE MACHINERY

You name it, we've got it.

Large business firms are online with their own computers around the globe; anything at all by way of telecommunications equipment, computers, copies, printers and what not is available.

If you are about to purchase new electronic equipment, be sure to choose the one that guarantees after-sales service! It is annoying to be told at every breakdown that the thing has to be sent overseas to be fixed, that a repairman has to come from Singapore or KL, or a part has to be ordered from somewhere else.

If your office is situated upcountry, check carefully on the electricity supply before installing sensitive equipment. It may be worth your while to purchase your own diesel generator.

BUSINESS GOLF

Business contacts are often made on the golf course, at dinner or cocktail parties, or at the club. Not more so than in other parts of the world is the opinion of most expatriate businessmen.

"We have a chat about some proposed deal on the golf course, why not? But he'll come and see me in my office if he's really serious."

It is generally felt that business entertaining is 'about the same as elsewhere' in East Malaysia. The towns are smaller, so each individual may get more turns than he would in New York or Tokyo.

Business dinners are often arranged at short notice. A foreign friend may have dropped in unexpectedly from Singapore. It is up to the guest whether or not he wants to accept an invitation at 3:00 pm for the same evening. Such spur-of-the-moment invitations do not usually include wives, who are presumed to need more notice to get their hair and wardrobe into dining-out trim.

DO YOU FEED THE CROCODILES?

'Feeding the crocodiles' is a euphemism for corruption. How bad is it in East Malaysia?

Some foreign residents in Sabah complain that they are expected to pay the man who comes to connect the power, the telephone, or turn on the water supply. If they decline, he will suddenly remember he has an urgent appointment elsewhere—and leave them without water for another day.

All these workmen have tags with names or numbers on their shirts. Ring up the relevant authority and make a complaint. The man will be back the next day, sulky and possibly menacing, so a woman should not be alone in the house when he comes. Many small-time extortionists count on the fact that a housewife or household helper on her own is a fairly helpless bit of prey. The sight of a husband turns them into perfect gentlemen in an instant!

One practice that some foreigners consider dishonest is that of discounting. The price for an article or service is quoted as RM 10,000. A favoured customer will get a discount of anything up to 30 per cent. This may be construed to mean that the real price is RM 7000, and the casual customer pays a 'penalty rate' of an extra RM 3000.

Looked at in this light, one might well consider commissions to be unlawful too.

No businessman, Malaysian or foreign, is prepared to say anything about corruption larger than slipping a 10-dollar bill to a traffic cop, which can misfire badly! They have all heard stories about large sums changing hands when lucrative big deals were being negotiated, but none is aware of exact details, and 'certainly our firm has never paid a bribe!'

TREAD SOFTLY, FRIENDS
Ghosts At Work?

Yes and no. You may never come across a supernatural problem in your whole tour of duty in Borneo. But you should know what's up if there is a "*Hantu*! *Hantu*!" scare. (*Hantu* is a ghost.)

Mass hysteria occasionally grabs the female staff of a large establishment. They are usually factory girls; once in a while the fever breaks out in a boarding school or a nurses' home, usually started by an underachiever a few weeks before exams.

The person 'saw something', preferably in the toilet because that is where she is safe from inquiring male eyes as well as male offers to 'deal with it'. Next minute, another 'saw something' too, and 3 minutes after that, a dozen or so are rolling on the floor kicking and screaming.

It is useless to tell them to 'snap out of it!' Once they have lost control, they cannot. Withdraw from the scene. Instruct your senior staff to send the screamers home, suitably escorted, and close down that section for the rest of the day.

A *bomoh* will be called in the next day to 'cleanse' the premises. Show your face during the proceedings as a mark of courtesy. You need not believe in spooks in the toilet, but ostentatious displays of scepticism will make you unpopular with the staff. Next time round, the hysterical girls may decide you are the ghost!

There is the occasional ghost at a worksite too. One of the chaps 'saw something', then half of them 'saw something'.

They will not burst into howls. They will inform their foreman, and may refuse to go to work until the 'something' has been dealt with by a competent professional.

You can be brave and modern and scientific and demand immediate resumption of work on pain of dismissal. Ignore the bloody ghost!

In times of high unemployment, you will probably carry your point, but you will have a very sulky work force on your hands and anything that goes wrong for the rest of that project is your fault! The ignominiously dismissed ghost can cause scaffolding to collapse, machinery to jam and tools to drop from great heights. Should there be a death on the worksite, the person who insulted the ghost (namely, you!) is held personally responsible.

Many large offices have a little shrine, somewhere out at the back, where the hungry ghosts are fed during the 7th month. Shades of those who died without relatives to care for their desolate graves, the hungry ghosts are entitled to a festival of appeasement once a year. If your office staff (most likely the non-Christian Chinese) want half a day off, weigh the worktime lost against the trouble a few bad-tempered ghosts can wreak among ditto humans.

OTHER WORK MATTERS
Patriotism
There are two kinds of patriotism around. One is the national feeling: pride in independent Brunei or Malaysia, loyalty to king and country. The White Rajahs and Baron von Overbeck may be good for tourism, but we do not see them as cultural heroes and tend to resent foreigners who do!

The other kind is 'local patriotism': that which makes an East Malaysian feel that West Malaysians, try as they may, are never quite up to it—ethically, morally and culturally—because educationally, financially and socially, the 'Westerners' usually have the upper hand.

East Malaysians like to complain about the treatment they get from the federal authorities. It is a kind of national pastime, like 'running down the guv'ment' elsewhere (the kind of remark Tasmanians make about 'that mob in

Canberra'), and it is a game only members can play!

If the chief minister of Sabah expresses a wish that a portion of a new multi-billion-dollar highway in already well-routed

"For the first three months, you keep your eyes and ears open and your mouth shut!" an Australian businessman in Sabah said, adding that he wished somebody had told him that when he first came out.

West Malaysia be transferred to Sabah, there is applause, respectful laughter and a witty headline in the papers the next day. If a foreigner blames the state of East Malaysian roads on the federal government, he will be set upon by all present. You keep out of this! We know very well some roads are lousy, but we do not need a foreigner to tell us so.

This goes for uncomplimentary remarks about federal (or state) politicians, leaders or policies. You keep out of this.

"In my country, we do it this way..." must always be tactfully expressed. If it comes out sounding like criticism of Malaysia, it will be badly received.

Humour in the Office

In nearly all cases, don't.

There is much fun and laughter in East Malaysia, and it is hoped that you will share in it often. But try to keep your comical talents right out of the office, especially while you're new. People probably will not understand; worse, they will misunderstand and feel hurt.

The Western sense of humour is often verbal. A pun is restricted to sharers of the same literary tradition, speech developments, slang, new movies and TV shows. Do not imagine your tribal deities are internationally known!

Much of Eastern humour is visual: people fall off things, things fall on people. It hinges on mistaken identities, misuse of gadgets, a thing in the wrong place, shrieking, fainting (into a huge bowl of curry for preference)—the silent movies of the 1920s still send East Malaysian audiences into gales of laughter.

If you want to be considered funny, drop your laptop into the tea urn 'accidentally' and then collapse backwards into a wastepaper basket. Guaranteed audience success, but is it quite what you had in mind?

Joking with a girl may be misunderstood as making a pass at her. She will feel offended, if you are lucky. If you are not, she will bring along her papa the next day to ratify the engagement.

Religion

You will first become aware of the significance of religion in East Malaysia and Brunei when you see female staff dressed in floor-length, long-sleeved gowns, and head coverings round their chins and over their foreheads. This lady is a Muslim of strict principle. Your comments about her medieval appearance will not be appreciated.

Muslims pray five times a day: Subuh at dawn, Zuhur at midday, Asar in mid-afternoon, Maghrib at sunset and Isyak (pronounced Ishak) after dark. Large offices have a prayer room where employees may perform the Zuhur and Asar prayers.

The exact prayer time varies with the seasons. Subuh and Maghrib are regulated by the rising and setting of the sun. All prayers are announced over the radio, so you can keep yourself informed of the time fluctuations. During the fasting month, you should know them.

Not all Muslims keep the strict routine, but they must be given time to do so if they wish. Do not call on a Muslim at the time of a prayer. If he is engaged in his devotions, you are intruding; if he is not so occupied, your call is seen as a reproach: "Caught you goofing off, eh?"

On a Friday, offices and schools shut before noon so people may go to the mosque. Staff return to work at 2:30 pm and stay on longer to make up for lost time.

During the fasting month of Ramadhan, Muslims are not permitted to eat, drink or smoke between sunrise and sunset. Office and school hours are adjusted, with a shorter lunch break and earlier closing hours in the evening.

Business goes on 'as usual' during the fast, but you have to be sensitive to certain changes. During Ramadhan, no drinks are offered to Muslim visitors. Some fast, some do not; some fast some of the time, but it is not your place to expose the remiss.

The query, "Are you fasting?" implies that he might not be; it demonstrates your care as a host, but it is less than complimentary to the guest. Do not offer cigarettes, and refrain from smoking while the visitor is with you.

Do not invite Muslims to business lunches during Ramadhan. Schedule meetings for the morning hours as much as is practicable. It is all right to invite people for a meal at night, well after sundown and Maghrib prayers. Many hotels have special 'break-fast' buffets and promotions which are well patronised, and can replace the 'business lunch' during Ramdhan.

In almost every office, there is a girl who faints by mid-afternoon and has to be taken home. Leave this matter entirely to her group. If a foreigner tells her, "Well, if you can't stick it, don't fast!", he is grossly insensitive and disrespectful. Her own friends are probably telling her the same thing. Persons who are ill or old and women who are pregnant or menstruating are excused from fasting, as are those who really cannot stand it. But this kind of advice has to come from the peer group, not from an outsider.

When inviting Muslims for a meal, at any time of the year, be sure you choose a restaurant that is *halal*. Malay and Indian establishments are acceptable; some of the bigger Chinese restaurants have separate kitchens. Rely on the advice of your senior Muslim staff member in this matter. He probably knows the place, or he may go along and inspect the *halal* kitchen. Inviting people to a meal of dubious purity is very bad policy!

Do not serve alcohol if most of your guests are Muslim. There are some who do not mind a drink, others who mind very much. Do not order a beer for yourself if all are imbibing tea or orange juice.

In a mixed group, offer a choice in a casual way. Never urge a Muslim to drink. You embarrass him, firstly by obliging him to decline his host's offer, and secondly by implying that you think he would take it if only he were pressed hard enough.

WORKING IN THE ULU

The East Malaysian *ulu* is another world. Literally, *ulu* means 'upriver', the headwaters of the big rivers. Foreigners who work here are likely to be doing research, implementing large-scale engineering or development projects, or are affiliated to various NGOs. They come into contact with the village and longhouse people 'at grassroots level'—people who may have little education, few experiences of the outside world, but great expectations as to what an outsider can do for them. Besides the standard professional skills, tact and sensitivity are essential qualities for an expat who works in the *ulu*.

Most of Borneo's population lives along the coastal plains, but a lot of development takes place in the *ulu*. Workers who are posted there need to be tough, resourceful and self-reliant. A lively sense of adventure helps, as does an interest in Borneo's native people. And a liberal dose of patience!

A stint in a longhouse is fun if you are a visitor. When faced with the same fun for two years, it may lose some of its appeal.

Housing in the Ulu

At a school, there are teachers' quarters; at a worksite, simple barracks, or Australian-style bungalows such as those put up for families at the big Batang Ai Hydro-dam project in Sarawak in the 1980s. It is best to go out expecting very little, and be pleasantly surprised.

If a work or study project only takes a few weeks or months, the personnel may be quartered in the local longhouse. This is not quite the same as being 'overnight guests', as most tourists are. Food, accommodation, sanitary facilities and social life may not be at all what the outsider is used to. He should try to adapt as far as possible; a complainer will soon be told, "This is our way of life. If you don't like it, you can go back to where you came from!"

Housing may be constructed of sawn timber or *kajang*, a kind of leaf mat. It is not insect-proof. Even if there is netting in the bedroom windows, use mosquito nets over each bed. A couple of rolls of insect screen and a handyman can make the rest of the house safe from the huge cicadas that like to fly into the pressure lamps at night.

In most places, there is 'night power', provided by a diesel generator from 7:00 pm to midnight. While the generator works, this is fine. When the thing is on the blink, it may

take several days to get the equipment or the mechanic to mend it. Do not blithely rely on 'night power'; learn to use those pressure lamps!

No electricity means no refrigerators, unless you can get a kerosene or gas-powered one. Learn how to service it, trimming the wicks or cleaning the jets.

Some *ulu* places are reached by (bad) road, others by river. 'River' means outboard-powered boat. Your employer probably provides drivers, but it is worth every foreigner's while to know how to drive a boat, and how to do basic repairs to the engine. You may never need to do either, but what if there is an emergency?

Water in the Ulu

There is always plenty of water—pouring from the sky and in the river. Some places have water piped in, some do not. Refer to Chapter Seven for hints on how to take a bath on a jetty in full view of the public. Your quarters probably have a latrine of sorts; use what power of persuasion you have to get indoor sanitary facilities. You will love them, and your successor to that house will bless your name!

Water in the *ulu*, even if it comes out of a tap in your kitchen, is not fit to drink. Boil a big kettle every morning, cool it and pour it into bottles which you cover with clean caps.

Clothing in the Ulu

Forget about fashion. You have to be comfortable and keep healthy.

Wear cotton, cotton, cotton! Long hours of walking or boating may be on your daily schedule. Trousers are best for women too; if your treks go through deep jungle, tuck them into the tops of your boots and tie the shoe-laces around them to discourage the leeches.

Around school, a pair of rubber sandals are all you need by way of footwear. Most fungal infections are caused by a hot, damp environment, such as the inside of a shoe. If your headmaster is fussy about 'proper' footwear, there are many kinds of perfectly respectable sandals around, for men as well as for ladies.

Find out where the longhouse people wash their clothes, and use the same spot. It is probably on a jetty, or on a stone protruding into the river.

Teachers in *ulu* schools usually have a girl to help them with their housework. This girl can be expected to sweep, dust and generally tidy up. She will also do the washing. She will use a lot of soap powder and a scrubbing brush powered by considerable human energy. You may find your clothes last longer if you attend to them yourself.

Home dressmakers can really shine in the *ulu*! Do not bring along an electrical sewing machine unless you are sure of power; pedal machines are available in the bazaars. Bring along your own patterns or learn to make them.

Health in the Ulu

It is usually advisable to take malaria prophylactics in the *ulu*, even if the disease has not been reported in your region recently. Travellers from across the border may bring it in; malaria is easy to contract but very hard to get rid of!

You are probably a long way from the next doctor. Stock up on general patent medicines for your own use. And be very particular about hygiene in the kitchen and the bathing place while travelling.

Be warned about 'playing doctor' in the longhouse. Many *ulu* people automatically expect a European to be a doctor; it can give the layman such a glow to be dispensing aspirins to admiring grandmothers. But if one of your 'patients' gets really ill, or dies, you are in big trouble!

Food in the Ulu

Food in the *ulu* is a problem. It is expensive. The nearby shop is as far from the next bazaar as you are, so the shopkeeper has to pay high transport fees to get the stuff there. What he has got will not be very varied in the first place: tinned goods, milk, some kinds of biscuits, sugar, coffee, flour, rice and salted fish.

Fresh vegetables are almost impossible to obtain in some *ulu* places. In school, there may be a gardening club from which you can obtain some produce. On a work site, give serious thought to raising a few vegetables yourself if you are going to live there for any length of time.

Learn how to make bread if you eat it regularly; if you rear chickens (not many *ulu* shops sell eggs), learn how to kill and clean them for the occasional curry. You can probably find a local person who will do it for you, but he is almost certainly not Muslim.

This is a problem Muslims find hard to cope with when they are posted to the *ulu*: where can we get *halal* meat? The answer is, you cannot buy it except tinned. For fresh poultry, buy live fowls or ducks and kill them yourself.

A West Malaysian teacher posted in an East Malaysian *ulu* school finds himself very much the centre of attention when he first comes there. A *cikgu* (pronounced '*che-gu*', teacher) from *sooo* far away! It should not take him long to make friends not only with his students, but with community elders, too. When a goat or buffalo is to be slaughtered for a festival, they will invite him to *sembeleh* the beast so he will be able to join in the feast.

This is a courtesy commonly extended to Muslims, be they casual guests or sojourners. They have to make themselves available, of course. One who takes one horrified look at these savage people and their surroundings and barricades himself in his room straight after work will not even know a buffalo is about to be slaughtered!

No Place for Women?

Expatriate couples posted to *ulu* places are surprised to find that many East Malaysian men leave their families in town and 'rough it' on their own.

"My wife couldn't stand it here!" Mr.Cheng from the Agriculture Department proclaims, eyeing Mrs Brown dubiously. "This is no place for women!"

Cheng is likely to be older than Brown, with children in school. And the nearest school from this project is 100 km (60 miles) downriver by boat—if the river is not flooded or dry or something!

Expatriate wives who have lived in *ulu* postings for years have won the respect and admiration of their husbands' workmates. At least one couple of anthropologists in Sarawak had their baby with them in the longhouse where they were doing research. And few foreign missionaries would consider being separated from their families.

It takes courage, good health and good sense to make it in East Malaysia's *ulu*. The Mrs Browns are advised to think about it seriously, and decide whether they can live without a lot of the basic comforts they have been used to all their lives.

But if they take the plunge—what an adventure!

FAST FACTS

'Statistics: To the layman a statistic is a piece of numerical information, often of a singularly useless variety; statistics are a multiplicity of these often assembled with the intention of baffling or confusing him, or concealing something underhand—witness the familiar slander 'lies, damned lies, and statistics'.'
—*Fontana Dictionary of Modern Thought*

Official Name

The island of Borneo comprises three countries: Brunei, Kalimantan (which is part of Indonesia) and East Malaysia (Sabah and Sarawak)

Brunei: Negara Brunei Darussalam
Indonesia: Republic of Indonesia
Malaysia: Malaysia

Capital

Brunei: Bandar Seri Begawan
Indonesia: Jakarta
Malaysia: Kuala Lumpur

Flag

Brunei: The Brunei flag is yellow in colour with one white and one black band stretching across diagonally. In the centre of the flag is the national emblem and on both sides of the emblem is an upraised hand

Indonesia: The Indonesian flag comprises two horizontal bands of equal width. The red bands sits on the top of the flag while the white band is on the bottom of the flag

Malaysia: The Malaysian flag has 14 horizontal red and white bands of equal width. A blue rectangle is located on the upper hoist-end of the flag. A crescent moon and a fourteen-pointed star sits inside the blue rectangle

National Anthem
Brunei: 'Allah Peliharakan Sultan' (God Bless His Majesty)
Indonesia: 'Indonesia Raya' (Great Indonesia)
Malaysia: 'Negara Ku' (My Country)

Time
West and Central Kalimantan
Greenwich Mean Time plus 7 hours (GMT + 0700)
South and East Kalimantan
Greenwich Mean Time plus 8 hours (GMT + 0800)
Brunei
Greenwich Mean Time plus 8 hours (GMT + 0800)
East Malaysia
Greenwich Mean Time plus 8 hours (+ 0800)

Telephone Country Code
Brunei	673
Kalimantan	62
Malaysia	60

Telephone Area Code
Brunei
Bandar Seri Begawan, Muara	2
Kuala Belait, Seria, Mumong, Penaga	3
Tutong	4
Temburong, Bangar	5

Kalimantan
Banjermasin	511
Pontianak	561
Samarinda	541
Tarakan	551
Balikpapan	542

East Malaysia
Kuching	082
Sri Aman	083
Sibu	084

Land
Borneo is the third largest island in the world. It is located in Southeast Asian archipelago, straddling the equator between the Malay Peninsula and the Philippines

Area
Borneo: 755,000 sq km (292, 000 sq miles) including adjacent islands
Brunei : 5,765 sq km (2,226 sq miles)
Kalimantan: 536,150 sq km (207, 009 sq miles)
East Malaysia: 198, 160 sq km (76, 150 sq miles)

Highest Point
Mount Kinabalu in Sabah (4,100m / 13,451.4 ft)

Climate
The climate for Borneo is generally tropical, hot, humid and rainy. All three countries are affected by the south-west monsoon (April–October) and the north-east monsoon (October–February, the wetter of the two)

Natural Resources
Crude oil, natural gas, timber, gold, coal

Population
Borneo's estimated populations is 16 million with about 12 million in Kalimantan, 4 million in East Malaysia and 300,000 in Brunei

Ethnic Groups
Brunei
Malay, Kedayan, Tutong, Belait, Bisaya, Dusun and Murut and other indigenous groups and Chinese

Kalimantan

Dayaks, Malays, Chinese, Madurese and other Indonesian ethnic groups

Sarawak

Iban, Chinese, Malays, Bidayuh, Melanau, Penan, Orang Ulu (with several sub-groups e.g. the Kayan, Kenyah), Kelabit, Lun Bawang and Indians

Sabah

Kadazan-Dusun, Murut, Rungus, Lundayeh and Bajau

Religion

Brunei: mainly Islam, with small groups practising Christianity, Buddhism and Animism
Kalimantan and East Malaysia: Buddhism, Christianity, Islam and Animism

Official Languages

Brunei : Malay
Kalimantan: Bahasa Indonesia
Malaysia: Bahasa Melayu
In all three countries, English is also spoken

Government Structure

Brunei: constitutional sultanate
Kalimantan: republic
East Malaysia: Malaysia is a constitutional monarchy but Sabah and Sarawak each have a governor, appointed by the Malaysian government

Administrative Divisions
Brunei

4 districts: Belait, Brunei and Muara, Temburong, Tutong

Kalimantan

4 provinces: Kalimantan Barat (West Kalimantan), Kalimantan Selatan (South Kalimantan), Kalimantan Tengah (Central Kalimantan) and Kalimantan Timur (East Kalimantan),

elegantly abbreviated to Kalbar, Kalsel, Kalteng and Kaltim in most official publications

Malaysia

13 states: Johor, Kedah, Kelantan, Melaka, Negeri Sembilan, Pahang, Perak, Perlis, Pulau Pinang, Sabah, Sarawak, Selangor and Terengganu; and one federal territory (*wilayah persekutuan*) with three components: the city of Kuala Lumpur, the administrative centre of Putrajaya and the island of Labuan off Borneo

Sarawak

11 administrative regions: Betong, Bintulu, Kapit, Kuching, Limbang, Miri , Mukah, Samarahan, Sarikei, Sibu and Sri Aman

Sabah

5 divisions which are further divided into 23 districts: Interior, Kudat, Sandakan, Tawau and West Coast. The Labuan district is federal territory

Currency

Brunei: Bruneian dollar (BND)
Indonesia: Indonesian rupiah (IDR)
Malaysia: Ringgit (MYR or RM)

Gross Domestic Product (GDP)

Brunei: US$ 6.842 billion (2003 est)
Indonesia: US$ 827.4 billion (2004 est)
Malaysia: US$ 229.3 billion (2004 est)

Products and Industries

Copra, firewood, hemp, pepper, rattan, resins, rice, rubber, sago, sugar cane, tannin extracts and timber, electronic assembly

FAMOUS PEOPLE
(late) Tun Jugan ak Barieng ('Apai') 1903–1981

Tun Jugah ak Barieng was born in the upper Rajang area in 1903. An energetic and charismatic personality, he served as local and regional leader. During World War Two, he took part in the guerilla movement against the invading forces.

Universally known as 'Apai' (father), Temenggong Jugah lent his authority and prestige to facilitate his people's acceptance of Malaysia; he was appointed federal minister for Sarawak Affairs in 1963. During the period of confrontation, 'Apai' courageously visited army posts along the border to encourage 'his boys'.

'Apai' was an indefatigable traveller. In remote village schools, he exhorted the youngsters to take their studies seriously. "All I can write is my own name!" he would tell them, chalking JUGAH on the blackboard, "you have a better chance than I ever had—make use of it!"

The Paramount Chief of all Ibans passed away in 1981.

His Majesty Paduka Seri Baginda Sultan Haji Hassanal Bolkiah Mu'izzaddin Waddaulah

His Majesty Paduka Seri Baginda Sultan Haji Hassanal Bolkiah Mu'izzaddin Waddaulah is the sultan of Brunei and the eldest son of the late Sir Omar Ali Saifuddin.

Born 15 July 1946 in Brunei Town, he became crown prince in 1961, and sultan in 1967 after his father's abdication.

Bolkiah's heir is his son with Queen Saleha, Crown Prince Al-Muhtadee Billah Bolkiah. The sultan has married a total of three times, the second marriage to a Bruneian air stewardess ending in divorce and his most recent to a former Malaysian lady occurring in August 2005.

Some magazines describethe Sultan as the world's richest man, an assertion which is not confirmed by official sources in Brunei.

Datuk Effendi Norwawi

Datuk Effendi Norwawi, a Melanau from the coastal area of Sarawak, was educated at the Malay College in Kuala Kangsar before completing his studies at the University of Tasmania, Australia. After a career in land development, he became chairman of the Sarawak State Economic Development Corporation; during his tenure, the SEDC won several prestigious management awards.

A man of flair and artistic tastes, Datuk Effendi is executive chairman of ENCROP Group, which has interests in media (ntv7 and Synchrosound Recording Studios), education [he founded the Center for Advanced Design (CENFAD) and the Malaysia University of Science and Technology (MUST) in collaboration with Massachusetts Institute of Technology (MIT)], property development (Encrop Systembilt Sdn. Bhd.), timber concessions and food production.

Datuk Effendi has recently become the Minister in The Prime Minister's Department (as of February 2006).

Tun Datu Haji Mustapha bin Datu Harun

Tun Datu Haji Mustapha bin Datu Harun was born on 31 July 1918 at Kampung Limau Limauan, Kudat. At the age of ten, he worked as a houseboy for the Resident of Kudat, E W Morell. 35 years later, he became Sabah's first governor, the man who led Sabah into Malaysia, thus securing its independence from the British.

Tun Mustapha's contribution to Sabah's political maturity is immeasurable. He died on 3 January 1995 and was buried in Putatan.

ALMOST A TO Z
Air

You probably like all the windows open, a fresh breeze through the house or wherever you are. Many of your local friends are convinced that 'wind' is bad for you and can make you ill; they will urge you to wrap up your head 'to keep the wind out' if you have recently been ill or had a baby. Most of the time this does not affect you, but please respect an elder person's request to shut the car windows if she is your passenger. If she believes the draft can make her ill, so it will!

Some people extend this theory to air-conditioning too, though on the whole we love to air-condition our houses, and particularly hotels and offices, to antarctic temperatures!

Brooms

Do not ever touch anybody with one, or even threaten to. Brooms are considered dirty! When you buy a new broom, put it in the boot of the car, not across the back seat.

Clothes

Light, cool, comfortable and reasonably demure. Children need a minimum of clothing at all times, so do mama and papa. For most daytime occasions, short-sleeved or sleeveless dresses will do fine; avoid short shorts, bum-riding skirts and jeans, strapless tops and the like in public.

Democracy

Yes...and no. You will not get servants crawling around on their knees here, or be much bothered by a sultan ordering your head to be cut off (though he can order what you may or may not wear to a palace reception). On the other hand, you will see large limousines parked where they have no business to be, hear senior politicians sing (and expect applause) at official parties and find that important people are always agreed with even if they talk errant nonsense. 'Democracy tempered with old-fashioned courtesy' might be the definition.

Energy

Until you are well acclimatised, you will have less energy than you were used to. Take things easy. Stroll, do not run; play one set of tennis, not five; keep out of the sun from 10:00 in the morning till 4:00 in the afternoon.

Fruit

Fruits are available all year round—delicious, fresh and inexpensive. Beware of urging a sick person to eat any, however! Fruits are considered 'cold' by the experts, and 'bad for you' if you are feverish, have a headache, a baby or anything else much other than broken bones.

Geography

No, people do not know where Luxembourg is, even if it is your home country. Many cannot tell a Swiss from a Swede; some New Zealanders are reduced to the grim fate of saying that they are from 'near Australia'! There is no need to work yourself into a lather each time you confront such ignorance. When did you first learn where Brunei is?

Hantu

Ghosties and ghoulies and all those things are not likely to bother you. Some of your local friends or employees do believe in them, however, and it is neither wise nor useful to try and talk them out of it. Just let them be and they will let you be.

Jokes

Be very, very careful in your early weeks and months. A sense of humour is a relative thing; local taste favours practical jokes that you may not see the point of. If somebody falls or hurts himself, his workmates burst into loud laughter! This is meant to help him 'get over it'; if you are the victim, try not to get annoyed. Do not attempt verbal humour in an unfamiliar language, or with people whose command of English does not match yours. You may be suspected of trying to 'make a fool' of somebody when you just wanted to create a happy atmosphere by cracking a few jokes.

Kisses

Not in public and not on helpless little children! Note that when local people 'kiss' toddlers, they actually smell their chubby faces. Never kiss a newly-bereaved widow; what you mean as condolence is taken as insult.

Language

It is Bahasa Melayu, and you might as well learn it. Many local people understand English, but their opinion of you will rocket if you can make yourself understood in their own language. When in Rome...

Medicine

Go easy on dishing out anything stronger than aspirin, or eucalyptus oil for rubbing on. Especially while travelling upcountry, you may be tempted to 'play doctor' with the few resources at your command. If your patient gets worse or dies, you face an instant malpractice suit in the form of well-armed, distressed and angry villagers. On the other hand, beware of accepting unfamiliar medicines from well-meaning friends if you are suddenly taken ill. Chicken soup with ginseng is harmless, other Chinese medicines are very potent and should be dispensed only by a qualified physician.

Noise

The listener's attitude makes noise music and vice versa. You will find stridently blaring loudspeakers in shops, on buses and longboats (where you have no way of escaping; if you are really lucky, they will play a frayed video tape of the blood-and-gore type as well), all over the beach and picnic spots. Wicked Western influence? The first half-hour of Chinese opera, traditional gongs, drums or a Malay *hadrah* band is music to most people, but what if the entertainment lasts 3 hours? Or 5 hours? The whole night? The survivor-type person develops thick skin over the eardrums. If the music, *music* or 'music' is played in your honour, you cannot very well pull faces and complain, can you?

Orang Putih

This is the 'white man'; he may also be called *ang mo* (red-hair; gradations of brown seem to escape the Asian retina), expat, foreigner or *Mat Salleh*. Basically, the local population is prepared to accept the *orang putih*. The one who makes an effort to get on, to learn about local culture, who has a word of praise for his host country and its products or institutions, gets on a lot better than the nose-in-the-air type. This applies to all expatriates, whatever their colour!

Pets

Few East Malaysians understand why you make such a fuss of a perfectly ordinary cat or dog, 'not even pedigree!' You may have to remind your helper to feed pets regularly; she does not mean to be unkind, she genuinely forgets. If your helper is Muslim, she should not be expected to touch the dog.

Queen

We have our own queen in Malaysia, the Yang di-Pertuan Agung's Consort. Say 'The Queen of England' or 'Queen Elizabeth' if that is who you mean; some local people resent the assumption of universality in 'The Queen' without a note of explanation.

Rumours

They exist here as anywhere else; the occasional official warning that the population is not to listen to rumours makes them more interesting of course. Do not take the rumours and gossip of a tightly-knit social community like the local club for more than what they are worth! The old hands say 'Never believe a rumour until it has been officially denied.'

Smells

Or should we say 'scents'? The best authorities notwithstanding, the Orient is not always quite so fragrant. Drains if extant are open, discarded rubbish starts to smell after a few hours and toilet arrangements in the rural areas are not always quite up to scratch. (Read 'non-existent' in some places.) It is very easy to give offence to your hosts by commenting, wrinkling a delicate nose, or worse. Never betray emotion about the smell of cooking or food. This can be taken very badly. Brief young children, leave them at home if they are likely to burst into a 'yuck, yeech!' chorus each time an unfamiliar scent assails their dainty little noses. In your own home, you are entitled to complain and take what action is necessary to establish your own olfactory standards.

Tantrums

Of course you try and avoid letting your children throw one in public, but if it happens, do not smack them (even if they need it!). Local people do anything to keep their darlings happy, including spoiling them shamefully. Your maltreated little one would be the centre of a crowd of pitying eyes, condemning you as an unnatural parent. Take him home fast, and make it plain that he will not be taken out again unless he behaves himself.

Uniforms

We love them! The local Women's Institute thinks nothing of putting its members into a regulation-pattern *batik*, girls involved with helping at a village festivity start off by getting the same outfits, even kindergartens uniform their scholars. The civil service in full fig looks like a concourse of South American generals from a particularly obscure banana republic. Your witty comments upon 'gold braid by the running metre' are not really necessary; of course you are allowed to think what you like.

Water

In the major urban centres, it is safe to drink from the kitchen tap which is always connected to the rising main. Bathroom and other taps may run from a roof cistern; such water should not be consumed (in Borneo or elsewhere!) though it is safe for tooth-brushing. When upcountry, insist on cool boiled water. If you are stationed at the *ulu*, you will soon have worked out a system of boiling a large kettle every morning and filling water bottles from it. If you are travelling, carry a sturdy bottle which you can get refilled each time you stop at a settlement.

Work Permit

Foreigners and West Malaysians need work permits to take up paid employment in East Malaysia. This formality is usually settled by the employer, prior to the employee's arrival here. Some work contracts specifically bar spouses and family members from working here. Read the small print!

CULTURE QUIZ

SITUATION 1

You are in a shop looking at blouses. You would like to see a different colour, and ask the shop girl to show you some. She replies, "Not got."

As you turn to go, you see half a dozen blouses in as many colours lying on the shelf just behind the girl.

Ⓐ You pull them out of the shelf and slam them on the counter, saying, "And what are these, heh? Are you too lazy to bring out things for people? How do you think your shop will do any business if you just stand there like a lamp post..."

Ⓑ You pull them out of the shelf, slam them on the counter, glare at the girl and stomp out.

Ⓒ You demand to see the shopkeeper, and proceed to inform him that his assistant is lazy, discourteous, useless, and you are not surprised if his shop is not making any money.

D You ask the girl, "Could I see those blouses in the shelf there?" and then make a leisurely selection.

Comments

A and **B** are out, unless you know you will never enter that shop again in your life.

C may be used as a last resort, if you honestly think the girl was deliberately being rude and lazy; it is likely that she did not understand a word you were saying to her in the first place.

If her English is poor, she will not understand things like, "Mmm, well, I wonder if you could possibly show me a somewhat larger selection." Just say, "Got any more like these, different colours?" **D** is the winning answer.

SITUATION 2

Your Indonesian household helper is often visited by a girl cousin. After a few weeks, you discover that the cousin is actually living in your helper's room; she may be working elsewhere, and you suspect she is in the country illegally.

A You walk into the girl's room late one evening when you know both are at home, and insist that the cousin leave the next morning. This is not a boarding house!

B You ask your helper about this cousin when you are alone with her. Ask her where the girl is working, how she is related; request details like her employer's name, work permit details, etc. If these particulars are satisfactory, you may consider permitting the girl to share your helper's room until she finds a permanent place to stay.

C Speak to your helper when you are alone with her, and insist the cousin be told to leave. Point out to her that the penalties for illegal entry are severe; she should advise the cousin to return to the home country, and re-enter in the proper way.

Comments

Please, not **A**! This embarrasses your helper unnecessarily. You may quite possibly lose her, at very short notice.

If there is good reason for not harbouring an unscheduled boarder, use **ⓒ**.

ⓑ is the correct procedure if on the whole you like the look of the guest. Ask a local friend to help you check out the employer, immigration details etc. very discreetly.

It is possible that she is there at your helper's invitation. Girls get lonely without a companion. Sometimes two good friends insist on being employed together, even if it means sharing one wage!

SITUATION 3

A storm has blown down a big branch of your neighbour's tree; it fell on your fence and has partly wrecked it. You ask the neighbour to have it removed, but he appears not to understand what you mean. As the sagging fence poses a bit of a security threat, you:

ⓐ Ask a friend who speaks the neighbour's language to ask him to remove the offending tree branch.

ⓑ Have another talk with the neighbour in which you threaten to ring the police (that's a word he does understand!)

ⓒ Enter the neighbour's yard armed with the necessary tools, cut the branch in half and mend the fence.

ⓓ Report the matter to your landlord and ask him to attend to it.

Comments

Your indignation is understandable, but **ⓑ** is a bad choice. The police could not do much about it unless you can report a robbery that was the direct result of a broken fence.

ⓒ involves a little loss of 'face' for you—the entire street would turn out to watch a burly European cut a bole of wood in half, while your neighbour would get sore jaws from grinning on his back teeth! If you do not mind that, go ahead. Admittedly, men do house repairs and gardening in the West, but it has not quite caught on in East Malaysia yet. Maybe you'll start a trend in your neighbourhood.

Depending on whether or not the neighbour is being deliberately difficult, choose between **ⓐ** and **ⓓ**. Your landlord, having a personal interest in the maintenance of his property, might speak somewhat sharply: he can do that, you cannot.

SITUATION 4

You are in charge of a major engineering project, and have just employed several hundred labourers. Some of the earth-moving is done by bulldozer; for other sections you have brought in wheelbarrows from your country.

On an inspection tour, you discover the barrows neatly piled up in a shed, while the earth is being carried in weird little wickerwork baskets.

Ⓐ You holler for the foreman at that section and give him a good dressing-down. "Do you think we are living in the Stone Ages? No wonder this country is so backward...if I see another of those bloody baskets next week, I'll sack the man who carries it!'

Ⓑ You speak to the foreman inside the works office, and ask him why the wheelbarrows are not used.

Ⓒ You check on the work progress with the site engineer. If it is up to schedule, let them carry the stuff any way they like! Arrange for the wheelbarrows to be sent to another of your company's projects.

Ⓓ You ask to have the men assembled, and give them a little pep-talk about the use of modern transport in a modern world.

Comments

Never **Ⓐ**! The foreman, all those of the workers who understand you and everybody who hears of it by and by (this sort of tale spreads) will have a very low opinion of you; you have insulted the nation as well as the men present at the moment.

Ⓑ and **Ⓓ** are harmless but not likely to be effective, though the workers will appreciate the little diversion created by **Ⓓ**. **Ⓒ** is the rational attitude to take. If the issue was essential safety equipment (i.e., helmets), you would of course have to insist that it be used, but ask the site engineer to enforce such rules.

SITUATION 5

On a visit to a longhouse, you are offered a meal of rice and several side dishes, one of them is a ragout of pieces of meat cooked in a dark sauce. Discreet inquiry discloses that the meat in question is monkey. You:

ⓐ Scream, leap to your feet, hastily gather your family to your bosom and scurry off.

ⓑ Make retching noises and inform those sitting near you that you think it is disgusting to eat such a thing.

ⓒ Try a little bit, but do not comment.

ⓓ Touch the edge of the plate with two fingers of your right hand when it is passed to you, but do not take any.

Comments

ⓐ and **ⓑ** make it clear that you do not appreciate the hospitality. Nobody will say anything much, but silently they will label you a person with shockingly bad manners.

ⓓ is what anybody, local or foreign, may do to refuse food. Many local people have 'food taboos' of various kinds; your hosts will not insist that you must eat this or that.

ⓒ is if you feel like it; do not make the mistake of loudly and insincerely praising the bouquet and aroma of the dish after you have tasted it. Upcountry people do not comment on their food. It is meant for eating, not discussing.

SITUATION 6

A fellow worker has invited you to a party at his parents' house; it is held to celebrate an elderly auntie's safe return from the pilgrimage to Mecca. He insists that it will be a big party, not confined to Muslims, and some of his mother's best curry dishes will be served—why not come along?

When the guest of honour enters, family members and some others come forward to bow and kiss her hand. When she comes near you, you:

ⓐ Bow and kiss the old lady's hand.

ⓑ Shake the old lady's hand.

❸ Bow and murmur a polite greeting.

❹ Quietly melt into the background.

Comments

❹ is really for family members and close friends; they will find it rather funny on a foreigner's part though they will not say anything.

❸ is all right if she extends her hand first. **❸** is what you are expected to do. **❹**, in a really large party, would be all right. Men do not generally shake (touch) hands with Muslim ladies; there are many exceptions to this rule, but you must leave it to the lady to choose.

SITUATION 7

You are working as a consultant with a large government department. A local businessman with whom you have become friendly visits your house at Christmas. He insists on giving your toddler an *ang pow*, a red packet containing money, because "this is our people's custom! Don't hurt my feelings by refusing!" etc.

After he has left, you discover there's a bundle of crisp new hundred-dollar notes in the packet!

This businessman has recently tendered for a lucrative contract with your department. The money can only be regarded as a bribe. What do you do?

❹ Monday morning, you bring the packet to your head of department and make a full report.

❸ Return the packet to the donor, tell him what you think of this revolting attempt at bribery, let him know that he is dealing with an honest man and that you could report him to the police.

❸ Ring the donor and tell him that he seems to have made a mistake (which he will laughingly deny). Inform him that you have nothing whatever to do with the awarding of contracts. Ask him if you might return the packet to him, or if you should donate it to the Red Cross or similar charity. Make it clear that you will not keep it.

❹ Report the matter to the police, surrendering the packet.

Comments

Only resort to **Ⓐ** and **Ⓓ** if you are convinced that your integrity is at stake. Is somebody trying to 'frame' you to get you into trouble? Otherwise keep the matter between yourself and this over-generous gentleman.

If you want to remain friends, use **Ⓒ**. He knows that you know that he tried and failed, but you are not making him lose 'face' in front of third parties.

Ⓑ is the end to a beautiful friendship; you also reinforce the local belief that foreigners are hot-tempered and uncouth.

SITUATION 8

Your driver's ailing grandmother, who stays in a village several hours' bus ride from where you live, is coming to town to seek medical advice. You have given permission for the old lady to put up at your house for a couple of nights, in the helper's room.

Granny turns up, visibly weak and ill, and spends almost all day waiting at the government clinic. The attendant who finally sees her tells her she is 'all right' and gives her a packet of little white pills which you suspect are simply aspirin.

Ⓐ You take the old lady to your own (private) doctor the next day.

Ⓑ You ring up a friend in the medical department and make another appointment for the old lady, this time to see a doctor.

Ⓒ You ring up the director of Medical Services and tell him what you think of him, his useless department and his negligent staff; inform him that the old lady could sue them all for malpractice, 'and in my country...'

Ⓓ Give the old lady a small present (money, a *sarong*) for her return journey and advise her to visit a clinic nearest her own *kampong* regularly. There isn't really any need to come all the way to town.

Comments

Beware of **Ⓐ** unless you are very rich! You have no idea what is wrong with granny, but once you have taken her on, her family, indeed her whole village, will hold you responsible for what happens next. Also consider the possible number of other invalids still at home...

B is fine if you have that sort of connection.

C is boorish as well as useless. You are insulting a man who is doing his job with the resources at his command. The threat of legal action is just a bad joke in this case—if the old lady could afford a lawyer, she could also afford to visit private clinics and specialists.

D sounds heartless to the average expat, but it is the best solution. Rural patients tend to flock to the major towns, overcrowding the hospitals there. If the patient needs nursing care, she may be better off in the sometimes half-empty wards of a district hospital.

SITUATION 9

You have given a cooking demonstration at your ladies' club. Carried away by success, you added a little impromptu talk and display considerable knowledge of local cooking and the principles underlying curry spice blending. The members thank and congratulate you. One particular friend assures you that you are an expert in the field who puts local ladies to shame; how ever did you manage to be so clever, etc.

A You thank her and add a few suitably worded compliments and praises to 'my good Malaysian friends who have taught me everything'.

B You decide to write a book on 'The Art of Curry Spice Blending'.

C You reprove your friend for insincerity and vain flattery. "Do you take me for a fool?!!"

D You change the topic as soon as is convenient, expressing much interest in next week's demonstration by Mrs Tan.

Comments

You are technically right with **C**, but do appreciate the group's attempt to make you feel good. If the dish you cooked was in any way edible, they will pronounce it a gastronomic delight.

East Malaysians consider foreigners their guests in a very direct way and would tell any number of white lies to keep them happy. If you want an honest appraisal, it would have to be a business proposition. Will the club president, owner of a fancy restaurant in town, give you a job as sous-chef? You will get a very straightforward answer to that, but not in public!

There is no harm in **B**, but do not expect to sell a cookery book on the sole testimony of a group of polite morning-coffee friends.

Depending on how large the gathering is, choose between **A** and **D**. **D** has the added advantage of easing out of the spotlight and letting it shine on Mrs Tan; such graciousness is appreciated in East Malaysia.

SITUATION 10

You are the only foreign member of an all-male jungle party. After several hours' march in difficult terrain, when you are sweaty, leech-bitten and exhausted, you come to a clear little river. You:

A Whoop with delight, tear off all your clothes and splash into the water, inviting the other fellows to join in.

B Invite everybody to have a quick dip; as they only strip to their undershorts, you leave yours on too.

C Suggest a refreshment stop to the party leader with a jolly: "Come on boys! Let's have a swim! We're all hot and tired."

D Suggest a refreshment stop to the party leader quietly.

Comments

Even in an all-male group, you will embarrass everybody with **A**.

With **B** and **C**, you take into your own hands the initiative that properly belongs to the group's leader, implying that he does not take proper care of his charges. You also reinforce the strong local belief that foreigners are 'softies' who cannot stand a few hours' walking. Playing in the water is for little boys!

D is the best solution. The leader is as hot as the rest of you; your polite appeal to his judgement makes him feel good—and he probably wanted a quick dip too.

If there are any crocodiles, leeches, water-snakes or other interesting natural phenomena in the river, you will be glad you asked before you jumped!

DO'S AND DON'TS

Compiling do's and don'ts is tricky, even embarrassing. Such a listing of the obvious can seem patronising; the implication is that the reader lacks commonsense, manners, or normal self-preservation instincts!

Your local friends will teach you what to do and what not to do in any given situation, pleasantly and informally. There is no fixed standard of human relations, in Borneo or anywhere else. You learn as you go, and you teach too. Many an interesting discussion is centered on social customs in my country, in your country, in their country...

Browse this list for general information and amusement; after six months in the country, you will be in a position to add margin notes, and cross out a few items!

DO'S

- Do wear light, cool and comfortable clothes, natural fibres for preference. If you live or work in an air-conditioned environment, you will need some warm things for 'indoors', but the minute you venture outdoors, you'll enjoy the tropical climate! Many local expatriates claim that the constant change from aircon-cold to natural-hot is what gives them colds!

- Do eat our local fruit, they're delicious! Imported apples, pears etc are always available and somewhat expensive, while the local products flood the markets according to their seasons. Beware, however, of urging a sick person to eat fruit, even if you're sure he could do with a few extra vitamins. Fruit, according to the experts, are 'cold', therefore 'bad for you' if you are feverish, have a headache, a baby or anything else much other than broken bones.

- Do learn Malay. It's the official language of Malaysia and Brunei, and even people who understand English will appreciate that you're making the effort.

- Do keep the more passionate displays of affection private, and be aware that random baby-kissing is not part of our culture. If you look carefully, you'll note that local people (usually relatives) who 'kiss' a baby are in fact smelling his chubby little face.

- Do show respect to local institutions. If you mean 'Queen Elizabeth of England', say so; many people resent the assumption of universality in 'the Queen' without a note of explanation. We have our own Queens, namely the consorts of our rulers, in both Malaysia and Brunei.

- Do drink the water...in town. In major urban areas, it's safe to drink from the kitchen tap, which is always connected to the rising main. Bathroom and other taps may run from a roof cistern; such water should not be consumed (in Borneo or elsewhere!) though it is safe for toothbrushing.

- When upcountry, insist on boiled water. When travelling, carry a sturdy bottle which you can get re-filled each time you stop at a settlement.

- Do be aware that any foreigner working here needs a permit; this applies to the spouses of contract officers as well as to household helpers and construction labourers! The formalities are usually settled by the employer before the employee enters East Malaysia or Brunei; some contracts specifically bar spouses or family members from taking up paid employment here. Read the fine print!

DON'TS

- Don't run—walk. Until you are well acclimatised, you have less energy than you were used to, so don't exert yourself unnecessarily. Play one set of tennis, not five; keep out of the noonday sun.

- When visiting a longhouse, it is very bad form to stride down the main passageway in front of the family rooms. In the old days, such behaviour was considered aggressive; only attacking enemies rush in, while visitors stroll decorously.

- Don't touch people with your hands unless there is a good reason; even hand-shaking with a person of the opposite sex is considered immodest by some really conservative folks of Borneo. Wait for the other person to extend his (or, more usually, her) hand before reaching out for a hearty shake. Greetings with a polite nod or slight bow are perfectly adequate.

- Never kiss a newly-bereaved widow; a token of condolence in one culture is an insult in another!

- Don't ever touch anybody with a broom—this is very insulting because a broom is dirty! Teachers may have to keep an eye on their students during classroom cleaning sessions, just in case latent rivalries are settled with a bit of broom-bashing. A few years ago, the local paper in Kuching carried an apology from Mdm.X to Miss Y, 'for having used a broom upon her in an uncalled-for manner.' The public never found out what provoked this broom-fight, but the combatants considered it serious enough to call in their lawyers!

- When you buy a new broom, don't put it across the back seat (where people will be sitting at other times); put it in the boot of your car instead.

- Don't open the windows in a house or moving vehicle unless all fellow-passengers are in agreement! Many of our local friends are convinced that 'wind' is bad for you and can make you ill. This doesn't have to be an actual draft; exposure to the open air is high on the danger list for people who are ill, convalescent, or have recently had a baby.

- Don't treat the general public to a excessive amount of cleavage, be it bosoms or bottoms. Low necklines, bum-riding jeans and skirts and the like are indeed in fashion, but the man-in-the-street considers them immodest amounting to indecent. The real admirers of so much bare skin are the mosquitoes...

- Don't get upset if people are woefully ignorant about geography in general, and your home country in particular. You may meet some who can't tell a Swiss from a Swede, and ask a Canadian whether he's from New York or Hollywood. New Zealanders are reduced to the grim fate of saying that they are 'from near Australia'. Come to think of it, when did you yourself first learn where Brunei is, and how many parts it consists of?

- Don't make scathing remarks when you are told of a haunted house, a ghost in the banyan tree, or the careful precautions necessary to keep the ghouls away from your work-mate's pregnant wife. Some local people believe in supernatural manifestations; it is neither wise nor useful (or even polite) to try and talk them out of it, or ridicule their superstitions. The best way to treat ghosts is to leave them alone, and they'll reciprocate.

- Don't crack jokes until you are sure of your surroundings. A sense of humour is relative; if somebody falls or hurts himself harmlessly, all bystanders are apt to burst into loud laughter. This is meant to help him 'get over it'. If you are the victim, try not to get annoyed.

- Don't attempt verbal humour in an unfamiliar language, or with people whose command of English doesn't match yours. You may be suspected of showing off your superior education or 'make a fool' of somebody, which is hardly what you intended!

- Don't dish out anything stronger than aspirins or eucalyptus balm to people who aren't feeling well. Especially when travelling upcountry, resist the temptation to become an instant medic! If your patient gets worse or dies, you may have an instant malpractice suit in the form of distressed, angry and well-armed villagers on your hands! On the other hand, beware of accepting unfamiliar medicines from well-meaning friends. Chicken soup with ginseng is harmless; other Chinese medicines are very potent and should be dispensed only by a qualified physician.

- Don't be upset by the general indifference to pets; few locals can understand why foreigners make such a fuss of a perfectly ordinary cat or dog, 'not even a pedigree!' You may have to remind your helper to feed pets regularly, she is more used to simply tossing them scraps once in a while.

- If your helper is Muslim she should not be expected to touch the dog.

- Don't take the rumours of tightly knit community, for instance the local club or college, for more than they are worth! The occasional official warning not to listen to rumours makes them more interesting, of course. If they appear to touch on a serious matter, make a few phone calls to the proper authorities and get the truth.

- Don't wrinkle a delicate nose each time the Orient is less fragrant than the tourist literature would have us believe. Yes, there are smelly drains and ditto rivers, and no not enough is done to clean the towns up. But the locals won't appreciate your ostentatious display of disgust and horror. You could sign up for the local neighbourhood-cleaning campaign.

- Never betray visible emotion about the smell of food and cooking; this can be taken very badly. You wouldn't like to see an Asian tourist pretend to retch when presented with a slice of ripe Limburger cheese, would you? Brief young children, or leave them at home if they are likely to burst into a 'yuck-yeech!' chorus each time an unfamiliar scent assails their dainty senses.

- Don't let your children throw tantrums in public places if it can possibly be avoided; but if it happens, do not smack them (even if they richly deserve it!). Local people do anything to keep their little darlings happy, up to the point of spoiling them. Your maltreated little one would be the centre of a crowd of pitying eyes, condemning you as an unnatural parent. Take him home fast, and make it plain he will not be taken out again until he learns to behave himself.

- Don't scoff at our penchant for uniforms—we love them! A group, any group, starts out by getting regulation shirts or blouses: the Women's Institute, the Cabinet Wives, political parties and government departments. School uniforms are standard throughout Malaysia, and there are even kindergarten uniforms. The Civil Service in full fig looks like a concourse of generals from one of more obscure banana republics. Your witty comments on 'gold braid by the running metre' are not really necessary, of course you are allowed to think what you like.

GLOSSARY

MALAY GREETINGS, QUESTIONS AND USEFUL PHRASES

Boleh kurang sedikit?	Can you reduce (price)?
Selamat tinggal	Goodbye (by the traveller)
Selamat malam	Good evening/night
Selamat pagi	Good morning
Selamat jalan	Have a good trip!
Itu berapa?	How much is this?
Sangat mahal!	Too much! (price)
Tolong hantar ambulan	Please send an ambulance!
Disini ada kemalangan (jalan raya).	There has been an (traffic) accident
Dua orang cedera.	Two people are injured.
Mana...	Where is ...
...*tandas?*	...the toilet?
...*stesyen bas? (perhentian bas?)*	... the bus station?
...*rumah sakit (hospital)?*	...the hospital?
...*steysen polis?*	...the police station?
...*stesyen keretapi?*	...the railway station?

SIGNS AND CURRENCY

Keluar	Exit
Masuk	Entry
Ringgit	Malaysian dollar
Wang	Money
Kedai/Pasar	Shop/Market

NUMBERS

Satu	One
Dua	Two

Tiga	Three
Empat	Four
Lima	Five
Enam	Six
Tujuh	Seven
Lapan	Eight
Sembilan	Nine
Sapuluh	Ten
Sabelas	Eleven
Duabelas	Twelve
Tigabelas (etc.)	Thirteen
Duapuluh	Twenty
Duapuluh-satu	Twenty-one
Duapuluh-dua (etc.)	Twenty-two
Tigapuluh	Thirty
Empatpuluh	Forty
Limapuluh	Fifty
Enampuluh (etc.)	Sixty
Seratus	One hundred
Dua ratus (etc.)	Two hundred
Seribu	One thousand
Satu juta	One million

ROAD SIGNS

Road sign symbols follow international standards: a yellow lozenge with a picture inside it means 'Beware of the buffalo, cow, train, etc.'; and a yellow sign with a skull and crossbones means 'Accident-prone area'.

Awas	Caution
Berhenti	Stop
Beri laluan	Give Way
Dilarang memotong	No Overtaking

Had laju	Speed Limit (*laju* means fast)
Ikut kiri	Keep Left
Kurangkan laju	Slow Down

Often seen at the scene of roadworks:

Jalan Sehala	One Way
Lencongan	Detour

DIRECTIONS

Barat	West
Selatan	South
Timur	East
Utara	North

SOME COMMON TERMS

Ang pau	'Red packet', gift of money given to children during Chinese New Year, or to the bride as wedding gift
Ang saman	'Red summons', a half-humorous way of describing wedding invitations, which are printed on red paper and which usually entail the obligation to cash up
Bomoh	Traditional healer, shaman, sometimes fortune-teller
Kampong	Village
Sarong	Wraparound type of skirt, worn by men or women

Umai	Raw fish speciality of the Melanau people
Baju kurung	Long overblouse, worn over a long skirt or sarung by Malay ladies
Pasar, bazaar	Market town
Padi	Unhusked rice grain

RESOURCE GUIDE

GENERAL

- http://www.livingabroad.com
- http://www.outpostexpat.nl.malaysia.html
  Two useful general websites which have lots of useful Malaysian links.

EMBASSIES

- http://www.newmalaysia.com
  Official embassies may be found in Brunei, or in Malaysia's capital Kuala Lumpur. Look up 'Government and Politics', then 'Foreign Embassies'.

- **Immigration Department**
  Kuching Tel: (082) 245-661
  Kota Kinabalu Tel: (088) 216-711

TOURIST INFORMATION

Tourism information is available on a number of sites. For information about Malaysia, look up:

- http://tourism.gov.my
- **Tourism Malaysia**
  Tel: (03) 2693-5188
  Email: tourism@tourism.gov.my

For information about Sarawak:
- **Sarawak Tourism Board**
  Tel: (082) 423-600
  Email: stb@sarawaktourism.com
  Website: http://www.sarawaktourism.com

For information about Sabah:
- **Sabah Promotion Corporation**
  Tel: (088) 212-121
  Email: info@sabahtourism.com
  Website: http://www.sabahtourism.com

EMERGENCY & HEALTH

- http://medics.virtulave.net/dir
  General information about public and private clinics in Malaysia.

Kuching

- **Sarawak General Hospital** (public hospital)
  Tel: (082) 275-555
  Website: http://sarawak.health.gov.my/sgh2
- **Normah Medical Centre** (private hospital/ outpatient)
  Tel: (082) 440-055
- **Timberland Medical Centre** (private hospital/ outpatient)
  Tel: (082) 234-991
- **Bintulu Hospital** (public)
  Tel: (086) 331-455

Miri

- **Miri General Hospital** (public hospital)
  Tel: (085) 420-033
- **Selesa Medical Centre** (private)
  Tel: (085) 437-755

Kota Kinabalu

- http://www.infosabah.com.my
  Provides general information about Sabah
- **Queen Elizabeth Hospital** (public)
  Tel: (088) 218-166
- **Sabah Medical Centre** (private)
  Tel: (088) 424-333
- **Damai Specialist Centre** (private)
  Tel: (088) 210-043

HOME AND FAMILY

Accommodation: Read the ads in the local newspapers. When you have spotted a place you might like, ask fellow workers or compatriots about the area: safety, drainage, services, etc. The same people may also recommend you to a reputable real estate broker.

Child Care

Look up the international schools on http://www.livingabroad. com Some such establishments, like the Shell school which teaches in English and Dutch, are restricted to the workforce of specific companies. Well-regarded private schools in East Malaysia include:

Kuching

- **Lodge Preparatory School** (to year 6)
  Tel: (082) 363-554, (082) 207-166,
  Email: lodge@cdc.com
- **Tunku Putra School** (to year 9)
  Tel: (082) 207-166
  Email: info@ tpis.cmsb.com.my

Miri

- **Sri Mawar School**
  Tel (085) 658-606, (085) 419-089

Kota Kinabalu

- **Kinabalu International School** (to year 13)
  Tel: (088) 224-526, 248-097
  Email: kismy@po.jaring.my

Maids

Agencies advertise in the *Yellow Pages*, and in the local newspaper. Be prepared for quite a lot of bureaucratic red tape!

MANAGING YOUR MONEY
Taxes

- http://www.newmalaysia.com/Government/Politics
  Look up the website and then the relevant ministry.

Insurance

- http://www.newmalaysia.com
  Lists a number of insurance companies, as does the *Yellow Pages*. Before leaving your home country, check whether

your (health, accident, etc) insurance is only valid inside your own country, or internationally.

Cash
In the towns, there are ATMs all over the place, most (not all) of them accept international cards.

Banking
Look up http://www.newmalaysia.com and the *Yellow Pages*. Credit cards are generally accepted in Malaysia's towns, in the larger establishments.

ENTERTAINMENT AND LEISURE
Look up the relevant links on the tourism sites, and ask around at your work place and among compatriots for the best supermarkets, bookshops, cinemas and the like. There is an entertaining night life in the bigger towns of East Malaysia, it may just take a bit of finding.

TRANSPORT AND COMMUNICATIONS
Telephone codes for East Malaysia (for calls from outside Malaysia add '6' first) Kuching (082), Sibu (084), Miri (085), Bintulu (086), Beaufort (087), Kota KInabalu (088), Sandakan (089), Tawau (089)

Internet Cafes
Available in the bigger towns.

Post Office
In every town of size, bazaars have a 'Mini-Post Office' in a shop (often a bookshop or stationers) or a postal agency. Utility bills can be paid in post offices.

Railway
The one and only railway in Borneo runs from Kota Kinabalu to Beaufort and then to Tenom, in Sabah.

FURTHER READING

The avid reader will soon find the bookshops, and figure out which ones carry a decent stock of Borneo books. Some studies, histories and compilations of purely local value are worth reading even if they are only printed in small editions and never make the foreign market!

Cookery books, collections of ethnic stories, 'Oldest Inhabitant Remembers' and the like belong to this category.

GOVERNMENT PUBLICATIONS

A few standard books of information are available from Malaysian government sources. Brunei has similar publications in respect of the sultanate. Each of the Borneo states has a Tourist Information Bureau that is only too happy to supply the public with reading matter of the colourful kind.

The Malaysian Official Yearbook
- Available from the Information Department and from selected bookshops.

Malaysian Statistics Handbook (bilingual). Department of Statistics, Kuala Lumpur.
- An annual Statistics Bulletin is also printed for each state; those who need accurate up-to-date information are referred to the monthly bulletins available straight from the department.

CLASSICS

There are a few Borneo classics that have been reprinted in paperback. As they are available and affordable, they are listed here; others, just as classic but out of print, belong to the rarefied world of the scholar or the bibliophile.

A Decade in Borneo. Ada Pryer. UK: Continuum International Publishing Group, 2002.
- The memoirs of a pioneer lady who stood at the cradle of today's Sabah.

Borneo Stories. Somerset Maugham. Kuala Lumpur: Heinnemann Educational Books, 1988.
- An informative summary of stories about expatriate Englishmen (and women) in an exotic setting; they are amusing to read as period pieces.

CultureShock! Malaysia. Heidi Munan. Singapore: Marshall Cavendish Editions, 2005.
- Companion volume to the one you are reading now, devoted to living happily ever after in West Malaysia.

Field Book of a Jungle Wallah. Charles Hose. US: Oxford University Press, 1986.
- One of the many works penned by this indefatigable naturalist and amateur anthropologist.

The Malay Archipelago. Alfred Russel Wallace. Singapore: Periplus Editions, 2000 (reprint).
- A travelogue of the very best kind. Wallace covered most of the East Indian archipelago, but he spent a fair while in Borneo.

My Life in Sarawak. Margaret Brooke. Singapore: Oxford University Press, 1986.
- A very readable account of late 19th century Sarawak written by the second Rajah's lady.

The Official Kuching Guide 2006, Wayne Tarman and Mike Reed.
- A booklet on how to live in Kuching, filled with useful and entertaining information; it is re-issued each year.

The Pirate Wind: Tales of the Sea-robbers of Malaya. Owen Rutter. Singapore: Oxford University Press, 1986 (reprint).
- This well-researched study deals with piracy in the Malacca Straits and around Borneo.

MODERN NON-FICTION

Modern titles include many hefty tomes of science, of interest to the scholar but hardly the general reader.

There is a new cottage industry devoted to the easy, cheap and plentiful production of political biography, a rather perishable article on the whole that depends on rapid turnover. The 'Any Three Books for $1' stall at the Sunday market may contain interesting selections.

Here are a few general works on East Malaysia:

The Birds of Borneo. Bertram E Smythies. (Revised by G W H Davison). Borneo: National History Publications, 1999 (4th edition).

- There is also a pocket-sized edition of this classic Borneo wildlife study, more convenient for carrying on bird-watching excursions.

People of the Weeping Forest: Traditions and Change in Borneo. Jan B Ave and Victor T King. Leiden: Rijksmuseum voor Volkenkunde (National Museum of Ethnology), 1986.

- A new and sensitive appraisal of the island of Borneo as a whole.

Mammals of Borneo. Charles M Francis, Junaidi Payne and Karen Phillipps. Kuala Lumpur: Sabah Society, 1985.

- A worthy companion volume to Smythies' Birds (see above).

Sabah: The First Hundred Years. C Leong. Kuala Lumpur: Percetakan Man Yang Muda, 1982.

- This is a history from the past into the future. Written in a fluent style, it covers the essential and omits the tedious.

The Sarawak Chinese. John M Chin. Kuala Lumpur: Oxford University Press, 1981.

- Sarawak from a Chinese point of view, with an interesting chapter on pre-Brooke history.

Sarawak Handicraft. Heidi Munan. Kuala Lumpur: Oxford University Press, 1988.

- A summary of a wide and fascinating field.

Sarawak's Heritage. L.Chin. Kuching: Sarawak Museum, 1980.
- An expertly-written work on the state's prehistorical and antique treasures as well as present-day material culture.

The Towkays of Sabah. Edwin Lee. Singapore: Singapore University Press, 1976.
- Veering towards the political, but a very interesting account of wealth and power in Sabah.

Beads of Borneo. Heidi Munan. Singapore: Archipelago Press, 2005.
- A lavishly illustrated work on one of the more colourful aspects of Borneo's material culture.

ORIENTATION LITERATURE
Shell Oil Company publishes some orientation materials for its new staff. 'Outsiders' may manage to borrow, steal or wheedle these delightfully-written and very informative booklets from their rightful owners. Two titles are:

Jungle Jaunts. Sarawak Shell Berhad, Miri (no date).

Making Out in Miri. Sarawak Shell Berhad, Miri, 1976.

ABOUT THE AUTHOR

Heidi Munan was born Adelheid Oettli in Switzerland. Her family migrated to New Zealand, where she attended university and teachers' college.

Fate in the person of Sidi Munan took her to Sarawak in 1965. The couple have two children.

Heidi Munan taught for a number of years but eventually retired to become a part-time journalist and full-time mother, daughter-in-law, aunt, niece, granny, cook, driver, nurse and general trouble-shooter to an over-extended family.

In her rare free moments, Heidi is a private researcher at the Sarawak Museum, and contributor to a number of local and overseas publications. She takes a keen interest in the varied cultures of her home state, particularly in the language and literature of the Iban people.

In collaboration with Malaysian composer Julia Chong, Heidi has produced Sarawak's first operetta, *Life in the Jungle*, and a number of shorter occasional pieces. She is also the author of *CultureShock! Malaysia*, *Cultures of the World: Malaysia* (both published by Times Media Pte Ltd), *Sarawak Crafts* (OUP), short collections of Borneo folk tales and *The Beads of Borneo* (Editions Dider Millet).

INDEX

264

Titles in the CULTURESHOCK! series:

Argentina	Hawaii	Pakistan
Australia	Hong Kong	Paris
Austria	Hungary	Philippines
Bahrain	India	Portugal
Barcelona	Indonesia	San Francisco
Beijing	Iran	Saudi Arabia
Belgium	Ireland	Scotland
Bolivia	Israel	Sri Lanka
Borneo	Italy	Shanghai
Brazil	Jakarta	Singapore
Britain	Japan	South Africa
Cambodia	Korea	Spain
Canada	Laos	Sweden
Chicago	London	Switzerland
Chile	Malaysia	Syria
China	Mauritius	Taiwan
Costa Rica	Mexico	Thailand
Cuba	Morocco	Tokyo
Czech Republic	Moscow	Turkey
Denmark	Munich	Ukraine
Ecuador	Myanmar	United Arab
Egypt	Nepal	Emirates
Finland	Netherlands	USA
France	New York	Vancouver
Germany	New Zealand	Venezuela
Greece	Norway	Vietnam

For more information about any of these titles, please contact any of our Marshall Cavendish offices around the world (listed on page ii) or visit our website at:

www.marshallcavendish.com/genref